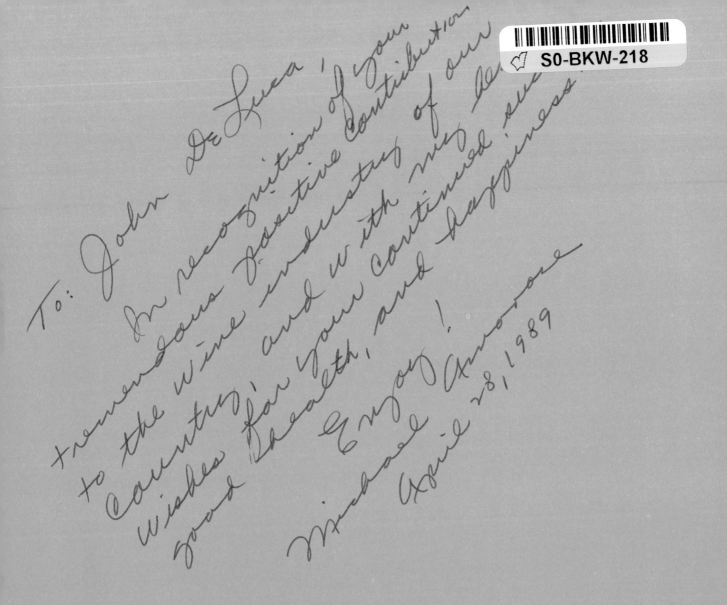

To: John DeLuca,

In recognition of your tremendous positive contribution to the wine industry of our country, and with my best wishes for your continued success, good health, and happiness.

Enjoy!

Michael Amorose
April 28, 1989

A
CATALOG
OF
CALIFORNIA
WINES

MICHAEL A. AMOROSE

6th EDITION

LIBRARY OF
WINE INSTITUTE

Photography Credits (in order of appearance):

Tom Vano, Portrait of Michael Amorose, dust jacket
Fred Lyon; wine glasses; page 13
Philip Wallick; grapevine sunrise; page 13
Lee Foster; green grape bunch; page 23
Linda A. Wiseman; glass, bottle, and pear; page 23
Ron Sanford; red grape bunch; page 129
Linda A. Wiseman; apple, bottle, and glass; page 129
George Olson; vineyard and mustard flowers; page 221
Philip Wallick; vineyards and mountains; page 221

Illustration Credits (in order of appearance):

David Bohn, dust jacket, title page
Jim Handrigan, pages 18 and 21
David Bohn, throughout listings

Book design, production and coordination
by Creative Concepts: Robert Ross, Tobie Vale,
Dona Turner, Stuart Bradford, Leslie Thulin.
Typography by Mercury Typography.

CONTENTS

ACKNOWLEDGMENTS

I am very gratified by the positive response my prior wine catalogs have received from many people in Arthur Young offices throughout the country. Some of these individuals have been a source of inspiration from the very beginning.

Special thanks to Bill Palmer, Chairman of Arthur Young's Construction Industry Group, for his steadfast support and encouragement over the years.

Thanks to Rita Shea, Arthur Young National Office, for her expert advice and overall support over the years. She is always there when I need her advice.

The internal team at our San Francisco office was absolutely tremendous—showing great enthusiasm for the project. Thank you, Phillippa Lack, for your expertise in word processing and in managing the internal production of this project. And special thanks to you, Jim Handrigan, for your invaluable advice and assistance with graphics and also for the illustrations on pages 18 and 21.

A very special thanks to you, Judy Berkowitz, for unselfishly using some of your many talents in editing the entire catalog. Your contribution to the quality of this catalog is significant. I am most appreciative.

To Jeanie Beatson, I appreciate your understanding and support throughout the project.

Thank you Gary Locke and Fred Foster for helping me acquire some of the special wines and for your advice and support over the years.

Thanks to my wine-tasting panel—"Club 33"—for their contribution to the evaluations of many of the wines included in this catalog.

Special thanks to Linda A. Wiseman for the photographs on pages 23 and 129.

Thank you Tom and Jon Vano for the photograph of me on the dust cover of this catalog.

Thanks to Robert Ross for the use of his creative talents in designing the entire catalog.

And a very special thank you to my wife Margaret, who has been a strong supporter of this project and my many wine-related activities. And to our children—Rick, Kathleen, David, Wendy, Matthew, Christopher, and Justin, each of whom made some direct contribution to this catalog.

Completing the catalog has been a major undertaking for me; however, I am very satisfied with the result. The sections on "Using This Catalog" and "All About Wine" were added with great enthusiasm. My thought was to gather interesting and useful information that would have some long-term value to you.

And as for the wines, I had fun with the tastings. Now it is your turn. Then, in a sense, we have shared. So sip, savor, and enjoy.

Michael Amorose
March, 1989
San Francisco

INTRODUCTION

It is January 1989 as I sit at my desk overlooking San Francisco Bay writing the introduction to the sixth edition of my Catalog of California Wines.

My book and I have come a long way since the first edition was published in 1978. That was a modest typewritten report intended for my colleagues in Arthur Young's San Francisco office. It contained evaluations of just 185 wines, and we printed (in our in-house print shop) a mere 100 copies. Now, a little more than ten years later, I am writing the introduction to this latest edition, encompassing more than 1,200 wines, with a print run of more than 40,000 copies. As in each prior catalog, the wines listed in this edition are completely new.

The reasons that prompted me to write the first catalog still hold. This edition, as has been the case in earlier editions, represents my response to friends and acquaintances who proposed that I update my evaluations of the numerous fine wines now available from California wineries. And now, I am even more motivated. With the significant increased interest in the prior catalog shown by Arthur Young personnel and our clients here and abroad, I want to produce a better catalog—one that will educate as well as inform. I have therefore included a section called "All About Wines," which includes materials I have developed for the seminars I conduct for professional and trade associations throughout the United States.

Responding to the suggestion of readers outside of California, I have included in this catalog, under the heading "Wineries," the name, address, and telephone number of virtually every winery listed in the critiques. If you are interested in a wine and cannot find it where you live, contact the winery directly. In most cases, vintners will be glad to oblige with direct shipments or give you the name of a local supplier. Certain states prohibit wine shipment across state lines; for specific information, ask your wine merchant and/or winery.

Over the past few years, I have increasingly emphasized the wine-with-food aspect of wine consumption. I have also focused on the subject of wine drinking and health. For the first time, I am covering these subjects in more depth, under separate sections captioned "Wine and Food" and "Wine and Your Health." Also included for

the first time are sections on how to buy, store, and serve wine, wine terminology, and other useful information.

In addition to the many California Wines, this catalog includes quite a number of very interesting wines from the Pacific Northwest. In 1978 there were about 200 wineries in California; today there are about 700, and wineries in the Pacific Northwest have also blossomed. In 1978 there were only a handful of wineries in the Pacific Northwest; today there are over 60 wineries each in Oregon and Washington, and about 10 in Idaho. Admittedly, many of these wineries are small. But, the overall quality is good, and it is getting better. Based on my limited experience with wines from this region, I am favorably impressed with the Rieslings, Chardonnays, and Cabernet Sauvignons from Washington; the Pinot Noirs, Rieslings, and Chardonnays from Oregon; and the Rieslings from Idaho.

Now, to the wines in the catalog. First, it is by no means a complete listing of wines for any period or for any winery. The California wines listed have distribution in at least some regional markets outside of California. Likewise, the wines from the Pacific Northwest have out-of-state distribution. All the wines listed were purchased in the San Francisco Bay Area.

Wines from other regions of the country are generally not available to me. Of course I can critique a bottle of wine from anywhere, but the evaluation will have more substance if, when explaining what is in that particular bottle, I know something about the winery and the region where the grapes are grown and the wines produced. I am always interested in learning more about wines from other regions of the country. And now and then a friend will give me a gift of a bottle or two from another region. In these cases I send a critique of the wine to the friend and also call the winery, if appropriate.

During the past two years I tasted approximately 1,450 wines; 1,254 appear in this catalog. I have included some wines where I tasted the varietal but not the specific vintage. In these cases my comments are based on discussions with friends who tasted the vintage in question, articles about the particular vintage, and my knowledge, gained over many years, of the styles of wine produced by the wineries in question.

This catalog's purpose is to assist in the selection of well-made wines, and I can honestly recommend every wine in this catalog. I tasted other wines, but did not include them because, in my opinion, they are either below average or their production and/or distribution is so limited that it would be pointless to include them. Also, I eliminated all light-bodied white wines prior to the 1986 vintage, since these have passed their peak in flavor, interest, and availability.

Many new wineries have been established during the past few years—and they are making excellent wines. The wines listed in this catalog represent only a modest number in proportion to the wines available from new wineries. Naturally, insofar as possible, I continue to list new vintages from those wineries I have become familiar with over the years.

Now, I will examine the number of wines in each varietal category included in this catalog and explain why I might generally favor one varietal over another. Following is a table of the categories and the number of wines in each.

Number of Wines in Catalog

White Wines	1989	1987	1985	1983	1980
Chardonnay	374	234	190	138	73
Sauvignon Blanc	116	108	58	58	25
Gewürztraminer	44	42	39	25	8
Johannisberg Riesling	41	50	29	40	28
White Zinfandel	22	33	0	0	0
Champagne	75	31	34	20	12
Chenin Blanc (included with Other White Wines in this catalog)	3	16	18	22	22
Other White Wines	11	26	23	24	13
	686	540	391	327	181
Red Wines					
Cabernt Sauvignon	290	168	128	84	60
Zinfandel	82	116	109	62	69
Pinot Noir	92	63	35	57	27
Merlot	78	40	41	19	14
Petite Sirah (included with Other Red Wines in the 1980, 1983, and 1985 catalogs)	20	36	3	1	18
Other Red Wines	6	22	15	22	9
	568	445	331	245	197
Total Wines	1,254	985	722	572	378

I group the wines by varietal (rather than by winery) for quick reference in comparing quality and price. Within each varietal category, the wines are listed alphabetically by winery, starting with the most recent vintage. In evaluating each wine, I use terms such as color, aroma, acidity, sugar, body, flavor, and astringency. I do this to aid the reader in making wine judgments, and hope, thereby, to improve wine selections and enhance enjoyment. An explanation of these terms is included in a separate section titled "Wine Terminology."

Chardonnay. The number of Chardonnays tasted has increased dramatically since the last catalog, which reflects the tremendous popularity of wines made from this varietal. It seems that most wine drinkers these days want to include Chardonnays as part of their life. And some of the recent bottlings are simply wonderful. As to my preference, I like the rich, fruity, California-style Chardonnay with oak in balance (not overpowering). My appreciation and respect for Chardonnays made in a more austere style— with the flavors presented in a more delicate composition—is continuing to develop.

Cabernet Sauvignon. It is incredible how the Cabernets continue to improve in quality. There are so many great wines out there, it is mind boggling. Many are accessible and enjoyable beginning about two years after vintage date. I hold a special regard, however, for wines produced for aging. There is always a special pleasure in sharing with friends a properly cellared, older wine. Some wineries produce specific varietals—one for early consumption and one to hold. This makes sense. If you have always purchased for current consumption, you may wish to consider cellaring a case or two. Refer to the section titled "Storing Wine" for information on cellaring.

Sauvignon Blanc. This is my favorite wine before dinner or with the first course. As for the popularity of this varietal, it is in stiff competition with the Chardonnay; however, I believe it is holding its own at present. I tend to taste Sauvignon Blancs from certain wineries time and time again. I prefer the moderately grassy fashion, but realize that grassiness is part of this varietal. Variations in flavor depend on the way the winemaker chooses to present the wine. Most wineries do an excellent job with this varietal.

Zinfandel. This catalog lists a smaller number of Zinfandels than the last edition. But oh, the quality! Many of them are wonderful to drink now. As with the Sauvignon Blanc, I tend to play favorites. I find this grape exciting because it generates so many interesting styles, ranging from the fresh raspberry flavor of a picnic wine to a rich, elegant vintage able to challenge a fine Cabernet. The Zin is faced with stiff competition from the Cabernet Sauvignon at present; however, it is holding its own. As for great red wine values, this is a good place to start.

Pinot Noir. The fourth edition (1985) of my catalog included sharp criticism of California Pinot Noirs. Then, for my fifth edition (1987), I tasted many more Pinot Noirs—and I noted great improvement. Well, that improvement continues. The new Pinots listed in this catalog possess more fruit, more character in the composition of the wine, and enough tannin for aging.

Johannisberg Riesling and Gewürztraminer. My interest in Johannisberg Riesling and Gewürztraminer continues, especially with some of the beautiful late-harvest offerings on the market today. I have included the residual sugar percentages for each wine when this information was available. The public's interest in the recent vintages of the early-harvest bottlings of Johannisberg Riesling has weakened in the past few years, while Gewürz seems to be holding its own. However, you might find a well-made dry Riesling a welcome partner to a lazy afternoon. Wine fashion is so serious; maybe we should all enjoy a few more lazy afternoons!

Merlot. Merlot continues to be the wine of choice at many dinners at home and in restaurants. Like the Zinfandel, the Merlot is made in styles ranging from light to heavy. I continue to be excited about the new Merlot offerings. There are some great wines critiqued in this category. Oftentimes this varietal is overlooked when selecting a red wine for a fine meal.

Petite Sirah. I like Petite Sirah and its attractive purple-inky color. Typically, wines made from this grape have been full and spicy, with aging a requirement. A mature, rich Petite Sirah is delicious with well-seasoned foods. Available now are recent bottlings ready for current drinking. Heavyweights are also available. The catalog lists some excellent Petite Sirahs at very good prices.

White Zinfandel. White Zinfandel continues to be very popular. Since this wine is made for early consumption, I have included only the latest vintages.

Champagne. The champagne category is much more interesting in this edition, principally due to the opening of several new champagne houses in California and their great variety of high-quality offerings. Champagnes are becoming increasingly popular for consumption with meals as well as at receptions and festive occasions. Refer to the section titled "Champagne" for a more detailed discussion.

Other Whites and Other Reds. "Other White Wines" and "Other Red Wines" are the remaining two categories. Included are some nice wines made from the Semillon grape and the Cabernet Franc grape. Watch for increasing interest in these varietals in the future.

I have eliminated Chenin Blanc as a category. There are a few nice Chenins available on the market, but the popularity of this varietal has waned in the past few years.

To benefit more fully from this catalog and to learn more about wines, I suggest that you first read the sections titled "Symbols" and "Wine Terminology." As for the critiques of the wines included in the catalog, they are a means for you to compare your taste to mine—and remember, it is your taste that counts!

Michael Amorose

USING THIS CATALOG

S Y M B O L S

The following symbols used in the critiques refer to the overall quality of the grape variety. For example, a Chardonnay rated "excellent" must possess characteristics of a Chardonnay—aroma, varietal flavor, etc.—and be more than just an excellent white wine. Price is not considered in the evaluations. For some, a Chardonnay at $12.00 per bottle might be a more desirable wine than a Chardonnay at $20.00 per bottle. You will have to make that decision yourself.

☆☆☆☆   Outstanding. Search for it.

☆☆☆   Excellent. Distinctive, memorable.

☆☆ ½   A good wine, with special attributes.

☆☆   Good. Fine example of wine type or style.

☆   Average. Well-made wine. Often very delightful.

🍷   Drinkable now. Might not get better.

🍷   Drinkable now. Will get better with further bottle aging. Includes wine that,
🍾   for some people, would be better after smoothing out for a year or two.

🍾   Hold for future drinking. Will improve with further bottle aging. Includes wines that, for most people, would be better after smoothing out for three years or more.

The following information will also help you in understanding the critiques.

NV   Nonvintage.

Year   The year grapes were harvested; e.g., 1986.

Price   Estimated California retail price for 750 ml. Other-sized bottles, e.g., 375 ml., indicated where applicable.

The following are the basic terms used to describe the level of sweetness in champagnes.

| Natural | 0% - 0.2% | Extra Dry | 1% - 2.0% | Semi-Dry | 4% - 6% |
| Brut | 0% - 1.5% | Dry | 2% - 4% | Sweet | 8% - 10% |

WINE TERMINOLOGY

The following is an explanation of the wine terms I used in my wine critiques. I suggest that you study this section carefully before seriously examining the critiques.

Acid, acidity — Sound, healthy grapes contain natural acidity, which give the wine its crisp, refreshing quality. Too much acidity will make the tongue curl; too little will make the wine taste flat.

Aftertaste — The flavors that sometimes remain in the throat and back nasal passages after a wine has been drunk.

Aging — Holding wines for a period of time to allow them to mature.

Alcohol — An essential component of wine, giving it body and backbone. There is no smell or taste as such, but a young wine would have a peppery nose from the alcohol. Adds a weighty feeling in the mouth, and warmth as the wine is swallowed.

Alcohol by volume — The percentage of alcohol contained in a wine. Table wines must be less than 15 percent alcohol.

Apéritif — Wine generally drunk before a meal.

Appearance — A category used in evaluating wines. Includes clarity, cloudiness, deposits, etc.

Aroma — The element of smell that derives from the grape.

Astringent — Having a bitter mouth-puckering effect due to excess tannin. Usually more noticeable in young red wines. Wears off as wine matures.

Aggressive — Overly lively in the nose and on the palate.

Austere — Used mainly in relation to taste. Hard and severe. Not necessarily a fault, but could mean wine is underdeveloped, lacking richness and charm.

Balance — A harmonious relationship between the taste and odor components of a wine.

Big — A robust wine, well endowed with vital elements, not just high in alcohol.

Bite — A substantial degree of acidity and/or tannins. Tolerable only in rich, full-bodied wines.

Bitter — A taste detected on the palate, on the back of the tongue in the finish. When in excess, unpleasant; in moderation, can add complexity and balance to wines of strong, fruity flavor. Usually attributable to seeds and stems.

Blanc de Blancs — Usually champagne made entirely from the Chardonnay grape.

Blanc de Noirs — A white wine made from black grapes, with a deeper tone than a white wine from white grapes. Frequently used for champagne.

Blend — Combination of wines of different varieties or lots to add interest or harmony to the finished product.

Body — The weight of wine in the mouth attributable to the alcoholic content and soluble solids. Wines from hotter climates tend to have more body than those from cooler climates.

Botrytis — Short for Botrytis cinerea. Known also as the "noble rot." A mold that shrivels the grapes, reduces the water content, and concentrates the sugar content. Honeylike taste and smell. Highly prized in white dessert wines but disastrous in red wines.

Bottle age — Maturity and development of a wine attributable to the length of stay in the bottle. White dessert wines bring out a honey quality. Red wines bring a softness and mellowness, or what I sometimes refer to as a red velvet quality.

Bottle fermented — A sparkling wine made by the méthode champenoise or the transfer method.

Bouquet — The element of smell that develops from aging the wine in a cask or bottle.

Briary — A stemmy character in a wine.

Bright — Used to describe appearance. Clarity.

Brut — Champagne that is quite dry but may still have a touch of sweetness.

Buttery — Self-descriptive. Could be smell or taste.

Caramel — A somewhat burnt, toffeelike odor or flavor.

Chocolaty — A chocolatelike smell or taste, usually attributable to heavy red wines.

Chewy — A term for big, heavy-bodied wines with enough viscosity to be almost chewable.

Clean — Absence of unpleasant odors or flavors.

Clear — Good clarity in the wine, but not brilliant. Does not have suspended solids.

Closed in	Usually refers to aromas. A wine that has yet to release its potential qualities.	**Hard**	Severe on the palate, probably from tannin. This is not a fault in a young wine.
Cloudy	A hazy appearance usually resulting from poor wine-making techniques.	**Harsh**	A wine high in astringency.
Coarse	Rough; lacks finesse.	**Hearty**	Generally refers to red wine. Robust, zestful, and warm.
Color	Derived primarily from the grape. White wines vary from pale straw to yellow to gold to amber. Reds vary from pink to claret to ruby to purple.	**Heavy**	High in alcohol. More than full bodied. Clumsy; lacks finesse.
Complex	A combination of odor and flavor elements not usually found in ordinary wines.	**Herbaceous**	Pleasant aroma somewhere between grass-like and flowery. Usually associated with young white wines, typically with the Sauvignon Blanc; however, to some extent associated with the Cabernet Sauvignon.
Corky	A negative smell or flavor attributable to fungus-infected or chemically tainted cork.		
Crisp	Firm, brisk, and refreshing. Indicates a good level of acidity, especially in dry white wines.	**Hot**	Alcohol content high. Slight burning sensation on the palate.
Cuvée	A specific blend of wines generally used in making sparkling wine but occasionally used in producing table wine.	**Jammy**	A sweetish berrylike aroma or taste, concentrated enough to suggest the flavor of jam.
Deep/Depth	Indicates underlying richness. Layers of flavors all interlocked.	**Legs**	The "tears" that fall down the inside of the glass after the wine is swirled.
Dry	Not sweet; fully fermented. Absence of residual sugar.	**Long**	Describes the desirable finish of a wine. Indicates quality.
Dull	Appearance not bright. The smell and taste lack interest.	**Maderized**	A term often used to describe wines with evidence of beginning oxidation. Correctly used, it describes caramel-like, baked flavors.
Earthy	Negative smells and flavors attributable to certain soils.	**Mature**	Most often applied to red wines to indicate that the wine has aged sufficiently for the tannin components to have softened, giving the wine a smooth taste and texture.
Elegant	Stylish, balanced, and refined quality.		
Extract	Soluble solids that add to a wine's substance.		
Finesse	An abstract qualitative term relating to refinement and elegance.	**Medium bodied**	Neither light nor heavy in alcohol or extract.
Finish	The end taste of a wine. Could be long or short. Smooth to rough; flat to puckery.	**Mellow**	Soft and mature; no rough edges.
Flat	Total lack of vigor on nose and palate. Lack of acidity.	**Nose**	A common term for the aroma and bouquet of a wine.
Flowery	An aroma or flavor that reminds one of flowers. Usually found in white wines.	**Nuance**	Having components reminiscent of specific smells and flavors.
Fresh	Attractive, youthful characteristics in nose and palate.	**Oaky**	Toasty or vanillin smells or flavors contributed by the oak during barrel aging.
Fruity	An aroma or flavor that comes from the grape.	**Odor**	The smell of the wine. Examples: flowery, fruity, herbaceous, musty, minty, citrusy, raisiny, peppery, nutty, woody, berrylike, appley, peachy, figgy, and melony.
Full bodied	High in alcoholic content and extract, filling the mouth.	**Off dry**	Slightly sweet.
Grassy	A flavor or aroma of some wines that in moderation adds interest. For example, a Sauvignon Blanc has inherent grassiness, which adds much interest when balanced with other aromas and flavors.	**Overripe**	The characteristic of wines made from overripe fruit. Raisiny.

Oxidized   When a wine is exposed to excess amounts of oxygen, flavor and aroma can be lost. Sometimes this is undesirable, other times desirable. For instance, the process may develop caramel-like flavors, which is a very desirable change for some people.

Powerful   This is self-explanatory. More appropriately used in the context of a big red wine.

Puckery   A tactile sensation in highly tannic wines.

Punt   The indentation in the bottom of some wine bottles.

Raisiny   Tasting like raisins. Generally characteristic of wine made from overripe grapes.

Residual sugar   Sugar that remains unconverted in the wine after fermentation.

Rich   To some extent, this is self-explanatory. However, it should not imply sweetness, rather a fullness of fruit flavors and alcohol.

Ripe   A synonym for mature. Ripe grapes give a wine a natural sweetness and richness.

Rough   Generally applies to young red tannic wines before they have begun to smooth out.

Round   A well-balanced, usually mature wine.

Sharp   A degree of acidity that goes beyond being attractively refreshing. Aging could correct this.

Short   Refers to length of flavor on the palate. This indicates lack of quality.

Silky   A firm, yet distinctly soft texture on the palate.

Slightly sweet   Containing a very minimal amount of residual sugar.

Smoky   Smell or taste overtones characteristic of some white grapes.

Smooth   Soft, mild texture; no rough edges.

Soft   Mellow. Tannin and acid fully absorbed.

Sparkling wines   Wines whose effervescence is produced by carbon dioxide captured during a second fermentation in the bottle or container in which it is made.

Spicy   Rich herblike aromas or flavors from certain grape varieties such as Gewürztraminer.

Spritz   A German word that is widely used to indicate a small amount of carbon dioxide in wine. Carbon dioxide levels are not sufficient to cause obvious bubbles, but gives a slight prickling sensation on the tongue.

Still wines   All wines made without effervescence.

Sturdy   Fairly tough; substantial.

Subtle   Richness and complexity not obvious.

Sulfur dioxide   The major preservative used in wine. It has a pungent and unpleasant odor when used in excessive amounts. Rarely detected in red wines. The more acidic the wine, the more obvious a given content of sulfur dioxide becomes. The aroma of many young wines is masked by a whiff of sulfur, which often wears out in a short while, after the wine has been poured.

Sweet   A wine with a high sugar content. This is the essential characteristic of any dessert wine.

Tannin   An essential preservative derived from the seeds, stems, and skins of grapes during fermentation. The presence of tannin dries the roof of the mouth and grips the teeth. However, it contributes to the longevity of the wine, and normally decreases as the wine ages.

Tart   High in acidity; sharp.

Thin   Deficient in the natural components of wine. Watery; lacking body.

Tired   An oxidized wine.

Ullage   Leakage or evaporation of wine from its container. Usually this results in oxidation and spoilage over a period of time.

Unbalanced   The major components in a wine are not matched. Overtannic, overacidic, lacking fruit, etc.

Vanillin   An extract of oak used in aging wines. Present in the smell or flavor.

Varietal   A distinctive aroma or flavor that is characteristic of a particular grape variety, such as Cabernet Sauvignon or Chardonnay.

Velvety   A textural connotation, related to silky and smooth.

Well balanced   The physical components of wine—fruit, acid, tannin, alcohol, etc.—are combined harmoniously.

Yeasty   A pungent, beery smell. In bottled wine, it is a sure indication of impending or secondary fermentation. Does not apply to champagne, where the secondary fermentation is part of the basic champagne-making process.

ALL ABOUT WINE

ALL ABOUT WINE

WINE AND YOUR HEALTH

In my seminars, I emphasize that wine should be consumed with food. This affords wine the opportunity to display itself properly. Equally important, it lowers the alcohol absorption rate.

When alcohol reaches an empty stomach, it passes directly into the bloodstream in a matter of 15 to 20 minutes. When alcohol reaches a full stomach, however, it may take up to two hours to enter the bloodstream. Further, studies have shown that when wine is consumed with a meal, the peak alcohol level is only one-half as high as when the same amount of wine is consumed on an empty stomach. Studies have also shown that heavy drinkers absorb more alcohol than moderate drinkers, with faster and higher peak blood-alcohol levels.

There are several ways we can decrease the alcohol absorption level. Sip, rather than guzzle. Drink moderate, rather than large, quantities of wine. Drink wine during the meal, accompanied by water. Consume wine with carbohydrates and fats rather than proteins.

Whether and how much alcohol to consume is an individual decision. Body weight and overall size determine the amount of alcohol tolerance. Some people can tolerate alcohol more than others, and there are those who cannot tolerate it at all. We should listen to our bodies. Twenty-five years ago I consumed twice as much wine per day as I do now. Over the years, my capacity has fallen from about 20 to about 10 ounces per day with meals. Some tolerance develops with frequent use; however, this tolerance tends to progressively decline as the body ages. The bottom line here is, be aware of your limitations and use common sense.

Some people complain that they have headaches after drinking wine. This is usually because they are dehydrated. At all my wine functions, I insist that room-temperature water be readily available (cold water anesthetizes the taste buds). I routinely drink a couple of glasses of water before bed, since I usually drink a couple of glasses of wine with dinner. This takes care of any dehydration problem.

It is true that I promote increased wine consumption in my talks to various groups. However, I am *not* encouraging regular wine consumers to drink more wine. Rather, I am trying to persuade others to learn to taste wine in a discriminating manner and, if they like it, to consume it in moderation with meals.

ENJOYING WINE

Of our five senses, we use three—sight, smell, and taste—to enjoy wine. (A fourth sense, touch, plays a lesser role.) The most important of these, in my opinion, is smell. Of course we want the wine to look attractive, but attractive appearance only invites us to examine the contents of the glass. I often get as much pleasure from the appearance of a wine and its aroma as I do in tasting it.

Our taste buds and olfactory senses are sharpest when we are hungry. However, I believe it is very important, for health reasons, that wine be consumed with some food. (See "Wine and Your Health.") So, if you taste wine prior to lunch or dinner, I suggest you have a supply of bread or unsalted crackers and water on hand.

The first element we examine in wine tasting is the aroma. There is no consensus as to categories of scents; however, I believe there are six commonly accepted aromas or smells that we can focus on— fruity, flowery, resinous, spicy, foul, and burnt. I have used, virtually throughout, the term "aroma," which is the element of smell that comes from the grape. There is another term, "bouquet," which is the element of smell that develops from aging the wine in casks and bottles. However, since the major part of this catalog is the evaluation of new wines, I use the term "aroma."

Suppose the wine has a fruity aroma. We then need to ask ourselves what kind of fruit. For instance, is it a tree fruit—cherry, apricot, peach, pear or apple; is it a berry fruit—blackberry, raspberry, strawberry, or black currant; is it a citric fruit—lemon, grapefruit, or orange; is it a tropical fruit—pineapple, banana, or melon? Or suppose the wine has a floral aroma. Is it jasmine, rose, or violet? Perhaps the wine has a spicy aroma, such as clove, cinnamon, or mint. Or perhaps the wine has resinous characteristics—scents of oak, cedar, or pine. Does the wine smell foul or burnt? If so, think in terms of earthy, vegetative, and chemical scents. Does the wine smell oxidized; that is, have the grape odors become lost somehow? If so, look for a caramel-like odor.

There are innumerable other scents that you might also think about; for example, butterscotch, honey, artichoke, black olive, green olive, or asparagus. While it is not necessary to be able to detect all of these, you should make an effort to detect as many as you can.

There are four basic taste sensations: sweet, sour, salty, and bitter. Combinations and varying degrees of these account for all the tastes we experience. Sweet and bitter tastes are commonly found in wines; sour is occasionally found; salt should not be found at all. Don't confuse taste with flavor. The flavor of a substance involves more than taste—it involves smell and temperature as well.

The taste of the wine, in most cases, confirms what you have already learned from the aromas. For instance, when the aromas are predominantly fruity, the flavor should be fruity. It may not be the same fruit; it may smell like cherries and taste like black currants. Or, if the predominant aroma is oaky, the wine will generally taste oaky, although probably not with the same comparative intensity; that is a judgment call.

Although our sense of smell is distinct from our sense of taste, our ability to smell (and, to a lesser extent, our ability to see), affects the flavor of things we taste. I have been to tastings where the participants were blindfolded and their noses stuffed with cotton or pinched closed. The flavors they then experienced were different from those experienced when they could both see and smell the wine. When the tasters were only blindfolded, the flavors they experienced were again different from those experienced when they could both see and smell, but only slightly.

T A B L E   W I N E

For more than two decades after repeal of prohibition, fortified wines such as Port and Sherry, which typically contain 18 to 20 percent alcohol, were especially popular with Americans. In recent years, however, natural dry wines, with an alcohol content of about 12 percent, have come to the forefront. The U.S. per capita consumption of these dry wines has doubled within the past 15 years, and the national average is now about 2.5 gallons per year. California's per capita consumption is about 4.5 gallons a year—still a far cry from approximately 25 gallons per person consumed by the French and Italians each year.

There are two basic classifications of dry wines: generic and varietal. A generic wine is typically produced from a variety of different grapes. A Burgundy might be a blend of several grapes such as Barbera, Petite Sirah, Zinfandel and Carignane. A Chablis might include Chenin Blanc, French Colombard, and certain of the Riesling varieties. A varietal wine is named after the grape that accounts for at least 75 percent of its content—Cabernet Sauvignon or Chardonnay, for example. Often the same grape varieties used in generic blends also make excellent varietal wines. In fact, some California wineries are noted for their fine Petite Sirahs and Zinfandels. Following is a brief description of the more popular California varietal wines.

White Wines

Chardonnay. One of the finest of all white wines; a medium-to-full bodied varietal wine renowned for its high quality and distinction. Look for sweet clove and appley, vanillin, lemony, buttery, and creamy characteristics. Depending on the intensity of the particular wine, usually accompanies well-seasoned fish, poultry, or white meat dishes.

Sauvignon Blanc (Fumé Blanc). Rich varietal aromas and complex flavors. Look for bell pepper, green olive, grapefruit, fig or melon (attributable to Semillon blend), and grassy and herbaceous characteristics. Usually made dry, with good acid balance. Goes well with rich seafood dishes.

Gewürztraminer. This wine ranges from delicate to quite intense, and dry to medium sweet. Aromatic, with a characteristic spicy taste. Often has enough grape intensity to enjoy with loin of pork, spiced meats, roast duck, or wild fowl.

Johannisberg Riesling. Made at different levels of sweetness. The lighter, less sweet wines go well with light meat dishes; the sweeter wines have intense citrus and floral aromas and go well with desserts. Look for peach, apricot, pineapple, and honey; also floral and citric characteristics.

Red Wines

Cabernet Sauvignon. Complex and distinctive. Look for peppercorn, green olive, and bell pepper; also herbaceous, spicy, and chocolaty characteristics. Sometimes grape flavors are complex and intense, in which case the wine should age a few years to smooth out. Depending on intensity, can accompany a wide range of meat dishes.

Zinfandel. Fruity, light bodied, and smooth. Sometimes made heavy. Look for raspberry and blackberry; also briary, herbaceous, jammy, minty, cedary, and chocolaty characteristics. The very best Zinfandels can be fine wines of distinction. Its flavor can be as heavy as a Cabernet or as fruity as a Beaujolais.

Pinot Noir. Rich in body, although delicate. Look for cherries and berries; also earthy, mushroomy, peppery, and floral characteristics. When made light and well-balanced, excellent with veal or fowl. Less frequently, wines from this grape are intense, with an overall elegance, and require highly seasoned foods for optimum enjoyment.

Merlot. A rich, complex wine with Cabernet Sauvignon characteristics in the flavors, and a softer dimension in the structure. Often used as a softening blend grape for Cabernet Sauvignon. When Merlot is made as a varietal, Cabernet Sauvignon is the blend grape to add backbone. Food suggestions similar to Cabernet Sauvignon.

Petite Sirab. A full-bodied, rich-tasting wine, with spicy flavors, and usually high in tannin. Some bottlings are soft and mellow with moderate acidity and superb bouquet. Usually best with spicy meat dishes.

Almost all premium California varietal wines are aged in oak barrels. (See section titled "Making Wine.") So, in addition to the aromas and flavors that have been included in the above varietal descriptions, one must consider what the additional dimension of oak flavoring does to the wine. As a consumer, I like an oaky flavor in wines. When I am drinking a light white or red wine, however, I prefer just a touch of oak so as not to overpower the grape flavor. With more intense white and red wines, such as the Chardonnay and Cabernet Sauvignon, I like more oak, as it adds complexity to the overall taste.

WINE WITH FOOD

Although there are no rigid rules about which wines to serve with which foods, I would like to share some thoughts that I hope will help you in selecting wines. Light foods require light wines. Spicy or flavorful foods require heavier wines. Protein balances the tannins usually found in red wines, and fat balances acid, usually found in white wines. Acid in the wine balances the alkaline in cheese. The acid in wine (in most cases white wine) will make seafood seem sweet. If the wine has some residual sugar, this sugar will balance salt and sharp spices. Remember that sauces can change the character of the food, and will therefore affect your selection.

Generally, sweet desserts need wines of similar sweetness. There are, however, exceptions to this, at least in my experience. For instance, a rich red wine with very mild tannins might go very well with a dessert of chocolate and fresh raspberries.

There are some clashes to be aware of. For example, mackerel, or any oil fish, does not go well with red wine; and vinaigrette salads or lemon desserts do not go well with any wine.

A well-known and widely observed rule for choosing wines is white wine with white meat and red wine with red meat. While this would be a safe bet in most instances, it should not be regarded as Scripture, and more and more Americans are learning to count instead on a more reliable criterion: their individual taste. There is no question that a crisp Chablis or Sauvignon Blanc is usually an excellent accompaniment to fish, or that a Pinot Noir or a Cabernet Sauvignon goes well with roast beef or steak. You can't go wrong with those choices. However, with turkey—a strong white meat that would usually call for a Chardonnay—some people prefer a very light Pinot Noir. Many like a light red wine with roast pork, while others prefer a spicy Gewürztraminer.

From my long experience in matching wines to foods, I've learned that whatever is pleasing to your palate is the way to go.

Women have had a profound influence on the drinking habits in this country (and in other wine-consuming countries as well). In the early 1970s, women began serving white wine at receptions and other social events, helping popularize white wine.

There is an interesting footnote to the white wine trend. Beginning in the early 1970s, roughly two-thirds of the grape vines under cultivation in California for wine production were earmarked for red wine, and one-third for white wine—the same ratio as in Europe for many years. By the late 1970s, the demand was reversed—two-thirds for white wine and one-third for red. This radical change in demand in such a short period had a tremendous effect on the wine industry. Red wines were on the market, in the making, and "on the vines," but the demand for red wine was diminishing while that for whites was surging. So what to do? Make white wine from red grapes. (See the section titled "Making Wine.") And that is what was done.

In the 1980s, the American public has become increasingly aware of, and interested in, ethnic foods as well as the many changes in our "national cuisine." And with this new awareness, food professionals (chefs, cookbook authors, and food consultants) increasingly recommend that wine be matched with food for increased enjoyment of the meal. I will add a footnote here—wine with food in moderation.

M A K I N G   W I N E

Through a process of fermentation, grape juice turns into wine. In this process, sugar, which is present naturally in the ripe grape, is converted to alcohol. After the grapes are crushed and the yeast is added, the fermentation process of changing sugar into alcohol begins. The fermentation process ends when all the sugar has been converted into alcohol, or the alcohol level has reached 15 percent, which kills the yeast. For every two parts natural sugar, approximately one part alcohol and one part carbon dioxide result. For example, if the grapes contain 24 percent sugar, the result would be approximately 12 percent alcohol.

Red wines are generally fermented with their seeds and skins in large wooden tanks. It is the skins that give color to the wine. The alcohol dissolves the pigmentation in the skins, making the wine red. After fermentation and a settling down period in which the wine is clarified, the wine is transferred to a smaller container for aging. Often this will be a 60-gallon oak barrel, which will soften the tannins and add a vanillin flavor to the wine. The wine will age in the oak barrel 6 to 18 months, sometimes longer, before being bottled.

White wines are generally fermented in temperature-controlled stainless steel tanks, without the seeds or skins. When aging in oak is not desired (e.g., White Zinfandels), after fermentation and a settling down period in which the wine is clarified, the wine is transferred directly to bottles. When a vanillin component (derived from aging in oak) is desired, the wine is transferred to oak barrels, where it is generally aged from three to six months, sometimes longer, before bottling.

The free juice from virtually all grapes is white. It is therefore possible to make a white wine from, say, a Cabernet Sauvignon or Zinfandel grape if the juice is fermented without the skins and seeds. If the skins are removed before the juice has a chance to pick up the red color, then a red (dark) grape will give you a white wine. It is also possible to make a pink wine by carefully limiting the exposure to the skins. You will notice that this catalog contains a section for Zinfandels (red) and a section for White Zinfandel. Both types are made from the same Zinfandel grape.

C H A M P A G N E

Champagne graces our tables at festive family gatherings, and it is increasingly being enjoyed with meals throughout the year. On very special occasions, such as a wedding or a 50th anniversary celebration, it performs a special magic—it raises our spirits. And champagne can be a wonderful accompaniment to an entire meal. (See the section titled "Serving Wine.")

You might be interested to know that the term "champagne" as used in this catalog is technically incorrect; the proper term is "sparkling wine." Champagne is truly "champagne" only when it comes from the Champagne district of France. Even sparkling wines produced in other areas of France are referred to as "vin mousseaux" (sparkling wine). In Germany, sparkling wine is called "Sekt"; in Spain, "Cava"; and in Italy, "Spumante." However, since most Americans refer to the bubbly as champagne, I see no reason to refer to it differently.

Basically, there are three techniques in producing champagne—méthode champenoise, the transfer method, and the charmat bulk process. The méthode champenoise requires that the wine be fermented in an individual bottle and that the secondary fermentation take place in that *same* bottle. This method takes time, requires special care, and is costly.

Less costly is the transfer method. Here the wine is fermented in individual bottles. All the bottles are then emptied into one pressurized tank, where the wine is filtered. The wine is then returned to the washed bottles.

The least costly method is the charmat bulk process. In this process, the wine is actually fermented in pressurized stainless steel tanks and then filtered from the tank directly to the bottles.

I have friends who marvel at the wonderful taste of the French sparklers, and who place the California product in a lower-quality category. Admittedly, the finest champagnes, to my knowledge, are French— and some are simply exquisite. However, California champagnes have been improving steadily during the past few years, and a number of wineries have been able to produce champagnes of excellent quality. (I am referring here to champagnes produced by the traditional méthode champenoise technique, which is the same technique that has been used in making fine champagnes in France for over 300 years.)

California champagnes are noted for their intense fruit flavors, and the makers have been able to marry rich, toasty, yeasty characteristics in the secondary fermentation. Further, a few of the wineries have been able to achieve additional dimensions of crispiness and complexity. It seems to me that the careful attention to detail, which carried California Chardonnay and Cabernets to world prominence, may, in time, do the same for sparkling wine. Following the future developments of California champagnes, both in quantity and quality, will be very exciting.

B U Y I N G   W I N E

One of the purposes of this catalog is to help you buy wines. As a general rule, the lighter white wines, such as Sauvignon Blanc, Gewürztraminer, Johannisberg Riesling, and White Zinfandel, are best enjoyed in their youth; say, within two years of bottling. The heavier white wines, such as a medium-full bodied Sauvignon Blanc or Chardonnay, should generally be consumed within two to four years of bottling. The fruity red wines, say some of the light Zinfandels and Pinot Noirs, should be consumed within one to three years. The heavier reds, such as the Cabernet Sauvignons and Petite Sirahs, should generally be consumed within three to five years. Of course, this is just a general rule. Many red wines have a long aging potential.

There are different factors to consider when buying wine for immediate consumption as opposed to wines that you wish to cellar for a period of time. A review of the sections "Wine and Food" and "Storing Wine" will help you here.

In addition to using this catalog, I suggest that you develop a relationship with a good wine merchant who can help you with your purchases. In the final analysis, however, you must be the judge. Keep in mind that quality is not always correlated to price; you may prefer a good wine at 5 dollars a bottle to an excellent wine at 20 dollars. The decision is yours.

S T O R I N G   W I N E

Storage is very important in developing and preserving good wine. Wine for aging should be kept in darkness, as light is harmful to the flavor and life of wine. The ideal temperature range is between 55 and 65 degrees Fahrenheit. Gradual fluctuations within this range are acceptable.

There are many storage units on the market today with temperature and humidity controls that meet the ideal standards for proper cellaring of wine. If you do not have a wine cellar or storage unit, you can probably find an adequate space in your home for storing wine for a limited period; say, two or three years. A dark area where the temperature does not go above 75 degrees Fahrenheit for any extended period and generally stays consistently under 70 degrees Fahrenheit will work fine. I would not recommend a closet for long-term cellaring unless ideal conditions can be met. However, most young wines are quite sturdy, and will store well for a limited period of time, even under less-than-ideal conditions.

Store the wines on the floor, in the original cardboard cartons. This will protect them from temperature fluctuations to some extent, and it will also keep out the light.

Maintaining the proper humidity is also very important in storing wines. If the air is very dry, some wine will evaporate through the cork over a period of time, allowing oxygen to enter the bottle and spoil the wine.

Above-ground, long-term storage can present major problems in most parts of the country, except the areas within a few miles of the Pacific Ocean. The summers are too hot and the winters too cold. An underground wine cellar may be satisfactory. For above-ground a storage unit with humidity controls may be the only answer.

The bottles should be stored on their side or upside down, to keep the corks moist and to maintain a tight seal at the neck of the bottle. Bottles with plastic or metal caps are an exception. Wine should not come in contact with this type of cap; therefore, these bottles should be stored upright.

This section on wine storage was written to make you aware of certain conditions necessary for the proper storing of wine. It will not give you all the answers. Hopefully it will help you make wiser decisions when it comes to buying wines for short- and long-term storage.

S E R V I N G   W I N E

A strong wine overpowers a delicate one. Therefore, do not serve a full-bodied wine before a lighter wine; for example, a Cabernet Sauvignon before a Pinot Noir. Also, do not serve sweet wine before dry; for example, a late-harvest Johannisberg Riesling before a Chardonnay.

As for champagne, it usually does not make a lot of sense to have champagne at the very end of the meal (except in some cases, a sweet champagne that might go well with a sweet dessert). Champagne can, however, accompany the entire meal. At the very beginning of a meal, try serving a champagne that is dry; proceed to a semi-dry, so that one can vary and harmonize the flavor sensations with the changing food; then end up with the sweetest champagne just before dessert.

Red wines should be served at higher temperatures than white wines. Red wines are generally best served at a temperature of 65-70 degrees, but a light red wine might be served at lower temperature.

White wines require chilling before opening. Generally, two hours in the refrigerator is enough. If necessary, you can chill a white wine in the freezer for, say, 20 minutes. It is better to serve it colder rather than warmer because the wine will always warm up after it is poured. As a basic rule, a light white wine should be served colder than a heavier wine. For instance, a rich Chardonnay will taste better at, say, 55 or 60 degrees than at 45 degrees, because as the wine gets warmer, the aromas and flavors develop further. Champagne should be chilled to about 45 degrees Fahrenheit to ensure that the bubbles are released slowly when the bottle is opened and the flavor is retained.

Here are some suggestions for opening a bottle of wine. First, the metal (or plastic) capsule must be removed. I suggest that you cut the foil (which covers the capsule) below the rim of the bottle. Then clean the area around the cork with a wet cloth; this prevents surface material from getting into the wine. To remove the cork, use a corkscrew or a two-pronged cork puller. I happen to prefer the latter. The beauty of the cork puller is that the risk of dropping pieces of cork in the wine is minimal.

If using a cork puller, push the prongs between the cork and the bottle, long prong first, in a downward, rocking motion. Some people lose the cork in the wine because they fail to use a rocking motion when pushing downward. You will have to apply a bit of strength if the cork is very tight. Keep pushing until the prongs are completely inside the bottle. Then remove the cork by pulling upward, in a clockwise or counterclockwise motion.

If using a corkscrew, choose one with the spiral at least two inches long. The spiral should also have a wide diameter (with the space inside the spiral at least big enough for a wooden matchstick to slip through) so that it can grip the cork without causing the cork to disintegrate. A cork with some type of leverage is best, although a direct-pull corkscrew can be satisfactory once you get used to it.

Some experts recommend that after removing the cork you let the wine breathe before serving. The benefits of exposing young wines to oxygen, either by letting the wine breathe in the bottle or by decanting, is being hotly debated. The old school believes that breathing develops bouquet and aroma and lessens the harshness of the young wine, making it more pleasant to drink. Now, a new school is developing, which believes that exposure to air lessens the wine's quality. However, both groups agree that exposure to oxygen can be a death sentence to a mature wine.

Finally, I would like to share some information on opening a bottle of champagne. I am including the instructions for those of you in the food and beverage industry as well as any others who may be interested. The instructions are for a right-handed person. If you are left-handed, the procedures for the left and right hands will be reversed; however, you must always serve with your right hand. If done correctly, opening a champagne bottle is an art form.

1. Remove the foil from the top of the bottle by cutting the foil just below the rim of the bottle and peeling the foil away.

2. Cradle the bottle in your left arm at a 45-degree angle, taking care never to point the bottle at another person. With your left forearm, brace the base of the bottle firmly against your body.

3. Hold the bottle with your right hand as you slide your left hand up the neck of the bottle. Hold the cork firmly with your left thumb and index finger. To get a firm grip on the cork, wrap your thumb and index finger around the side of the cork, angling your thumb so that part of it rests on the top of the cork. This prevents the cork, which is under extreme pressure, from shooting out of the bottle unexpectedly.

4. With your right hand, remove the cage (wire net) that covers the cork. Loosen the cage by turning the wire loop at the base of the cage counter-clockwise (five half-turns); then lift off the cage. As you lift off the cage with your right hand, you will have to release your left-hand grip on the cork momentarily.

5. After lifting off the cage, with your right hand cover the cork with a napkin. The napkin will help you hold down the cork and keep the champagne from spilling or spraying.

6. Firmly grip the napkin and cork with your right thumb and index finger, with the other fingers of your right hand loosely around the upper neck of the bottle. You can now slide your left hand back down the neck of the bottle. Make sure the bottle is still at a 45-degree angle.

7. With your left hand gripping the bottle at the base of the neck and your right thumb and index finger firmly gripping the cork, turn the bottle clockwise with your left hand. The first couple of turns may be difficult because the cork is tightly sealed.

8. After the seal between the cork and bottle is broken, continue turning the bottle clockwise. If the cork feels tight, loosen it by pulling on it slightly with your right hand. If, however, you feel the cork coming out on its own, this means that considerable pressure has built up inside the bottle and you must keep a tight grip on the cork with your right hand.

9. When the cork is almost free of the bottle, release the remaining pressure inside the bottle by momentarily holding the cork at a slight angle.

10. You are now ready to pull out the cork and pour the champagne.

While this is the proper way to open a bottle of champagne, you don't *have* do it this way; there are many variations possible. Some people rest the bottle on a table instead of cradling it in their arm. Some rotate the cork instead of the bottle. Some use a champagne bottle opener. Whatever method you choose, be aware of the pressure inside the bottle and follow the above-mentioned safeguards.

WINE GLASSES

Centuries ago, when glass-blowing was a novelty, glasses were looked upon as an art form. Cups and bowls were the principal shapes, colors and glazes the principal interest. As artisans learned to decorate in colored glass, wine glasses were etched, monogrammed, and enameled. In this period, it was just as well this was the norm; the less the drinker saw of the wine, the better. Now that wines are brilliantly clear, and their eye appeal rivals their taste appeal, clear glass without any surface ornamentation or color is the ideal choice.

The wine glass should be thin and smooth, with polished edges, and tapered slightly inward at the top. The stem should be reasonably long, for holding the wine up to the light. The base should be solid, for setting down the glass. Flared and bell-shaped glasses, which were the predominant shapes for centuries, are now giving way to the tulip shape that curves "in" at the top rather than "out." This allows the fragrance of the wine to gather in the upper part of the bowl.

Adequate size is a relatively new develoqment. About 20 years ago, the wine growers of California designed a 9-ounce glass with a short stem and a tulip-shaped bowl as their choice for the all-purpose wine glass. It seemed large at the time, but now it is smaller than average. A line drawing of this glass appears here. I use a wine glass of similar design and size in all of my wine tastings. This type of glass is widely available in the United States in the more economical grades.

The average size of the wine glasses now used throughout the country is closer to 10 ounces. Increasingly, popular sizes are reaching 14, or even 20, ounces. Two commonly used glasses are the Bordeau glass, which is generally used for white wines (refer to photo on page 23), and the Burgundy balloon, which is used mostly for red wines (refer to photo on page 129.) There is no set size for a drinking glass, and any size will do, provided the glass is clear and has a stem.

No wine glass should ever be filled to the top because this would prevent you from swirling the wine to develop bouquet. I suggest that when pouring the wine you fill the glass no more than half way.

That brings us to the next point—should you use an 8- to 10-ounce all-purpose glass for dinner? I generally do for everyday dinners. Many people understandably choose fine crystal glasses for serving their best wines. If you use crystal, I suggest that you avoid cut crystal, because the elaborate design hides the color of the wine.

When selecting the size of the wine glass, use a larger glass (if there is more than one size) for a red wine. Red wines respond to contact with the air, and give off additional bouquet when served in a larger glass. The richer white wines, such as heavy Chardonnays, also display changing and attractive aromas as they warm up in the glass, and will benefit from being served in a larger glass. Other white wines respond to contact with the air to a lesser extent.

As for champagne glasses, flat, dish-shaped glasses are traditionally used for celebrations. The dish shape shows the bubbles, but also causes the champagne to go flat more quickly. (I often tell the participants in my seminars around the country that it is better to use this type of glass for bread pudding.) I suggest using *flutes,* which are lovely slim, tall glasses. Some flutes have a diamond cut in the hollowed-out stem, which causes the bubbles to rise in a single stream.

Washing wine glasses correctly is very important. For tasting purposes, glasses are always washed in very hot water, then drained on a clean cloth or suspended in a rack to dry. Using a drying cloth may give the glass a hint of unwanted flavor. Many wine connoisseurs never allow detergent to come in contact with their tasting glasses. However, I feel we do not have to go to these extremes. I use a dishwasher for 8- to 10-ounce glasses, and for the more delicate glasses—the large ones—I will use a detergent but take great care that plenty of hot water is used to rinse the glasses thoroughly.

Storing glasses correctly is also very important. Some people store their frequently used glasses suspended above a sink; others store them in a cupboard. I store my glasses in a cupboard with the open side up. Whichever method you choose, make sure that the glasses are not kept near polished wood or foods with strong aromas, because these aromas may be picked up by the glasses. For example, if your shelf is lined with a porous paper and you keep your glasses open side down, the glasses may pick up a chemical smell, which will taint the wine served in those glasses.

Here is a suggestion for longer-term storage of glasses. For our special sets of wine glasses at home, we have discovered plastic-covered boxes, with 12 full-length dividers and lids that zip closed. Glasses can be stored with either end up, and do not pick up unusual odors or collect dust. When guests arrive unexpectedly, it isn't necessary to hastily polish glasses—nor need you be concerned about odors and flavors transmitted to the wines you serve.

WINE LABELS

The Bureau of Alcohol, Tobacco, and Firearms (referred to as "BATF" or "ATF") is a multimission Treasury bureau responsible for carrying out compliance and law-enforcement duties in alcohol, tobacco, firearms, and explosives. As part of its alcohol responsibilities, BATF approves grape wine labels and viticulture areas.

Following are terms commonly found on wine labels and the criteria that must be met before the terms may be used.

Estate Bottled. The winery must own or control 100 percent of the vineyards from which the wine was produced, and this appellation (specifically designated area) must be shown on the label. Further, the wine must be made in one continuous process from fermentation through bottling, at no time leaving the winery premises.

Viticultural Area. At least 85 percent of the grapes used to produce the wine must have been grown within the specified area.

Vintage Dated. At least 95 percent of the wine must have been produced from grapes harvested in the stated year.

Varietal Name. The wine must contain at least 75 percent of the grape variety listed. The label must state an appellation of origin, which indicates where the grapes came from.

Produced and Bottled by. Seventy-five percent of the grapes must be fermented, cellared, and bottled by the listed producer.

Every wine label should have a brand name, which, in most cases, would be the name of the vineyard.

A statement of alcohol content and percent by volume appears on most labels. As an alternative, some bottlers prefer to label wine with an alcohol content between 7 and 14 percent as "table wine" or "light wine."

The label number can be a plus-or-minus 1.5 percent of the alcoholic content in the wine.

Finally, the net contents of the bottle must be printed on the label or blown in the glass.

WHITE WINES

CHARDONNAY

☆☆ ½ **Acacia Winery, 1986 Napa Valley** $12.50

Appealing, medium-intense aromas of spice, apples, and toasty oak. Medium-full bodied. Moderately rich citric fruit on the palate, with ample oak, in perfect balance. Pleasant, lingering finish. Try with baked salmon or turkey with apple-sage dressing.

☆☆ ½ **Acacia Winery, 1987 Napa Valley—Carneros** $16.00

Forward pineapple and honey aromas, with clove and lemon overtones. Medium-full bodied. Slightly viscous and rich on the palate, with the pineapple, spice, and oak flavors in nice balance with the acid. Pleasant finish. Enjoy with sautéed scallops or sea bass with ginger and lemon.

☆☆☆☆ **Acacia Winery, 1986 Napa Valley—Carneros** $15.00

A Chardonnay to age! Forward floral, buttery, and lemony aromas, with toasty oak throughout. Medium-full bodied. The deep Chardonnay fruit flavors are perfectly balanced with oak and acid, in a clean, firm structure. Good aging potential for, say, five more years. Enjoy this superior wine with sautéed scallops, sea bass with ginger and lemon, or chicken with pistachio sauce. Good value.

☆☆☆☆ **Acacia Winery, 1986 Napa Valley—Carneros, Marina Vineyard** $16.50

A great wine! Intense aromas of ripe, appley, and buttery fruit, with floral, herbal, and spicy tones, nicely framed in vanillin oak. Medium-full bodied. Rich, deep fruit on the palate, with citric nuances, and substantial oak, in a harmonious presentation. This superior wine has depth and breadth, and will improve for a number of years. Try with veal or pork roast with rosemary.

☆☆ **Acacia Winery Vin de Lies, 1986 Napa Valley** $9.00

Very appealing aromas of apples and toast, with honey tones. Medium bodied. Moderately deep fruit impression on the palate, with the appley/oaky impressions in perfect balance. Try as an accompaniment to sea bass with ginger and lemon.

Adler Fels, 1986 Sonoma County, Nelson Vineyards $10.00

Forward, appealing ripe varietal fruit and toasty oak aromas, with nutty scents. Medium-full bodied. Deep fruit impression on the palate, with a full oaky dimension. Slightly bitter finish. Try with fowl or veal dishes.

 Alderbrook Winery, 1987 Dry Creek Valley $9.75

Nice aromas of apples and apricots, with toasty oak tones. Medium bodied. Generous sweetish fruit on the palate, with nice oak in support. Fruity finish. Fine with moderately seasoned poultry dishes. Can also be enjoyed on its own.

 Alderbrook Winery, 1986 Dry Creek Valley $9.25

Golden yellow color. Moderately intense appley fruit in the nose, joined by creamy oak. Medium-full bodied. Ripe, rich, fleshy fruit on the palate, with tropical fruit nuances, and a nice touch of sweet oak. Lingering finish. Try as an accompaniment to sea bass with ginger and lemon. Good value.

 Alexander Valley Vineyards, Wetzel Family Estate, 1987 Alexander Valley $11.00

Brilliant. Nice straw color. Moderately intense appley fruit in the nose, with vanillin scents. Medium bodied. Medium-intense melon and banana flavors on the palate, with a touch of spice. Slightly tart finish. Fine with moderately seasoned fish dishes.

 Alexander Valley Vineyards, Wetzel Family Estate, 1986 Alexander Valley $11.00

Nice floral and lemony aromas, with scents of juniper berries and spice. Medium bodied. Moderately intense citrusy and oaky fruit flavors on the palate, in a good structure. Sharp finish. Try with grilled sea bass or sautéed scallops.

 Amity Vineyards, Estate Bottled, 1986 Willamette, Oregon $15.00

Bright. Light gold color. Appealing sweetish apple and melon aromas, with vanillin scents. Medium bodied. Ripe appley fruit flavors on the palate, with moderate oak and acid. Smooth finish. Try as an accompaniment to chicken breasts in a cream sauce.

☆☆ **S. Anderson Vineyard, 1986 Napa Valley** $16.00

Appealing sweetish appley fruit in the nose, with oaky overtones. Medium bodied. Attractive fresh apple and grapefruit flavors on the palate, with ample acid and oak, in a good structure. Tart finish. Try with Rex sole or sand dabs.

☆☆½ **S. Anderson Vineyard, 1985 Napa Valley** $14.00

Appealing ripe apricots and apples in the nose, with citric scents, and a nice oaky dimension. Medium-full bodied. Moderately intense appley and lemony fruit flavors on the palate, with ample oak and acid. Sharp finish. Best with rich seafood or poultry dishes.

☆☆ **Beaulieu Vineyard Beaufort, 1986 Napa Valley** $9.50

Medium intense appley aromas, with melony and herbal scents. Medium bodied. Moderate appley fruit flavors on the palate, with citric nuances, in a clean presentation. Enjoy with filet of sole meuniere.

☆☆½ **Beaulieu Vineyard Beaufort, 1985 Napa Valley** $10.00

Light yellow color. Brilliant. Moderately intense aromas of nutmeg and oak. Medium-full bodied. Rich, properly focused varietal fruit on the palate, with oak and acid in perfect balance. Enjoy with moderately seasoned white meats.

☆☆½ **Beaulieu Vineyard Reserve, 1986 Los Carneros** $11.00

Appealing, moderately intense floral and appley aromas, with buttery and oaky scents. Medium-full bodied. Supple in the mouth, with generous appley fruit flavors, and a nice dimension of toasty oak through the finish. Try with sautéed scallops or chicken with pistachio sauce.

☆☆ **Belvedere Winery, 1986 Carneros** $12.00

Moderately intense appley and peachy aromas, with floral and spicy tones. Medium bodied. Nice appley fruit on the palate, with spicy oak and citrusy nuances, in a good structure. Crisp finish. Try with petrale sole.

☆☆½ **Beringer Private Reserve, 1985 Napa Valley** $14.00

Complex floral and fruit aromas, with a nice dimension of toasty oak. Medium-full bodied. Moderately intense appley fruit in the mouth, with butterscotch nuances, and ample oak. Finishes a bit astringent. Try with chicken in a light sauce or veal piccata.

Beringer Vineyards, 1986 Napa Valley $10.50

Very attractive appley, floral, and spicy aromas with butterscotch scents, and a nice dimension of sweet oak throughout. Medium-full bodied. Quite big on the palate, with the generous toasty fruit flavors balanced with an ample citric dimension. Try with rich seafood dishes and chicken.

Bonny Doon Vineyard, 1987 Monterey County, La Reina Vineyard $15.00

Very attractive appley and lemony aromas, with earthy tones. Medium-full bodied, complex flavors of apples, nectarines, and lemons, perfectly balanced, in a good structure. Finishes a bit tart. Give this wine a year or so for the parts to further integrate, then enjoy with well-seasoned poultry or seafood dishes.

Bonny Doon Vineyard, 1986 Monterey County, La Reina Vineyard $14.00

Appealing spicy, oaky, lemony, and appley aromas. Medium bodied. Generous appley and oaky flavors on the palate, with a fair lemony dimension into the finish. Slightly bitter finish. Best with well-seasoned fish dishes.

Bonny Doon Vineyard, 1985 Monterey County, La Reina Vineyard $13.00

Forward lemony Chardonnay aromas, with toasty oak and cinnamon scents in support. Medium-full bodied. Slightly rich and buttery fruit flavors in the mouth, with a nice citric dimension, and an oaky finish. Good depth. Try with sea bass and lemon, chicken with pistachio sauce, or pork roast with rosemary.

Bouchaine, 1986 Napa Valley $13.50

Attractive appley and toasty oak aromas. Medium-full bodied. Generous appley fruit and toasty oak flavors on the palate, with lots of acid. This is an excellent wine that needs a couple of years to smooth out. Enjoy with lobster Newberg, swordfish, or grilled salmon.

Bouchaine, 1985 Napa Valley $13.50

Forward pineappley aromas, with nice toasty oak. Loads of rich fruit fill the mouth, with acid and oak in perfect balance. A very fine wine for current consumption with broiled fish or chicken in a light sauce.

☆☆☆ ***Buena Vista Private Reserve, 1986 Carneros*** $16.50

Very attractive, medium-intense appley fruit and sweet oak in the nose. Medium-full bodied. Deep fruit impression on the palate, with the rich fruit flavors perfectly balanced with acid and oak. Clean, lingering finish. Several years of improvement can be expected. Try this superior wine with rich seafood or poultry dishes.

☆☆½ ***Buena Vista Private Reserve, 1985 Carneros*** $14.50

Appealing appley, floral, and oaky aromas. Medium bodied. The fruit flavors are deep and well-focused on the palate, with oak and acid in good balance. Finishes a bit sharp. Try with cracked crab or sea bass with ginger and lemon.

☆☆ ***Buena Vista Winery, 1987 Carneros*** $10.00

Appealing appley fruit in the nose, with pears, flowers, and citrus in the background. Medium bodied. Nicely focused, clean fruit on the palate, in a firm structure. Crispy finish. Try with sautéed petrale sole or scallops.

☆☆ ***Buena Vista Winery, 1986 Carneros*** $10.00

Moderately intense herbal fruit in the nose. Medium bodied. Modest pineappley fruit in the mouth, with a fair acid dimension. Sharp finish. Best with well-seasoned fish dishes.

☆☆½ ***Buena Vista Winery, 1985 Carneros*** $10.75

Ripe appley fruit aromas, with butterscotch and toasty oak overtones. Medium-bodied. Clean lemony fruit on the palate, with good structure. The finish is a bit sharp. Try as an accompaniment to sea bass with ginger and lemon.

☆☆☆ ***Burgess Cellars, 1986 Napa Valley, Triere Vineyard*** $14.00

Beautiful, forward appley fruit and toasty oak in the nose, with lemony scents. Medium-full bodied. Loads of ripe fruit and oak on the palate, in a firm structure. Crispy finish. This is a Chardonnay with aging potential; say, five more years of improvement. Just enjoy!

☆☆½ ***Burgess Vintage Reserve, 1985 Napa Valley*** $13.00

Attractive medium gold color. Complex, buttery, appley, and spicy aromas, with a fair dimension of rich oak. Medium-full bodied. The fruit flavors are firm and deep on the palate. The finish is long and a bit sharp. Best with rich seafood dishes.

Davis Bynum Reserve Bottling, 1985 Sonoma County **$10.00**

Appealing apple and floral aromas. Medium bodied. Nice fruit flavors in the mouth upon entry, with a slightly bitter dimension. Finishes tart. Fine with fish dishes.

 ### Byron Vineyard, 1985 Central Coast **$9.00**

Pleasant tropical fruit aromas, with vanillin oak overtones. Medium-full bodied. Ripe, slightly fat, lemony fruit in the mouth, with ample acid. Mildly tart finish. Best with well-seasoned fish dishes.

 ### Byron Vineyard Reserve, 1985 Santa Barbara County **$13.00**

Medium-intense appley and buttery aromas, with nice oak in support. Medium-full bodied. Nice toasty and lemony flavors on the palate, in a good structure. Fine with well-seasoned fish dishes.

 ### Cain Cellars, 1986 Napa Valley **$10.00**

Attractive, medium-intense appley, floral and spicy aromas, nicely supported by sweet oak. Medium-full bodied. Appealing applelike flavors on the palate, with moderate oak, and a citric dimension through the finish. Try with sauteeed scallops or sea bass with ginger and lemon. Good value.

 ### Cain Cellars, 1985 Napa/Sonoma, 36% Napa County, 64% Sonoma County **$10.00**

Light yellow color. Pleasant pearlike fruit aromas, with citric and vanillin oak scents. Medium-bodied. Moderately intense appley and lemony flavors on the palate, with a touch of oak. Finishes sharp. Best with moderately seasoned fish dishes.

 ### Cakebread Cellars, 1986 Napa Valley **$18.50**

Medium-intense appley, citrusy, spicy, and oaky aromas. Medium bodied. Generous ripe fruit and oak on the palate, with a fair lemony dimension throughout. Crisp finish. This is a well-made Chardonnay that is enjoyable now, and will improve for a couple of years. Try as an accompaniment to grilled salmon with mustard sauce.

 ### Calera, 1985 Santa Barbara County **$11.75**

Attractive, intense ripe appley fruit aromas, with butterscotch scents, and a full dimension of toasty oak. Medium-full bodied. Buttery flavors on the palate, and nice acid for balance. Fine as accompaniment to sautéed chicken breast with cream or veal roast with rosemary.

☆☆ *Callaway, Calla-lees, 1987 Temecula* $9.75

Medium intense appley and pineappley aromas, with floral and herbal scents. Medium bodied. Attractive melony fruit on the palate, with citric nuances, in a firm structure. Sharp finish. Try with filet of sole meuniere or light luncheon foods.

☆☆ *Carneros Creek Winery, 1987 Los Carneros* $12.50

Forward buttery and toasty oak aromas, with floral and pearlike scents. Medium-full bodied. Generous fruit on the palate, with ample oak and acid. Tart finish. Try with cracked crab or stuffed clams.

☆☆ *Carneros Creek Winery, 1986 Los Carneros* $13.00

Medium-intense appley fruit in the nose, with caramel scents, and ample oak in support. Medium bodied. Generous oak-enriched fruit in the mouth, with nutty nuances. Slightly bitter finish. Try with fowl or veal dishes.

☆☆ ½ *Carneros Creek Winery, 1985 Los Carneros* $10.50

Moderately intense green apple fruit, with citrusy and pineappley scents, framed in sweet oak. Medium-full bodied. Generous fruit and oak on the palate, with a substantial acidic dimension into the finish. Fine with cracked crab.

☆☆ *Carneros Creek Winery, 1984 Los Carneros* $10.50

Pleasant appley and lemony aromas, with ample oak in support. Medium-bodied. Moderate toasty Chardonnay fruit, with lemony nuances. Finishes slightly hot. Best with well-seasoned fish dishes.

☆☆ *Caymus Vineyards, 1985 Napa Valley* $12.00

Attractive floral and appley aromas, with hints of apricots and pineapples. Medium bodied. Medium intense fleshy fruit on the palate, with spicy nuances, and acid in balance. Tart finish. Fine with moderately seasoned fish dishes or chicken in a light sauce.

☆☆ *Chalk Hill Winery, 1987 Sonoma County* $8.00

Light gold color. Pleasant tropical fruit and buttery aromas, with toasty oak tones. Medium bodied. Creamy texture, with nice toasty fruit flavors on the palate, and a touch of lemon in the finish. Pleasant, lingering aftertaste. Best with moderately seasoned fish dishes. Good value.

Chalk Hill Winery, 1986 Sonoma County
 $7.00

Appealing, delicate fruit aromas, and nice oak in support. Medium bodied. Modest citric flavors in the mouth, with a slight bitterness in the finish. Best with moderately seasoned fish dishes.

 ### Chalk Hill Winery, 1985 Sonoma County
 $8.00

Forward appley, herbal, and lemony aromas. Medium-full bodied. Assertive varietal flavors, with a buttery character, and nice oak. Lingering aftertaste. Fine with shellfish or moderately seasoned chicken dishes. Excellent value.

 ### Chalone Vineyard, 1987 Chalone
 $22.00

Complex aromas of pears, butterscotch, and lemons, with nice toasty oak in support. Medium-full bodied. The fruit flavors are beautifully integrated on the palate, in an elegant presentation. Excellent potential. Suggest consuming beginning in 1992 for optimum enjoyment.

 ### Chalone Vineyard, 1986 Chalone
 $22.00

Abundant oak in the nose, with weedy and musty scents. Medium-full bodied. Big and full on the palate, with the herbal fruit dominated by the oak. Harsh finish. This is a powerful wine that requires highly seasoned dishes.

 ### Chateau Montelena, 1986 Alexander Valley
 $18.00

Golden yellow color. Medium-intense aromas of apples, pears, ripe tropical fruit, and toasty oak. Medium-full bodied. Rounded feel in the mouth, with the ripe fruit and attractive oak in perfect balance. Excellent for current consumption, and will improve for a few years. Try with stuffed clams, sautéed chicken breast with cream, or lobster Newburg.

 ### Chateau Montelena, 1985 Alexander Valley
 $16.00

This is a classic! Wonderfully proportioned aromas of fresh appley, lemony, and spicy fruit, with floral, buttery, and creamy oak overtones. Medium-full bodied. Youthful rich flavors of apples and lemons fill the mouth, with tropical nuances, and just the right proportion of oak. This superb wine can accompany grilled salmon with mustard sauce, lobster Newburg, or veal roast with rosemary.

☆☆☆ **Chateau Montelena, 1986 Napa Valley** $18.00

Forward, attractive, nicely focused varietal fruit and oak in the nose. Medium-full bodied. Generous rich fruit and ample oak flavors on the palate, with lemony elements, in a firm structure. Sharp finish. Fine with cracked crab, swordfish, or frogs' legs.

☆☆☆ **Chateau Montelena, 1985 Napa Valley** $18.00

Moderately intense appley fruit and toasty oak aromas. Medium-full bodied. Rich, concentrated lemony fruit gives a deep palate impression, with ample acid for structure. Tart finish. Needs a couple of years to open up. Be patient, then try with baked salmon, broiled abalone, or monkfish in parchment with vegetables.

☆☆ **Chateau Potelle, 1986 Napa Valley** $13.00

Attractive, medium-intense appley fruit and toasty oak in the nose, with citrusy scents. Medium bodied. Round on entry, with the moderate fruit and oak in balance, in a clean presentation. Crispy finish. Try with filet of sole meuniere.

☆☆ **Chateau Potelle, 1985 Napa Valley** $11.50

Light yellow color. Medium-intense appley and oaky aromas. Medium-full bodied. Round on entry, with moderate juicy fruit, and ample oak. Finishes tart. Fine with well-seasoned fish dishes.

☆☆ ½ **Chateau St. Jean, 1985 Alexander Valley, Belle Terre Vineyard** $16.00

Moderately intense appley and toasty oak aromas, with hints of tropical fruit and peaches. Medium-full bodied. Ripe, buttery fruit on the palate, with lemony nuances, and abundant oak. Slightly harsh finish. Try with rich seafood dishes.

☆☆ ½ **Chateau St. Jean, 1985 Alexander Valley, Robert Young Vineyards** $18.50

Attractive appley, floral, spicy, and toasty aromas. Medium-full bodied. Rich, fleshy tropical fruit flavors on the palate, with lemony nuances, and sweet oak in balance. This is a delicious wine on its own. Also try with white meats in a light sauce.

☆☆ **Chateau St. Jean, 1986 Sonoma County** $11.00

Moderately intense melony and appley aromas. Medium bodied. Lean fruit on the palate, with a citrusy dimension. Tart finish. Try with Rex sole.

Chateau St. Jean, 1985 Sonoma County **_$10.00_**

Light yellow color. Moderately intense lemon and pear aromas, with hints of apricots. Medium-full bodied. Clean, lively, citric flavors in the mouth, with nice oak in balance. Finishes tart. A fine wine for current consumption. Enjoy with a wide range of fish dishes.

 Chateau Ste. Michelle, 1986 Washington **_$11.00_**

Green-gold color. Forward aromas of fresh apples and pears, with floral and oaky scents. Medium bodied. Creamy texture, with the moderately intense appley fruit and spicy oak flavors nicely balanced with acid, in a firm presentation. Long finish. Try with baked salmon or sautéed Pacific scallops.

 Chateau Ste. Michelle Limited Bottling, **_$13.00_**
1986 Cold Creek Vineyard, Washington

Beautiful honeyed apple aromas, with perfumed vanilla tones. Medium bodied, with generous fruit on the palate, in a firm structure. Finishes clean and crisp. Try with petrale sole or sand dabs.

 Chateau Souverain, 1986 Sonoma County **_$8.00_**

Appealing, medium-intense floral and pineappley fruit aromas. Medium bodied. Moderate fruity and oaky flavors on the palate, with minimum acid. Finishes slightly flat. Will go well with moderately seasoned fish dishes.

 Chateau Souverain, 1985 Sonoma County **_$8.50_**

Medium-intense, attractive aromas of flowers, nutmeg, and oak. Medium-light bodied. Moderate appley fruit flavors on the palate, with melony and herbal nuances, and a touch of oak. This is a well-made wine that can accompany moderately seasoned fish dishes.

 Chateau Souverain Reserve, **_$12.00_**
1986 Carneros—Sonoma County

Attractive appley, floral, and buttery aromas, with apricoty and pineappley scents, nicely supported by sweet oak. Medium-full bodied. Rich tropical fruit flavors on the palate, with citric nuances, in a soft structure. Well made. Fruity finish. Very enjoyable on its own or with light luncheon dishes.

Chestnut Hill, 1986 Sonoma County
 $8.50

Medium-intense aromas of nicely focused varietal fruit and vanillin oak. Medium bodied. Generous ripe fruit on the palate, with rich oak, and ample acid for structure. Fine with a wide range of fish dishes.

Chimney Rock Wine Cellars, 1986 Napa Valley
 $14.00

Appealing green apple aromas with oaky overtones. Medium bodied. Nice appley fruit on the palate, with good oak and acid, in a firm structure. Tart finish. A well-made wine that will go well with oysters on the half-shell.

The Christian Brothers, 1985 Napa Valley
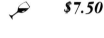 **$7.50**

Medium-intense aromas of green apples, with buttery and vanillin scents. Medium bodied. Moderate, clean fruit flavors on the palate. Crispy finish. Fine with most moderately seasoned fish dishes.

The Christian Brothers Private Reserve, Barrel Fermented, 1986 Napa Valley, Oak Knoll Ranch
 **$12.00**

Moderately intense, nicely focused varietal fruit in the nose, with spicy oak in support. The fruit on the palate is generous and clean, with spicy oak elements in good balance. Fruity finish. Try this well-made wine with moderately seasoned light meats, seafood, or poultry.

Christophe Vineyards, 1987 California
 **$6.50**

Attractive, medium-intense aromas of appley fruit and sweet oak. Medium-full bodied. Good fruit depth on the palate, with nice oak, and ample acid. Crispy finish. Enjoy with a wide range of fish dishes. Good value.

Christophe Vineyards, 1986 California
 **$6.00**

Light gold color. Moderately intense aromas of green apples, with lemony scents. Medium bodied. Modest, but appealing, Chardonnay fruit flavors, with acid and oak in balance, in a clean presentation. This is an easy-drinking wine that will go well with light luncheon foods. Good value.

Clos du Bois Barrel Fermented, 1987 Alexander Valley
$11.00

Appealing apple and butterscotch aromas, with vanillin oak tones. Medium bodied. Attractive green apple and vanillin oak flavors on the palate, in a clean, well-balanced presentation. Enjoy with well-seasoned fish dishes, chicken, or veal piccata.

Clos du Bois Barrel Fermented, 1986 Alexander Valley

$10.00

Moderately intense herbal, butterscotch, and citric aromas, with a nice touch of oak. Medium bodied. The aromas follow into the flavor in a clean, well-balanced presentation. Try with cracked crab or lobster. Good value.

 ### Clos du Bois Calcaire, 1987 Alexander Valley

$16.00

Most appealing appley, buttery, and sweet oak aromas. Medium bodied. Rich and complex flavors of pineapples, honey, and peaches, with nice buttery oak in support. Finishes long and smooth. Will improve for several years. Enjoy with well-seasoned fish dishes or moderately seasoned white meats.

 ### Clos du Bois Calcaire, 1986 Alexander Valley

$16.00

Very attractive, moderately intense bright green apple aromas, with scents of flowers, butterscotch, and tasty oak. Medium-full bodied. Slightly viscous on the palate, with loads of lemony fruit flavors and buttery nuances. Slightly tart finish. Another superior bottling, consistent with prior vintages. Fine with shellfish or whatever suits your fancy. Just enjoy!

 ### Clos du Val, 1986, Carneros—Napa Valley

$12.00

Pleasant, medium-intense, nicely focused appley fruit in the nose, with oak in full support. Medium-full bodied. Moderately intense appley fruit flavors in the mouth, with citric nuances, and ample oak. Slightly harsh finish. Best with rich seafood or fowl dishes.

 ### Clos du Val, 1985 Napa Valley

$11.50

Medium-intense, distinct Chardonnay aromas, with hints of pineapple, and a touch of oak. Medium bodied. Smooth entry in the mouth, with nice lemony fruit and oak. Long, crisp finish. Try this very fine wine with Rex sole or petrale.

 ### Clos Pegase, 1985 Alexander Valley

$12.00

Moderately intense aromas of apples and toasty oak. Medium bodied. Well-defined fruit character of moderate intensity on the palate, with some toasty oak. Slightly sharp finish. Fine with lightly seasoned orange roughy.

 ### Clos Pegase, 1986 Los Carneros

$15.00

Appealing sweetish fruit and creamy oak in the nose, with floral and herbal scents. Medium-full bodied. Generous juicy fruit on the palate, nicely balanced with acid. Long, flavorful finish. Try with sautéed chicken breast or pork roast with yams.

B. R. Cohn Winery, 1986 Sonoma Valley, Olive Hill Vineyard **$12.00**

Moderately intense appley and buttery aromas, joined by ample spicy oak scents. Medium bodied. Ripe and round in the mouth, with the medium-deep fruit flavors and oak in good balance. Slightly bitter aftertaste. Try this fine wine as an accompaniment to mousseline of crab with chives, wrapped in Pacific sole.

 Columbia Crest Vineyards, 1986 Columbia Valley, Washington **$8.00**

Very attractive appley and floral nose. Medium bodied. The fresh appley fruit dominates the taste, with sufficient acid for structure. Try this very pleasant wine with moderately seasoned fish dishes or chicken in a light sauce. Good value.

 Concannon Selected Vineyards, 1986 California **$8.00**

Very appealing appley fruit and creamy oak aromas. Medium-full bodied. Lush feel in the mouth, with the buttery fruit and oak flavors in nice balance, in a good structure. Enjoy with well-seasoned shellfish or poultry. Good value.

Congress Springs Reserve, Barrel Fermented, 1986 Santa Clara County, San Ysidro Vineyard **$15.00**

Beautiful aromas of rich, ripe appley fruit, honey, pineapples, and toasty oak. Medium-full bodied. Fleshy fruit flavors and a full oaky dimension fill the mouth. This is a big wine that will improve for a number of years. Enjoy with rich seafood or poultry dishes.

 Congress Springs Vineyards, 1987 Santa Clara County **$12.00**

Medium-intense appley, buttery, and toasty aromas. Medium-full bodied. Nectarinelike fruit on the palate, with nutty nuances, and abundant oak and acid. Tart finish. Try with grilled swordfish steak.

 Congress Springs Vineyards, 1986 Santa Clara County **$11.00**

Forward aromas of ripe appley fruit and toasty oak, with hints of grapefruit and herbs. Medium-full bodied. The wine is round at entry, with generous fruit flavors, and ample oak and acid. Finishes a bit harsh. Try with well-seasoned pork or veal dishes.

 Cosentino, The Sculptor, 1986 Napa Valley **$17.00**

Appealing appley, floral, toasty, and lemony aromas. Medium bodied. Generous lemony fruit flavors on the palate, with oak in balance, in a firm structure. Tart finish. Try with baked sea bass.

Cronin Vineyards, 1986 Alexander Valley **$14.50**

Beautiful aromas of apples, pineapples, and melons, with a full dimension of toasty oak in support. Medium bodied. Generous appley fruit on the palate, with abundant oak through the finish. Slightly coarse in the finish. This wine will improve for a number of years. Fine with rich seafood or fowl dishes. Very limited availability.

 Cronin Vineyards, 1986 Monterey County, Ventana Vineyards **$14.50**

Very intense ripe fruit, butterscotch, and toasty oak in the nose. Full bodied. Rich and viscous in the mouth, with bold fruit and oak flavors. This is a big wine that will improve for a few years. Try with well-seasoned fowl or veal dishes.

 Cronin Vineyards, 1986 Napa Valley **$14.50**

Lots of toasty oak and ripe apples in the nose, with smoky scents. Medium-full bodied. Very attractive rich Chardonnay fruit flavors on the palate, with ample oak and acid, in a firm structure. Fine as an accompaniment to tenderloin of pork with mustard sage sauce or turkey with sage dressing.

 Crystal Creek Proprietor's Reserve, 1986 Monterey County **$4.50**

Medium intense appley and buttery aromas, with artichoke scents. Medium bodied. Moderate appley fruit on the palate, with a citric dimension through the finish. Fine as an apéritif or with light luncheon dishes. Good value.

 Cuvaison, 1987 Napa Valley **$13.50**

Very appealing apple and peach aromas, with toasty oak overtones. Medium bodied. Generous, clean fruit in the mouth, with oak and acid in balance, in a firm structure. Tart finish. A well-made wine that needs a little time for the parts to come together. Try with grilled salmon or Cornish hen with herbs and wild rice.

 Cuvaison, 1986 Napa Valley **$13.00**

Moderately intense green apple aromas, with nice oak in support. Medium bodied. Crisp, clean fruit on the palate, with good depth. An excellent wine for current consumption with baked sea bass or sautéed chicken breasts with cream.

Cuvaison, 1985 Napa Valley

 $13.00

A big winner! Forward, deep appley fruit aromas, nicely complemented with buttery and citrusy scents, and framed in creamy oak. Medium-full bodied. Generous appley/oaky fruit in the mouth, with lively acid, in perfect balance. Pleasant, lingering aftertaste. Try this superior wine as an accompaniment to grilled salmon with mustard sauce, veal or pork roast with rosemary, or turkey with apple-sage dressing. Excellent value.

De Loach Vineyards, 1987 Russian River Valley

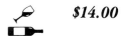 $14.00

Forward appley, spicy, toasty, and oak aromas, with hints of tropical fruit. Medium-full bodied. Lush on the palate, with the ripe fruit and toasty oak in nice balance with acid. Lemony and oaky finish. Try this superior wine with baked sea bass, chicken with pistachio sauce, or pork roast with yams.

De Loach Vineyards, 1986 Russian River Valley

 $14.00

Assertive ripe apple aromas, with butterscotch and pineapple scents, framed in a nice dimension of toasty oak. Medium-full bodied. Ripe, appley fruit flavors in the mouth, with citric nuances, and ample sweet oak in the presentation. Long, fruity finish. Try with veal or pork roast with rosemary.

De Loach Vineyards OFS, 1986 Russian River Valley

$20.00

Assertive ripe fruit aromas, with butterscotch scents, framed in creamy oak. Medium-full bodied. Fleshy, expansive, viscous feel in the mouth, with the tropical fruit flavors in nice balance with oak. A rich wine that will go well with chicken in a flavorful cream sauce.

De Moor Winery, 1985 Napa Valley

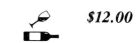 $12.00

Moderate buttery and toasty aromas. Medium-full bodied. Rich appley fruit flavors in the mouth, with lemony nuances, and ample oak. Pleasant lingering aftertaste. Best with rich seafood or poultry.

Dehlinger Winery, 1987 Russian River Valley

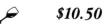 $10.50

Nice pineapple, fig, and honey aromas, with toasty oak scents. Medium-full bodied. Beautifully layered fruit on the palate, with ample buttery oak, in a firm structure. This excellent wine will improve for several years. Excellent value.

☆☆½   *Dehlinger Winery, 1986 Russian River Valley*   **$11.00**

Attractive green apple aromas, with nice toasty oak in support. Medium-full bodied. Medium-deep Chardonnay fruit flavors on the palate, with citric nuances and ample oak, in a firm structure. Will improve for a few years. Try with swordfish steak or sautéed chicken breasts.

☆☆☆   *Dehlinger Winery, 1985 Russian River Valley*   **$10.00**

Elegant aromas of toasty oak and pineapples. Medium-full bodied. Generous juicy fruit flavors, with citric nuances, and ample oak, in a firm presentation. Clean, crisp finish. Has good aging potential. Try as an accompaniment to sea bass with ginger and lemon, grilled salmon with mustard sauce, or chicken with pistachio sauce. Excellent value.

☆☆   *Devlin Wine Cellars, 1986 Monterey County, La Reina Vineyard*   **$8.00**

Lots of ripe apples, toast and spice in the nose. Medium-full bodied. Fat on entry, with the broad fruit flavors dominated by oak through the finish. Best with fowl and veal dishes. Good value.

☆☆½   *Domaine Laurier, 1986 Sonoma County*   **$13.50**

Very appealing aromas of apples and pears. Medium bodied. Fresh fruit flavors follow directly from the aromas, with a nice dimension of lemon, in a clean presentation. Crisp finish. Try with Rex or petrale sole.

☆☆   *Domaine Laurier, 1985 Sonoma County*   **$13.00**

Restrained green apple aromas, with herbal and melony scents. Medium-full bodied. Moderately intense appley and lemony flavors on the palate, with a slight toasty character, in a firm structure. Enjoy with baked snapper.

☆☆   *Domaine Potelle, 1986 California*   **$6.00**

Appealing, clean, pineappley fruit in the nose, with a touch of oak. Medium bodied. Moderately intense appley fruit flavors, with moderate oak and acid, in good balance. Fine with a wide range of fish dishes. Good value.

☆   *Domaine St. George, 1986 Sonoma County*   **$4.50**

Light yellow color. Moderate herbal fruit in the nose, but not distinctly varietal. Medium bodied. Low intensity fruit flavors, with acid in balance, in a clean presentation. Fine with moderately seasoned fish dishes. Good value.

★★ ½ **Dry Creek Vineyard, 1986 Sonoma County** $10.00

Moderately intense, nicely focused Chardonnay fruit in the nose, with spicy, herbal, and oaky scents. Medium bodied. Medium-deep appley fruit flavors in the mouth, perfectly balanced with oak and acid. Pleasant, long finish. Try with sautéed scallops.

★★ **Dry Creek Vineyard, 1985 Sonoma County** $10.00

Pleasant blossomy fruit aromas, with toasty and buttery scents, and creamy oak in the background. Medium-bodied. Moderately deep appley fruit on the palate, with buttery elements and a citric dimension. Crisp finish. Enjoy with rich seafood.

★★ ½ **Edna Valley Vineyard, 1986 San Luis Obispo** $12.00

Forward toasty oak and butterscotch aromas. Medium-full bodied. Nipe ripe fruit in the mouth, with ample acid and oak. The wine is rich, and will best accompany highly seasoned fish dishes or poultry.

★★ **Estancia, 1986 Alexander Valley** $6.50

Medium-intense appley, floral, lemony, and herbal aromas. Medium bodied. Moderate fruit flavors on the palate, with a pronounced citric dimension, and modest oak. Crisp finish. Fine with a wide range of fish dishes. Good value.

★★ **The Eyrie Vineyards, 1986 Yamhill County, Willamette Valley, Oregon** $15.00

Forward ripe Chardonnay fruit and toasty oak in the nose. Medium-full bodied. Full and round on entry, with the rich fruit and oak flavors in nice balance, in a good structure. Try with rich seafood and fowl dishes.

★★★ **Far Niente Winery, 1987 Napa Valley** $26.00

Appealing pineapple and butterscotch aromas, with toasty oak tones. Medium bodied. Complex flavors of pineapple, grapefruit, honey, and spice on the palate, with ample vanillin oak. Crisp, long finish. Give this superior wine a couple of years for further improvement, then enjoy.

★★ **Far Niente Winery, 1986 Napa Valley** $22.00

Moderately intense ripe melony fruit aromas, with spicy and earthy scents, and oaky overtones. Medium bodied. Generous varietal fruit in the mouth, with citrusy nuances, and oak in a firm structure. Slightly tart in the finish. Fine with cracked crab or grilled salmon.

Gary Farrell, 1985 Sonoma County

 $11.00

Light golden yellow color. Moderately intense appley fruit aromas, with spicy and oaky scents. Medium-bodied. Slightly rich appley flavors on the palate, with spicy nuances, and oak in balance. Finishes crisp. Enjoy this fine wine with rich seafood dishes.

Ferrari-Carano Winery, 1986 Alexander Valley

$14.00

Beautiful, intense, rich Chardonnay fruit and toasty oak in the nose, with lemony tones. Medium-full bodied. Loads of ripe fruit and rich oak fill the mouth, with a citrusy dimension, in a lively structure. Try this superior wine with Cornish game hen or salmon in parchment with vegetables and tarragon.

Ferrari-Carano Winery, 1985 Alexander Valley

$13.00

Very attractive, complex aromas of apples, spice, lemons, and sweet oak. Medium-full bodied. Smooth and supple in the mouth, with the rich, lemony fruit flavors in perfect balance with the oak. A superior product from this new winery. Just enjoy.

Fetzer Barrel Select, 1985 California

$8.50

Very attractive appley, melony, and floral aromas, with a nice touch of toasty oak. Medium-bodied. Juicy tropical fruit flavors in the mouth, with lemony nuances. Fine with moderately seasoned fish dishes.

Fetzer Barrel Select, 1986 Mendocino

$8.50

Very appealing, medium-intense, perfumed aromas of lemons, pineapples, and peaches, with hints of nutmeg and nice sweet oak throughout. Medium bodied. Soft and supple in the mouth, with tasty delicate fruit through the finish. Fine with moderately seasoned fish dishes. Good value.

Fetzer Special Reserve, 1985 California

$12.00

Ripe, rich, buttery fruit in the nose, with herbal and lemony scents, and nice toasty oak in support. Medium-full bodied. The wine is fleshy and round in the mouth, with generous honeyed fruit and ample oak. Slightly harsh finish. Fine with sautéed chicken or sea bass with ginger and lemons.

Fetzer Special Reserve, 1986 Mendocino County

$14.00

Most attractive, intense ripe appley fruit and toasty oak aromas, with floral and spicy tones. Medium bodied. Round and full in the mouth, with the juicy fruit and rich oak balanced in a soft structure. A wonderful wine for current consumption. Try as an accompaniment to sautéed chicken breast with cream or baked sea bass.

★★ *Fetzer Sundial, 1986 California* $6.50

Moderate aromas of pears and melons. Medium bodied. The fruit flavors are soft and medium, in a clean presentation. A fine wine for early consumption with a wide range of fish dishes. Good value.

★★ *The Firestone Vineyard, Tenth Anniversary Bottling, 1985 Santa Ynez Valley* $10.00

Forward ripe varietal fruit in the nose, with floral, buttery, and oaky overtones. Medium bodied. Somewhat viscous on the palate, with the moderately deep fruit and oak flavors in balance, with ample acid through the finish. Try with baked halibut or chicken in a cream sauce.

★★½ *Fisher Coach Insignia, 1986 Sonoma County* $17.00

Appealing, medium-intense appley fruit and creamy oak in the nose, with herbal and lemony tones. Medium-full bodied. Loads of concentrated tropical fruit flavors fill the mouth, with a nice dimension of handsome oak, in a good structure. Best with rich seafood or fowl dishes.

★★½ *Fisher Coach Insignia, 1985 Sonoma County* $16.00

Attractive toasty, appley, fruit aromas, with citric scents. Medium-full bodied. The wine is rounded on the palate, with the rich appley and lemony fruit flavors in nice balance with the ample oak. Slightly tart finish. Fine as an accompaniment to turkey with sage dressing or stuffed lobster.

★★ *Fisher Vineyards, 1986 Napa/Sonoma* $11.00

Moderately intense ripe varietal fruit and sweet oak in the nose. Medium-full bodied. The moderately intense ripe fruit flavors and oak are in balance, in a firm presentation. Best with well-seasoned fish dishes.

★★½ *Flora Springs, 1986 Napa Valley* $14.00

Forward aromas of ripe apples and oak, with floral and butterscotch scents. Medium-full bodied. Round and full in the mouth, with the buttery fruit and rich oak in nice balance. Pleasant, lingering finish. Try with sautéed scallops or chicken breast with a pistachio sauce.

★★½ *Flora Springs, 1985 Napa Valley* $14.00

Attractive golden color. Pleasant varietal fruit and toasty oak in the nose. Medium-full bodied. Generous, buttery, young fruit on the palate, nicely balanced with acid and oak. High alcohol (13.8%) does not detract. Enjoy this fine wine with stuffed lobster, veal piccata, or game birds.

Flora Springs Barrel Fermented, 1986 Napa Valley   **$20.00**

Beautiful, intense, buttery fruit and toasty oak in the nose. Medium-full bodied. Deep and expansive rich fruit and toasty oak flavors on the palate, with a nice lemony element, in a firm structure. This is a Chardonnay that will improve for five more years. Try with lobster Newburg, grilled salmon with mustard sauce, or frogs' legs.

 Thomas Fogarty Winery, 1986 Edna Valley   **$15.00**

Medium-intense green apple aromas, with herbal and citric scents, fully supported by vanillin oak. Medium-full bodied. Generous lemony fruit on the palate, with ample acid and oak. Tart finish. Fine with rich seafood dishes and fowl.

 Thomas Fogarty Winery, 1985 Monterey      **$15.00**

Ripe appley fruit in the nose, with spicy scents, nicely supported with toasty oak. Medium-full bodied. Generous, lively fruit in the mouth, with ample oak through the finish. Enjoy this fine wine with highly seasoned fish or white meats.

 Thomas Fogarty Winery, 1986 Napa Valley—Carneros      **$15.00**

Medium-intense aromas of ripe apples and creamy oak, with tropical fruit and herbal tones. Medium-full bodied. Round and full on the palate, with the rich fruit and oak in balance, in a good structure. Slightly sharp finish. Try with grilled swordfish steak or sautéed chicken breasts.

 Thomas Fogarty Winery, 1985 Napa Valley—Carneros, Winery Lake Vineyards   **$15.00**

Appealing honey/oaky nose. Medium-full bodied. The wine enters the mouth round and supple, with the moderate fruit flavors matched with a full dimension of sweet oak. Finishes oaky. Try with veal roast, swordfish steaks, frogs' legs, or turkey.

 Thomas Fogarty Winery, 1986 Santa Cruz Mountains   **$16.50**

Light gold color. Appealing, moderately intense varietal fruit in the nose, with a nice dimension of oak in support. Medium-full bodied. Generous apricoty fruit on the palate, with citric nuances, and oak in balance, in a good structure. Try as an accompaniment to sea bass with ginger or turkey with sage dressing.

☆ ☆ ½   ***Thomas Fogarty Winery,***
1985 Santa Cruz Mountains $16.50

Loads of toasty oak and ripe fruit in the nose. Medium-full bodied. Moderately intense appley and citrusy flavors on the palate, with a full dimension of creamy oak, in a good structure. Finishes a bit rough. This is a big wine that goes well with hearty dishes.

☆ ☆ ½   ***Folie á Deux Winery, 1985 Napa Valley*** $13.50

Pleasant aromas of apples, honey, lemons, and spice, with pronounced oaky overtones. Medium-full bodied. Rich, round, buttery fruit on the palate, with ample oak. This wine has some power. Try with rich seafood dishes.

☆   ***Louis J. Foppiano Winery, 1986 Sonoma County*** $9.00

Medium-intense pearlike fruit in the nose, with a touch of oak. Medium bodied. Moderate fruit flavors on the palate, with oak in balance, in a clean presentation. Crisp finish. Enjoy with fish dishes.

☆ ☆   ***Louis J. Foppiano Winery, 1985 Sonoma County*** $8.50

Moderate appley fruit in the nose, with citric scents and oaky overtones. Medium-light bodied. Lemony fruit on the palate, with a nice touch of oak. Sharp finish. Fine with well-seasoned fish dishes.

☆ ☆ ½   ***Forman Vineyard, 1987 Napa Valley*** $18.00

Nicely focused appley, buttery, and spicy fruit aromas, with vanillin and lemony tones. Medium-full bodied. Generous toasty, buttery fruit on the palate, in a good structure. Crisp finish. Fine with well-seasoned fish dishes.

☆ ☆ ½   ***Franciscan Vineyards, 1986 Napa Valley,***
Oakville Estate $9.25

Attractive, forward appley and oaky nose, with tropical fruit tones. Medium bodied. Citrusy fruit on the palate is nicely balanced with oak. Clean finish. Try with grilled salmon or sautéed scallops. Good value.

☆ ☆   ***Franciscan Vineyards, 1985 Napa Valley,***
Oakville Estate $10.00

Medium-intense appley fruit aromas, with oaky tones. Medium bodied. The varietal fruit is firm on the palate, with oak and acid in balance. Crisp finish. Try with cracked crab or shad roe.

☆☆☆   **Freemark Abbey Winery, 1986 Napa Valley**   *$15.00*

Attractive aromas of apples and peaches, with floral tones. Medium-full bodied. Lots of sweetish apple fruit on the palate, with melony and buttery nuances, and nicely integrated oak throughout. Smooth finish. A great wine. Enjoy.

☆☆ ½   **Freemark Abbey Winery, 1985 Napa Valley**   *$14.00*

Moderately intense lemony and tropical fruit aromas, with earthy tones. Medium-full bodied. Lush fruit impression on the palate, with ample oak and acid, in a firm structure. Finishes slightly hot. Best with rich seafood dishes.

☆☆ ½   **Freemark Abbey Winery, 1984 Napa Valley**   *$14.00*

Nicely focused applelike fruit in the nose, with buttery and toasty oak overtones. Medium-full bodied. Generous ripe fruit flavors in the mouth, with good acidity and oak in balance. Clean finish. Can accompany sea bass with ginger and lemon as well as sautéed chicken breast with cream.

☆☆   **Fritz Cellars, 1987 Dry Creek Valley**   *$9.00*

Medium-intense lemony and floral aromas. Medium bodied. Moderately deep herbal fruit flavors on the palate, with citric elements, in a firm structure. Tart finish. Nice with filet of sole meuniere or light luncheon dishes.

☆☆   **Fritz Cellars, 1987 Russian River Valley**   *$10.00*

Appealing floral and honeysuckle fruit aromas. Medium bodied. Moderate tropical and lemony fruit flavors on the palate, in a good structure. Finishes short. Fine with moderately seasoned fish or poultry dishes.

☆☆   **Fritz Cellars, 1986 Russian River Valley**   *$9.00*

Light gold color. Forward, clean lemony fruit in the nose. Medium bodied. Slightly viscous on entry, with the moderate citrusy fruit flavors and acid in good balance. Crisp finish. Try with Rex or petrale sole.

☆☆   **Fritz Cellars Private Reserve, 1986 Russian River Valley**   *$12.00*

Moderately intense lemony fruit and oak in the nose. Medium-full bodied. Generous, but firm, appley and citrusy fruit flavors on the palate, with ample oak and acid. Lean finish. Try with filet of sole meuniere.

☆☆☆☆ **_Frog's Leap, 1987 Napa Valley_** 🍷 **_$14.00_**

Nice pineapple fruit in the nose, with scents of clove, and ample oak in support. Medium bodied. Silky smooth texture, with the generous fruit flavors in nice balance with spicy oak and acid. Lovely pineapple flavors in the long finish. A wonderful wine for current consumption. Just enjoy.

☆☆ **_Frog's Leap, 1985 Napa Valley_** 🍷 **_$12.00_**

Light yellow color. Medium-intense aromas of apple, butterscotch, and nutmeg. Medium-light bodied. Moderate apple and peach flavors on the palate, with a pronounced citric dimension. The wine finishes tart. Best with well-seasoned fish dishes.

☆ **_Geyser Peak, 1986 Sonoma County_** 🍷 **_$7.00_**

Produced by Trione Vineyards. Modest, clean, sweet fruit aromas, with floral and herbal scents. Medium-light bodied. Soft on the palate, with moderate lemony fruit, and acid in balance. Crisp finish. Best with most fish dishes.

☆☆☆ **_Girard Winery, 1986 Napa Valley_** 🍷 **_$13.50_**

Very attractive, intense pears and pineapples in the nose, with lemony tones, and an abundance of toasty oak. Medium-full bodied. Rich and lush on the palate, with the lemony fruit and oak in good balance, in a firm structure. Try this superior wine with rich seafood or fowl dishes.

☆☆ **_Girard Winery, 1985 Napa Valley_** 🍷 **_$13.50_**

Moderately intense lemony and buttery aromas, with butterscotch scents, and pronounced oaky tones. Medium-full bodied. Ripe fruit flavors in the mouth, with a substantial dimension of oak throughout. Slightly bitter finish. Best with well-seasoned fish dishes or poultry.

☆ **_Glen Ellen Proprietor's Reserve, 1987 California_** 🍷 **_$5.00_**

Light yellow color. Medium-intense aromas of tropical fruit, peaches, and flowers. Medium bodied. Moderately intense floral fruit flavors, with a touch of residual sugar, in a soft structure. Not Chardonnaylike, but pleasant as an apéritif or with light luncheon foods. Good value.

☆☆½ **_Glen Ellen Winery, 1985 Sonoma Valley—Carneros_** 🍷 **_$9.00_**

Assertive, youthful, appley fruit in the nose, with citric scents, and abundant toasty oak. Medium-full bodied. Generous buttery fruit on the palate, nicely balanced with oak and acid. Crisp finish. Excellent with well-seasoned fish dishes. Good value.

☆   **Gran Val, 1986 California** $8.50

Produced by Clos du Val. Medium-intense varietal fruit aromas, with earthy tones, and toasty oak. Medium bodied. Moderately intense fruit on the palate, with earthy nuances and ample oak and acid, in a firm structure. Will go well with most fish dishes.

☆☆☆   **Grgich Hills Cellar, 1986 Napa Valley** $22.00

Appealing appley, buttery, and oaky aromas. Mcdium-full bodied. Nice weight and substance in the mouth, with the generous apple, apricot, and lemon flavors nicely supported by ample oak. Pleasant, oaky finish. A superior wine by any standard. Just enjoy.

☆☆☆   **Grgich Hills Cellar, 1985 Napa Valley** $22.00

Attractive buttery, lemony, and herbal aromas, with nice toasty oak overtones. Medium-full bodied. The wine is expansive in the mouth, with the buttery and spicy fruit flavors perfectly balanced with oak and acid, in a firm structure. Long, crisp finish. Enjoy with veal dishes, turkey, stuffed lobster or broiled salmon.

☆☆☆   **Groth Vineyards, 1986 Napa Valley** $12.00

Attractive floral and appley fruit aromas, with oaky tones. Medium-full bodied. Intense flavors of ripe apples and lemons on the palate, enhanced by rich oak, in a good structure. Try this excellent wine with turkey, stuffed lobster, or roast goose.

☆☆½   **Groth Vineyards, 1985 Napa Valley** $11.00

Appealing, ripe Chardonnay fruit in the nose, with tropical fruit nuances, and nice toasty oak in support. Medium-full bodied. Rich and full on the palate, with the ripe fruit flavors, oak, and acid in balance, in a firm structure. Try with grilled salmon, Cornish hen with herbs and wild rice, or veal piccata.

☆   **Guenoc Winery, 1986 North Coast** $8.50

Moderate varietal fruit in the nose, with herbal scents. Medium bodied. Modest fruit flavors on the palate, with good acid, in a clean presentation. Enjoy with a wide range of fish dishes.

☆☆½   **Guenoc Winery, 1985 North Coast** $10.50

Nice toasty oak and appley fruit aromas, with lemony and earthy overtones. Medium-full bodied. The wine is creamy on entry, with appley/spicy fruit flavors nicely balanced with acid and oak. Try with sautéed orange roughy or baked chicken.

☆☆ **_Gundlach-Bundschu Special Selection,_** $12.00
1986 Sonoma Valley, Sangiacomo Ranch

Appealing, medium-intense floral, herbal, and citrus aromas,
with a nice touch of oak. Medium bodied. A bit hard in the
mouth, with a clean grapefruit dimension throughout.
Crisp finish. Best with well-seasoned fish dishes.

☆☆ ½ **_Gundlach-Bundschu Winery, 1986 Sonoma Valley_** $9.75

Very attractive appley, floral, citrusy, and herbal aromas, with a
nice oaky dimension throughout. Medium-full bodied. Deep fruit
impression in the mouth, with nice toasty fruit flavors through
the finish. A well-proportioned Chardonnay, with a clean finish.
Fine with well-seasoned fish dishes. Good value.

☆☆☆ **_Hacienda Clair de Lune, 1986 Sonoma County_** $12.00

Very attractive appley, buttery, and toasty aromas. Medium-full
bodied. Round and full on the palate, with the rich lemony fruit
in nice balance with the acid. Long, flavorful finish. Enjoy with
stuffed lobster or frogs' legs. Good value.

☆☆ ½ **_Hacienda Clair de Lune, 1985 Sonoma County_** $11.00

Appealing appley aromas, with butterscotch and oaky overtones.
Medium bodied. Rich, toasty flavors in the mouth, in a nice
structure. Enjoy this fine wine with well-seasoned fish dishes or
poultry in a light sauce.

☆☆ **_Hafner Vineyard, 1986 Alexander Valley_** $12.00

Bright. Light golden color. Attractive floral, appley, and
pineappley aromas, with nice sweet oak in support. Medium
bodied. Appealing appley and melony fruit on the palate in
perfect balance with sweet oak, in a smooth presentation.
Try with grilled salmon or baked turkey.

☆☆ ½ **_Handley Cellars, 1986 Dry Creek Valley_** $13.00

Appealing, medium intense floral fruit aromas, with butterscotch
scents, and toasty oak overtones. Medium bodied. Lots of
buttery fruit on the palate, with ample oak, in a good structure.
Try with rich seafood dishes.

☆☆ ½ **_Handley Cellars, 1985 Dry Creek Valley_** $12.50

Intense sweet oak in the nose, joined by nice appley fruit.
Medium-full bodied. Deep appley fruit impression on the palate,
with citric nuances, and ample oak. Long, sharp finish. This
wine will improve for several years. Try with well-seasoned fish
dishes or poultry.

☆☆ ½   ### Hanna Winery, 1985 Sonoma County $13.50

Complex, delicate aromas of pears, peaches, and flowers, with a nice touch of oak. Medium bodied. The aromas carry into the flavors in a smooth presentation. Pleasant, lingering aftertaste. Try as an accompaniment to salmon in parchment with vegetables or sautéed chicken breast with cream.

☆☆ ½   ### Hanzell Vineyards, 1984 Sonoma Valley $20.00

Aggressive aromas of ripe appley fruit, toasty oak, and honey, with herbal and spicy overtones. Full bodied. Deep, somewhat oxidized fruit flavors fill the mouth, with a full dimension of oak. High alcohol (14%) contributes to a somewhat harsh finish. This is a fine wine that is best enjoyed with savory foods.

☆   ### Haywood Winery, 1985 Sonoma Valley $9.50

Pleasant aromas of peaches, lemons, and flowers. Medium-full bodied. The fruit flavors are lean on the palate, with citric nuances. Sharp finish. Fine with a wide range of fish dishes.

☆☆☆   ### William Hill Reserve, 1986 Napa Valley $17.00

Forward toasty oak in the nose, joined by floral and butterscotch tones. Medium-full bodied. Generous appley fruit in the mouth, with ample oak, in a good structure. Lingering finish. This wine will improve for several years. Best with rich seafood and fowl dishes.

☆☆   ### William Hill Reserve, 1985 Napa Valley $17.00

Golden yellow color. Medium-intense green appley fruit aromas, with herbal and earthy scents. Moderate lemony fruit flavors on the palate, with a fair oak dimension. Finishes tart. Try with grilled salmon.

☆☆   ### William Hill Silver Label, 1986 Napa Valley $10.00

Medium-intense, nicely focused varietal fruit aromas, with honey scents, and creamy oak in support. Medium bodied. Moderate fruit flavors in the mouth, with a full dimension of oak. Slightly bitter in the finish. Best with well-seasoned fish dishes.

☆   ### Hogue Cellars, 1986 Washington $8.00

Very appealing floral aromas. Medium bodied. Moderately intense tropical fruit aromas, with acid in balance. Crisp finish. Fine with fish dishes.

☆☆½ ***Hogue Cellars Reserve, 1986 Yakima Valley, Washington***  $11.00

Attractive green apple fruit and rich toasty oak aromas. Medium-full bodied. Round and full in the mouth, with nice spicy fruit flavors, and ample oak. Best with well-seasoned fish dishes or poultry.

☆☆½ ***Husch, 1986 Mendocino*** $9.75

Very appealing, fresh, nicely focused varietal fruit in the nose, with sweet oak in the background. Medium-full bodied. Lush fruit in the mouth, with oak and acid in perfect balance. Try this very attractive wine with sautéed scallops or monkfish in parchment with vegetables. Good value.

☆☆ ***Husch, 1985 Mendocino*** $9.75

Moderately intense green apple aromas, with toasty oak scents. Medium bodied. Deep fruit impression on the palate, with lemony and oaky elements in firm structure. Tart finish. Fine with a wide range of fish dishes.

☆☆½ ***Inglenook Reserve, 1987 Napa Valley*** $15.00

Beautiful appley, flowery, and spicy oak in the nose. Medium-full bodied. Ripe spicy fruit flavors on the palate, with honey and pear nuances, and a nice oak/acid balance, in a firm structure. Try with cracked crab or baked sea bass.

☆ ***Inglenook Vineyards, 1985 Napa Valley*** $9.00

Modest green apple fruit in the nose, with herbal and oaky scents. Medium-bodied. Moderately intense citric flavors in the mouth, with a touch of oak. Finishes clean. This is an enjoyable Chardonnay that will go well with moderately seasoned fish dishes.

☆☆ ***Innisfree, 1986 Napa Valley*** $9.00

Appealing appley, floral, and citrusy aromas, with a touch of oak. Medium bodied. Moderately intense fruit flavors on the palate, with moderate oak, in a clean presentation. Fine with moderately seasoned fish dishes or poultry.

☆☆½ ***Iron Horse Vineyards, 1987 Sonoma County— Green Valley*** $15.00

Medium-intense blossomy fruit and sweet oak aromas. Medium bodied. Moderate floral fruit and oak on the palate, with citric nuances, in a firm structure. Finishes slightly sharp. Best with rich seafood dishes.

★★½ Iron Horse Vineyards, 1986 Sonoma County— Green Valley

$12.00

Moderately intense, clean, pineappley, and oaky aromas. Medium bodied. Nice green apple flavors in the mouth, with crispiness through the finish. Try with sautéed scallops or chicken with pistachio sauce.

★★ Iron Horse Vineyards, 1985 Sonoma—Green Valley

$12.50

Pleasant, delicate green apple and citric aromas, with nice oak in the background. Medium-bodied. The modest fruit in the mouth is nicely balanced with acid and oak. This is a somewhat austere, delicate Chardonnay. A fine wine that will go well with sautéed scallops.

★★½ Jekel Private Reserve, 1984 Arroyo Seco, Home Vineyard

$14.50

Attractive honeyed varietal fruit aromas, with herbal and toasty oak overtones. Medium-full bodied. Generous fruit flavors in the mouth, with a full dimension of oak. This is a rather big wine that will improve for a couple of years. Try as an accompaniment to salmon in parchment with celery, carrots, and tarragon.

★★ Jekel Vineyard, 1985 Arroyo Seco

$10.50

Assertive buttery and oaky aromas, with earthy scents. Medium-full bodied. Deep fruit impression of ripe apples, and rich oak. Slightly coarse finish. Try with well-seasoned fish dishes or poultry.

★★½ Jekel Vineyard, 1984 Arroyo Seco

$10.50

Very appealing aromas of oak and butterscotch, with herbal overtones. Medium-full bodied. The fruit, acid, and oak combine in a creamy texture. Smooth finish. Fine with soft-shelled crab or poached salmon.

★★½ Jepson Vineyards, 1986 Mendocino County

$11.00

Appealing buttery fruit and toasty oak in the nose. Medium-full bodied. Rich honeyed fruit on the palate, with toasty and spicy nuances, in a good structure. Try with grilled salmon or sautéed chicken breast with cream.

★★½ Jordan Vineyard, 1985 Alexander Valley

$17.00

Moderately intense ripe varietal fruit aromas, with butterscotch scents, and toasty oak throughout. Medium-full bodied. Supple and full on the palate, with good fruit flavors, dominated by oak through the finish. Try with swordfish steak or turkey with sage dressing.

Karly, 1985 Santa Maria Valley $12.00

Pleasant appley fruit in the nose, nicely supported with creamy oak. Medium-full bodied. Deep appley impression on the palate, with ample oak and acid, in a firm presentation. Best with rich seafood dishes and poulty.

Robert Keenan Winery, 1986 Napa Valley $12.00

Pleasant, medium-intense appley, lemony, and spicy aromas, with sweet oak in support. Medium-full bodied. Loads of ripe appley fruit and sweet oak in the mouth. Slightly coarse finish. Enjoy with rich seafood or poultry dishes.

Robert Keenan Winery, 1985 Napa Valley $11.00

Moderately intense appley fruit aromas, with scents of nutmeg, mint, and lemon. Medium bodied. The pineappley and lemony flavors are nicely balanced with oak. Pleasant, lingering aftertaste. For an entrée try sea bass with ginger and lemon.

Kendall-Jackson Proprietor's Reserve, 1986 California $17.00

Forward appley fruit and floral aromas, with toasty oak overtones. Medium-full bodied. Loads of lively tropical fruit flavors on the palate, with lemony nuances, and a nice oaky dimension. Smooth finish. An excellent wine for current consumption with white meats.

Kendall-Jackson Proprietor's Reserve, Barrel Fermented, 1985 California $16.00

Attractive appley and lemony fruit aromas, with hints of butterscotch, and toasty oak in support. Medium-full bodied. Nice tropical fruit flavors in the mouth are favorably balanced with sweet oak. Lingering aftertaste. This wine will improve for several years. Try as an accompaniment to grilled salmon with mustard sauce or turkey with sage dressing.

Kendall-Jackson Vintner's Reserve, 1986 California $9.00

Appealing appley fruit in the nose, with floral scents, and sweet oak. Medium bodied. Ripe, juicy fruit on the palate, with nice acid. Crisp finish. Fine with a wide range of fish dishes.

Kenwood Vineyards, 1986 Sonoma Valley, Beltane Ranch $15.00

Very appealing appley, floral, and spicy oak aromas. Medium-full bodied. Generous lemony fruit and toasty oak aromas, in a firm structure. Slightly harsh finish. Give it a year to smooth out, then enjoy with rich seafood dishes or poultry.

Kenwood Vineyards, 1985 Sonoma Valley, Beltane Ranch $12.50

Moderately intense floral fruit and toasty oak in the nose, with earthy scents. Medium bodied. Narrow fruit flavors on the palate, with acid in balance. Crisp finish. Try with sautéed orange roughy.

  Kenwood Vineyards, 1985 Sonoma Valley, Yulupa Vineyard $11.00

Refined appley, lemony, and oaky aromas. Medium bodied. The low-key aromas follow into the mouth, with the flavors nicely balanced with acid, in a clean presentation. This is a fine wine for early consumption with moderately seasoned fish or chicken dishes.

  **Kinneybrook, 1986 Sonoma Valley, Estate Bottled** $15.00

Produced by Sebastiani Vineyards. Light golden yellow. Medium-intense floral and tropical fruit aromas, with ample oak. Medium bodied. Subdued fruit flavors in the mouth, with a strong oaky element throughout. Slightly bitter finish. Best with well-seasoned fish dishes.

  Kistler Vineyards, 1985 California, Dutton Ranch/Winery Lake Vineyard $15.00

Bright. Light yellow color. Forward aromas of ripe apples and pineapples, with sweet oak in support. Medium-full bodied. Rich fruit flavors fill the mouth, with a nice dimension of toasty oak, in a smooth presentation. This is a superior wine that will improve for several years. Enjoy with fowl, veal, or well-seasoned white meats.

  Kistler Vineyards, 1987 Russian River Valley, Dutton Ranch $18.00

Very appealing appley and spicy aromas, with a touch of vanillin oak. Medium-full bodied. Complex flavors of apples, pears, and butterscotch in perfect balance with sweet oak. Rich and crisp. Will improve for several years. Try as an accompaniment to Cornish hen with an apple-sage dressing.

  Kistler Vineyards, 1986 Russian River Valley, Dutton Ranch $16.00

Medium-intense toasty and earthy aromas, joined by nice appley fruit scents. Medium-full bodied. Deep appley fruit impression on the palate, with lemony nuances, and a full dimension of oak. This wine will improve for several years. Enjoy with fowl or veal.

Kistler Vineyards, 1987 Sonoma Valley, Durell Vineyard **$16.00**

Assertive appley and pineappley aromas, with buttery and toasty tones. Medium-full bodied. Lots of rich fruit in the mouth, nicely balanced with ample acid, giving good structure. Will improve for several years. Try this superior wine with rich seafood or poultry dishes.

Kistler Vineyards, 1986 Sonoma Valley, Durell Vineyard **$14.50**

Abundant appley aromas in the nose, with nice oak in support. Medium-full bodied. Loads of ripe fruit on the palate, with buttery and spicy nuances, and ample oak, in a good structure. Citric finish. Try this superior wine with lobster Newburg, frogs' legs, or sautéed chicken breasts.

Kistler Vineyards, 1986 Sonoma Valley, Kistler Vineyards **$18.00**

Here is a winner! Forward honeyed, appley fruit and toasty oak in the nose, with hints of melons, butterscotch, and lemons. Medium-full bodied. The wine is big and expansive on the palate, with the layers of rich fruit, nicely balanced with oak and acid, in a firm structure. Try this superior wine with roast pork, veal piccata, or cold duck.

Charles Krug Winery, 1986 Napa Valley, Los Carneros **$9.00**

Appealing, clean aromas of green apples and lemons, with a touch of toasty oak. Medium bodied. Nice appley fruit on the palate, with oak and acid in good balance. Slightly tart finish. Enjoy with light pasta dishes, chicken in a white sauce, or moderately seasoned fish dishes. Good value.

La Crema, 1987 California **$13.00**

Medium intense appley fruit in the nose, with minty and herbal tones. Medium bodied. Lots of lively young fruit flavors on the palate, with the apple and oak components in good balance. Crisp finish. Try with grilled salmon.

 La Crema, 1986 California **$11.00**

Medium-intense lemony fruit aromas, with nice oak in support. Medium bodied. Restrained fruit flavors in the mouth, with ample oak, in a firm structure. Fine with well-seasoned fish dishes.

★★½ La Crema, 1985 California $10.50

Light golden yellow color. Medium-intense aromas of ripe appley fruit, with hints of butterscotch and lemon in the background. Medium-full bodied. Rich, buttery fruit on the palate, with a full dimension of toasty oak. Fine with rich seafood or fowl dishes.

★★★ La Crema Reserve, 1986 California $16.00

Powerful aromas of ripe tropical fruit and toasty oak, with nice buttery tones in support. Full bodied. Lush fruit on the palate, with the abundant appley/lemony fruit flavors and rich oak in balance, in a good structure. This is a big wine. Try as an accompaniment to veal or pork roast with rosemary.

★★★ La Crema Reserve, 1985 California $15.00

Powerful aromas of ripe fruit and toasty oak. Medium-full bodied. The wine enters the mouth round and full, with the rich fruit and oaky flavors nicely supported with ample acid. This is a powerful Chardonnay that will go well with rich seafood dishes.

★★½ Lakespring Winery, 1986 Napa Valley $11.00

Medium-intense peach and pear aromas, with herbal scents. Medium bodied. Lots of toasty fruit on the palate, with butter-scotch nuances, and crisp acidity. Try with grilled salmon or pasta in a cream sauce.

★★½ Lambert Bridge, 1986 Sonoma County $12.00

Very appealing floral and appley fruit aromas. Medium bodied. Nice green apple and vanilla flavors on the palate, with spicy nuances, in a firm structure. Finishes clean and slightly tart. Best with well-seasoned fish or poultry dishes.

★★½ Lambert Bridge, 1985 Sonoma County $11.00

Attractive, intense appley fruit, with a nice touch of toasty oak. Medium-bodied. Deep fruit impression on the palate, with green apple and oaky nuances, nicely balanced with acid, in a clean presentation. Tart finish. Try with grilled sea bass or snapper in parchment with soy and ginger.

★★ Landmark Vineyards, 1985 Sonoma County $10.00

Light gold color. Moderately intense floral and citrusy aromas, with herbal scents. Medium bodied. Soft, slightly weedy fruit flavors in the mouth, with citric nuances. Tart finish. Fine with well-seasoned fish dishes.

Leeward Winery, 1987 Central Coast $8.00

Enticing aromas of butterscotch, bananas, and toasty oak. Medium-full bodied. Generous ripe, sweet, lemony fruit on the palate carries through the finish. Try as an accompaniment to sautéed chicken breast with cream. Good value.

Leeward Winery, 1986 Central Coast $8.50

Appealing ripe apricots and pineapples in the nose. Medium-full bodied. Rich tropical fruit flavors in the mouth, with moderate acid. Try as an accompaniment to linguine with clams or Cantonese chicken and almonds.

Leeward Winery, 1985 Edna Valley, MacGregor Vineyard $14.00

Light golden color. Pleasant tropical fruit aromas, with toasty oak overtones. Medium-full bodied. The wine enters the mouth soft and smooth, continuing the tropical fruit and toasty oak elements through the finish. This is a softly structured wine that will go well with a wide range of fish dishes.

J. Lohr Winery, 1986 Monterey County, Greenfield Vineyards $10.00

Fragrant aromas of tropical fruit and orange blossoms. Medium bodied. Generous, somewhat sweet, juicy fruit on the palate, with moderate acid. Nice as an apéritif or with light lunches.

Lolonis Winery, 1985 Alexander Valley $12.50

Moderately intense ripe apple and toasty oak aromas. Medium-full bodied. Lots of rich fruit on the palate, balanced with sweet oak, in a good structure. Clean, lingering finish. Enjoy this fine wine with shellfish, veal piccata, or baked chicken.

Long Vineyards, 1986 Napa Valley $26.00

Most attractive apple and butterscotch aromas, with nice toasty oak in support. Medium-full bodied. Full and rich on entry. Good depth. Attractive flavors of spicy pear, butterscotch, and lemon, in an elegant presentation. This superior wine will improve for several years. Just enjoy.

Long Vineyards, 1985 Napa Valley $26.00

Pleasant green apple aromas, with nice toasty oak in support. Medium-full bodied. Attractive varietal fruit in the mouth, with a full dimension of creamy and toasty oak throughout. Enjoy with well-seasoned shellfish or white meats.

MacRostie Winery, 1987 Carneros $14.50

Appealing pearlike and buttery aromas, with a nice dimension of
toasty oak in support. Medium-full bodied. Most attractive pineapple, peach, and apple flavors on the palate, nicely balanced
with oak and spice, in a firm structure. This is the initial offering
from this winery. They are off to a fine start. Enjoy with sautéed
scallops or baked chicken.

Mark West Vineyards, 1985 Russian River Valley $10.00

Appealing floral and appley aromas, with nice sweet oak
overtones. Medium-bodied. Generous juicy fruit flavors in the
mouth, with spicy and oaky nuances, and ample acid. Finishes
sharp. The wine will hold for a few years. Enjoy with well-
seasoned seafood dishes. Good value.

Mark West Vineyards, 1986 Sonoma County $11.00

Appealing, medium-intense pineappley and lemony fruit
aromas, with nice toasty oak in support. Medium bodied.
The pineappley/lemony fruit flavors are nicely balanced
with moderate oak, in a clean presentation. Slightly tart finish.
Best with well-seasoned fish dishes.

Markham Vineyards, 1986 Napa Valley, Markham Vineyard $12.00

Pleasant, medium-intense green apple and floral aromas.
Medium bodied. Assertive lemony and toasty flavors on the
palate, in a firm structure. Flinty finish. A well-made wine in a
somewhat austere style. Enjoy with Rex sole or sand dabs.

Markham Vineyards, 1985 Napa Valley, Markham Vineyard $12.00

Forward sweet oak in the nose, joined by appley and floral
scents. Medium bodied. Generous appley fruit on the palate,
with ample oak and spice, in a well-structured presentation.
Sharp finish. Fine with tasty fish or poultry dishes.

Masson Vintage Selection, 1987 Monterey County $6.50

Appealing appley fruit in the nose. Medium bodied. Generous
peach flavors on the palate, with honey nuances, in a firm
structure. Clean and brisk in fruity finish. Fine with Rex sole or
sand dabs. Excellent value.

Matanzas Creek Winery, 1986 Sonoma County **$17.50**

Appealing fresh varietal fruit in the nose, with spicy scents, nicely supported with sweet oak. Medium-full bodied. Firm and deep on the palate, with the intense Chardonnay fruit flavors nicely balanced with oak and a citric element. Long, crispy finish. A fine candidate for several years of aging. Try with oysters on the half-shell or shad roe.

 ### Matanzas Creek Winery, 1985 Sonoma County **$16.50**

Assertive ripe apple aromas, with spicy, lemony, and oaky overtones. Medium-full bodied. Deep, vibrant appley fruit flavors on the palate, with spicy and lemony nuances, and ample oak, in a firm structure. Try this elegant wine with baked sea bass or chicken with pistachio sauce.

 ### Mazzocco Vineyards Barrel Fermented, 1987 Sonoma County **$11.00**

Assertive tropical fruit and lemony aromas, with ample toasty oak in support. Medium-full bodied. Generous applelike fruit flavors on the palate, with moderate oak and acid, in a good structure. Slightly sharp finish. Best with well-seasoned fish dishes.

 ### Mazzocco Winemaster's Cuvée, 1986 Sonoma County **$10.00**

Medium-intense ripe varietal fruit aromas, with buttery and weedy scents, and a touch of toasty oak. Medium-full bodied. Attractive, complex flavors of peach, lemon, and oak, with sufficient acid for structure. Crisp finish. Best with rich seafood dishes.

 ### McDowell Valley Vineyards, 1986 McDowell Valley **$11.00**

Medium-intense, clean, citrusy fruit aromas, with sweet oak tones. Medium bodied. Well focused, but somewhat austere, Chardonnay fruit flavors on the palate, with moderate oak, in a clean presentation. Crisp finish. Fine with well-seasoned fish dishes.

 ### Meeker Vineyard, 1986 Dry Creek Valley **$11.00**

Forward aromas of ripe Chardonnay fruit and spicy oak. Medium-full bodied. Rich buttery fruit on the palate, and a full dimension of spicy oak. Slightly bitter in the finish. Try with rich seafood or fowl dishes.

Meridian Cellars, 1985 Napa Valley *$11.00*

Light yellow color. Pleasant aromas of lemons and butterscotch, with nice oak in support. Medium-bodied. Clean, appley and lemony flavors on the palate, with a rich oak dimension, in a firm presentation. Has enough structure to hold for a few years. Fine with fresh lobster or swordfish steak.

 Merlion, 1986 Napa Valley *$12.50*

Medium-intense spicy apple, citric, and floral aromas. Medium-full bodied. A good depth of ripe fruit flavors on the palate, with ample oak, in a firm structure. Clean finish. Fine with well-seasoned fish dishes.

 Merryvale Vineyards, 1986 Napa Valley *$20.00*

Moderately intense buttery fruit in the nose, with herbal and earthy scents, and toasty oak overtones. Medium-full bodied. Moderately deep apple fruit flavors in the mouth, with ample oak, in a firm structure. Slightly bitter finish. Fine with veal piccata or chicken breasts in a cream sauce.

 Merryvale Vineyards, 1985 Napa Valley *$16.50*

Light gold color. Assertive toasty oak in the nose, joined by peach and apple aromas. Medium bodied. The fruit is firm on the palate, with a full dimension of oak through the finish. Give this wine a couple of years for the fruit and oak to blend further, then enjoy with well-seasoned fish dishes or poultry.

 Milano Reserve, 1985 Mendocino County, Hopland Cuvée *$18.00*

Appealing, medium intense creamy fruit aromas, with minty tones. Medium bodied. Lots of juicy fruit in the mouth, with sufficient acid for structure. Try with sautéed chicken breasts in a cream sauce.

 Milano Winery, 1985 Sonoma County, Vine Hill Ranch *$18.00*

Forward appley fruit and toasty oak aromas. Medium-full bodied. Generous, very ripe apples and apricot fruit on the palate is combined with a fair dimension of lively acid. Big and firm in the mouth. Fine with baked turkey or veal piccata.

 Mirassou Vineyards, 1986 Monterey County *$8.00*

Medium-intense, clean, green apple aromas, with delicate floral and licorice scents. Medium bodied. Moderate lemon/grapefruit flavors on the palate, in a clean presentation. Crisp finish. Fine with lightly seasoned fish dishes.

Mirassou Vineyards, 1985 Monterey County, Fifth Generation Family Selection

 $8.00

Light yellow color. Brilliant. Pleasant floral Chardonnay aromas, with a nice touch of oak. Medium bodied. Moderate fruit, with caramel nuances, and acid in the balance. This is an appealing wine for current consumption with moderately seasoned fish dishes.

Robert Mondavi Reserve, 1985 Napa Valley

 $25.00

Forward toasty oak in the nose, joined by scents of flowers, spice, and butterscotch. Medium-full bodied. Generous ripe fruit on the palate, with a full dimension of oak. Consistency over the years is the hallmark here, both in quality and style. Enjoy with veal roast, cold roast goose, swordfish steak, or turkey.

Robert Mondavi Winery, 1987 Napa Valley

 $16.00

Forward rich oak fills the nose, joined by ripe appley fruit. Medium-full bodied. Round and full at entry, with the ripe fruit and toasty oak in nice balance. Slightly hot finish. Give this wine a year or so for further improvement, then enjoy with baked swordfish or sautéed chicken breasts.

Robert Mondavi Winery, 1986 Napa Valley

 $13.50

Aggressive toasty oak aromas fill the nose, joined by a complex blend of ripe fruit tones. Medium bodied. The taste follows consistently from the aromas, with the rich fruit flavors on the palate dominated by the oak throughout. Try as an accompaniment to grilled salmon with mustard sauce or turkey with apple-sage dressing.

Robert Mondavi Winery, 1985 Napa Valley

 $12.50

Pleasant toasty oak in the nose, with nutty and butterscotch scents. Medium bodied. Moderate fruit in the mouth, with considerable oak, and a fair acidic dimension. Clean finish. Fine with a wide range of well seasoned fish dishes.

Monterey Classic, 1987 Monterey County

 $5.00

Medium-intense appley and oaky aromas. Medium bodied. Moderate pearlike fruit and oak flavors in good balance. Short finish. Fine with a wide range of fish dishes. Good value.

Monticello Cellars, 1986 Napa Valley, Corley Reserve

 $16.50

Forward rich aromas of appley fruit and creamy oak, with buttery and spicy tones. Medium-full bodied. Round and full in the mouth, with loads of ripe fruit nicely balanced with toasty oak and acid. Try this very fine wine with grilled salmon.

Monticello Cellars, 1985 Napa Valley, Jefferson Ranch
 $10.00

Medium-intense toasty Chardonnay aromas. Medium-full bodied. Smooth feel in the mouth, with the lemony fruit flavors nicely balanced with sweet oak. Try as an accompaniment to chicken with pistachio sauce or pork with rosemary. Good value.

 ### *Monticello Corley Reserve, 1985 Napa Valley*
 **$14.00**

Forward ripe appley and spicy nose, with toasty oak overtones. Medium-full bodied. Lush appley fruit on the palate, with butterscotch nuances, and nice spice and oak. Smooth finish. Try with sautéed chicken in a cream sauce.

 ### *Morgan Winery, 1987 Monterey County*
 **$15.00**

Appealing buttery and lemony fruit aromas. Medium-full bodied. Lots of well-defined lemony varietal fruit on the palate with oak in balance. Slightly sharp finish. Try with moderately rich seafood or fowl dishes.

 ### *Morgan Winery, 1986 Monterey County*
 $14.00

The string of superior Chardonnays from this winery continues. Most attractive buttery, appley, lemony, spicy, and toasty oak in the nose. Medium-full bodied. Beautiful, rich appley fruit flavors in the mouth, with floral nuances, and oak in perfect balance. This wine will improve for at least five more years. Enjoy! Good value.

 ### *Mount Eden Vineyards, 1986 Santa Cruz Mountains*
 $25.00

Intense ripe, buttery fruit and toasty oak in the nose. Full bodied. Powerful oak-enriched fruit in the mouth, with butterscotch and vanillin elements, and good acid for structure. This is a big Chardonnay that will go with rich seafood or fowl dishes.

 ### *Mount Eden Vineyards, 1985 Santa Cruz Mountains*
 $25.00

Intense ripe Chardonnay fruit in the nose, fully supported with toasty oak. Medium-full bodied. The wine is broad and mouth-filling on the palate, with the lemony fruit flavors nicely balanced with rich oak. Try as an accompaniment to veal with rosemary, pork roast with yams, or turkey with sage dressing.

 ### *Mount Veeder Winery, 1985 Napa Valley*
 $13.50

Forward ripe fruit and buttery aromas, with citric scents, and abundant oak in support. Medium-full bodied. Rich tropical fruit flavors in the mouth, with a nice dimension of toasty oak. Try as an accompaniment to veal roast with rosemary or chicken with pistachio sauce.

Murphy-Goode, 1986 Alexander Valley $8.00

Forward sweet oak in the nose, joined by appley, lemony, floral, and buttery scents. Medium-full bodied. Generous buttery fruit flavors on the palate, with citric elements, and ample oak and acid. Try this fine wine with grilled salmon or turkey with sage dressing. Good value.

Murphy-Goode, 1985 Alexander Valley $9.00

Pleasant appley aromas, with hints of grapefruits. Medium-full bodied. Ripe, juicy appley flavors, with citric nuances and nice oak. Tart finish. Fine with well-seasoned fish dishes.

Napa Ridge Winery, 1986 North Coast $5.00

Pleasant floral fruit aromas. Medium bodied. Soft, juicy fruit on the palate, with a slightly sweet element. Smooth finish. Serve as an apéritif or with light meals. Good value.

Nevada City Winery, 1986 Napa Valley $12.00

Moderately intense Chardonnay fruit in the nose, with herbal and earthy scents. Medium bodied. Lively pineapple fruit flavors in the mouth, with toasty oak, in a firm structure. Long finish. Try with well-seasoned fish dishes or poultry.

Newton Vineyard, 1985 Napa Valley $14.00

Most attractive aromas of blossomy fruit and toasty oak, with yeasty scents. Medium bodied. Round at entry, with the nicely focused fruit and oak flavors in balance with the acid, in a good structure. Will improve for several years. Try this superior wine with rich seafood and poultry dishes.

Neyers Winery, 1986 Napa Valley $12.50

Medium-intense appley fruit in the nose, with yeasty scents, and ample oak in support. Medium-full bodied. Moderate Chardonnay fruit in the mouth, with a substantial oaky element. Slightly bitter finish. Best with highly seasoned fish dishes.

Neyers Winery, 1985 Napa Valley $11.75

Forward appley fruit aromas, with spice and butterscotch scents, and toasty oak in the background. Medium-full bodied. Fleshy fruit on the palate, with acid in balance, and ample oak. Finishes somewhat harsh. Fine with rich seafood dishes or well-seasoned poultry.

Niles, 1986 Sonoma Valley, Estate Bottled $17.00

Produced by Sebastiani Vineyards. Forward honeyed apple aromas, with toasty oak overtones. Medium-full bodied. Ripe, buttery fruit on the palate, with nice sweet oak, in a firm structure. Very enjoyable now and will improve for a few years. Try as an accompaniment to sea bass with ginger and lemon.

Parducci Wine Cellars, 1986 Mendocino County $8.00

Appealing, medium-intense green apple aromas, with citrusy scents. Medium bodied. Round in the mouth, with moderately intense citric fruit flavors, and a hint of sweetness, in a clean and pleasant presentation. Enjoy with moderately seasoned fish dishes. Good value.

Parsons Creek Winery, 1986 Sonoma County $9.00

Medium-intense peach and melon aromas, with a touch of oak in the background. Medium bodied. Round on entry, with the moderately intense youthful fruit flavors and oak in good balance. Slightly tart finish. Best with moderately seasoned fish dishes.

Robert Pecota Winery, 1987 Alexander Valley, Canepa Vineyard $16.00

Loads of ripe fruit in the nose, with smoky and toasty oak tones in full support. Medium-full bodied. Full and rich in the mouth, with the generous ripe fruit in nice balance with the toasty oak. Lovely honeylike finish. This is a superior wine that will improve for several years. Just enjoy.

Robert Pecota Winery, 1986 Alexander Valley, Canepa Vineyard $16.00

Assertive green apple fruit aromas, with citric scents. Medium-full bodied. Deep fruit impression on the palate, with the rich, oaky fruit flavors in balance with the acid. Lingering aftertaste. Try as an accompaniment to sea bass with ginger and lemon or chicken with pistachio sauce.

J. Pedroncelli Winery, 1987 Sonoma County $8.00

Attractive fresh fruit aromas, with a touch of oak. Medium bodied. Lively apple and lemon fruit on the palate, enriched by sweet oak, in a clean presentation. Slightly sharp finish. Enjoy with shellfish, frogs' legs, or most fish dishes. Excellent value.

J. Pedroncelli Winery, 1986 Sonoma County $8.00

Light yellow color. Medium-intense appley fruit aromas, with a touch of oak. Medium bodied, nicely focused appley fruit in the mouth, with toasty oak in balance, in a clean presentation. Enjoy with moderately seasoned fish dishes. Good value.

J. Pedroncelli Winery, 1985 Sonoma County $7.75

Appealing appley aromas, with nice toasty oak in support. Medium-full bodied. Deep fruit impression on the palate, with oak and acid in balance. A tasty wine. Enjoy with shellfish, frogs' legs, or sautéed chicken breasts. Excellent value.

Robert Pepi Winery, 1985 Napa Valley $12.00

Ripe peachlike fruit aromas, with buttery scents, and rich oaky overtones. Medium-full bodied. The wine is soft and round in the mouth, with the rich fruit and oak in nice balance. Structure is a bit soft. Enjoy with poultry in a rich sauce.

Joseph Phelps Vineyards, 1985 Carneros District, Sangiacomo Vineyard $14.00

Medium-intense floral fruit aromas, joined by nice sweet oak. Medium-full bodied. The wine is round and full in the mouth, with the appley fruit in nice balance with oak and acid. Sharp finish. Fine with well-seasoned fish dishes or poultry.

Joseph Phelps Vineyards, 1986 Napa Valley $14.00

Medium-intense appley, buttery, and toasty oak aromas. Medium bodied. Generous ripe fruit and toasty oak flavors, with a strong citric dimension, in a firm structure. Best with rich seafood dishes.

Joseph Phelps Vineyards, 1985 Napa Valley $14.00

Appealing varietal fruit and oak aromas, with some earthy tones. Medium-full bodied. Crisp, lemony fruit on the palate, with nice oak, in a firm structure. Clean, fruity finish. Fine with a wide range of fish dishes.

Joseph Phelps Vineyards, 1984 Napa Valley $12.75

Attractive ripe varietal fruit aromas, with herbal scents, and nice toasty oak. Medium-full bodied. The wine enters the mouth smooth and round, with the juicy fruit and oaky oak in nice balance. Long, pleasant aftertaste. Try with sautéed chicken breasts, veal roast with rosemary, or frogs' legs.

R. H. Phillips, 1986 California $6.00

Forward ripe appley aromas, with a moderate oaky element. Medium bodied. Moderately intense ripe citrusy fruit flavors in the mouth, with a touch of oak. Clean finish. Fine with a wide range of fish dishes. Good value.

Pine Ridge Winery, 1987 Napa Valley, Knollside Cuvée

$15.00

Nicely forward varietal fruit aromas, with lemony tones, and toasty oak in support. Medium-full bodied. Deep impression of apple and peach flavors on the palate, with oak and acid in nice balance. Try as an accompaniment to sea bass with ginger and lemon or sautéed chicken breast with a cream sauce.

Pine Ridge Winery, 1986 Napa Valley, Pine Ridge Stag's Leap Vineyard

$19.00

Moderate lemony fruit and oaky aromas. Medium bodied. Delicate lemony fruit on the palate, with butterscotch nuances, and ample oak in a firm structure. Try with sautéed orange roughy filet.

Pine Ridge Winery, 1985 Napa Valley, Pine Ridge Stag's Leap Vineyard

$18.00

Golden yellow color. Rich buttery and toasty aromas, with lemony scents. Medium-full bodied. The wine enters the mouth clean and round, with a nice impression of lemon, peach, and toast, in a smooth presentation. Fine with broiled salmon or chicken with pistachio sauce.

Plam Vineyards, 1985 Napa Valley

$12.00

Appealing buttery fruit aromas, with nice toasty oak in support. Medium-full bodied. Generous tropical fruit flavors on the palate, with citrusy nuances, with ample oak and acid, in a good structure. Slightly bitter finish. Best with well-seasoned fish or poultry dishes.

Ponzi Vineyards Reserve, 1986 Willamette Valley, Oregon

$15.00

Bright. Pretty gold color. Very appealing apple, honey, and butterscotch aromas. Medium-full bodied. Generous ripe apple fruit on the palate, with clove and artichoke nuances, and a fair dimension of oak throughout. Oaky finish. Try with veal piccata, turkey with sage dressing, or roast pork with pineapple.

Preston Wine Cellars, 1986 Washington

$8.00

Light gold color. Clean aromas of fresh fruit and flowers. Medium bodied. Moderate sweet fruit flavors on the palate, with a touch of lemon and oak. Slightly tart finish. Fine with light luncheon dishes.

Quail Ridge Cellars, 1985 Napa Valley

$14.00

Light yellow color. Moderate aromas of pears, apricots, and green apples. Medium-bodied. The fruit flavors are properly focused and lean, with ample acid. Tart finish. Best with fish dishes.

☆☆ ***Raymond California Selection, 1987 California*** $9.50

Lots of young juicy fruit and sweet oak in the nose. Medium-full bodied. An abundance of fresh fruit in the mouth, with a nice touch of oak in a clean presentation. Fine for current enjoyment with moderately seasoned chicken dishes.

☆☆½ ***Raymond Private Reserve, 1985 Napa Valley*** $18.00

Attractive, medium-intense appley, floral, and rich oak aromas. Medium-full bodied. Generous sweetish varietal fruit on the palate, with ample toasty oak. Slightly buttery in the finish. Best with rich seafood and poultry dishes.

☆☆½ ***Raymond Vineyard, 1987 Napa Valley*** $13.00

Appealing tropical fruit, spicy, and lemony aromas. Medium bodied. Loads of bright appley fruit on the palate, with a touch of oak, and crisp acidity. Clean, youthful, and lively. Try with sautéed scallops or baked chicken.

☆☆☆ ***Raymond Vineyard, 1986 Napa Valley*** $12.00

Very appealing floral, appley, and citrusy aromas. Medium bodied. Moderately rich fruit flavors in the mouth, with nice oak and acid, in a smooth presentation. Consistency is the hallmark here. Try as an accompaniment to sautéed chicken breast with cream or monkfish in parchment with vegetables. Good value.

☆☆☆ ***Raymond Vineyard, 1985 Napa Valley*** $12.00

Appealing appley and lemony aromas, with rich oak in support. Medium-bodied. Rich generous fruit on the palate, with handsome oak and acid in perfect balance. An excellent wine that may be enjoyed with shellfish, turkey, or veal piccata. Good value.

☆☆½ ***J. Rochioli Vineyards, 1986 Russian River Valley*** $12.00

Medium-intense aromas of apples, lemons, spice, and toasty oak. Medium-full bodied. Generous appley and pineappley fruit flavors in the mouth, with citric nuances, and moderate oak. Crispy finish. Try with filet of sole meuniere.

☆☆ ***Rodney Strong, 1985 Chalk Hill, Chalk Hill Vineyard*** $9.00

Nice blossomy fruit and sweet oak in the nose. Medium bodied. The wine enters the mouth smooth and round, with a moderate grape impression throughout, and fair acid. Tart finish. Try with filet of sole meuniere.

Rodney Strong, 1986 Sonoma County $6.00

Appealing appley fruit aromas, with nice floral and toasty oak scents in support. Medium bodied. Nicely focused fruit on the palate, with oak and acid in perfect balance. This is a very fine wine for early consumption with a wide range of fish dishes. Excellent value.

Rombauer Vineyards, 1986 Napa Valley $14.50

Appealing spicy fruit in the nose, with floral and earthy scents, and nice oaky overtones. Medium-full bodied. Generous spicy fruit flavors on the palate, with lemony nuances, and ample oak through the finish. Try with pasta and shellfish.

Rombauer Vineyards, 1985 Napa Valley $14.50

Appealing appley fruit in the nose, with some herbal scents and oaky overtones. Medium-bodied. Moderately intense varietal fruit flavors on the palate, with a fair dimension of oak, and generous acid. Crispy finish. Fine with rich seafood dishes.

Rombauer Vineyards, 1986 Napa Valley, French Vineyard $12.50

Nice apple and pearlike aromas, with floral scents. Medium bodied. The flavors consistently follow the aromas, moderately deep on the palate, in a firm structure. Tart finish. Fine with a wide range of fish dishes.

Rombauer Vineyards, 1985 Napa Valley, French Vineyard $13.50

Light golden yellow color. Moderate appley, herbal, and toasty oak aromas. Medium-bodied. Soft vanilla and butterscotch flavors in the mouth, with ample oak and tannin. The finish is oaky and tart. Try with rich seafood dishes or poultry.

Round Hill, House, 1987 California $6.00

Moderately intense green apple and oaky aromas. Medium bodied. Mild appley fruit and oaky aromas, nicely balanced, in a clean presentation. Fine with moderately seasoned fish dishes. Good value.

Round Hill Vineyards, 1986 North Coast $6.75

Pleasant, medium-intense appley fruit aromas, with a touch of oak. Medium bodied. The wine is round upon entry, with moderate fruit and oak, in a clean presentation. Fine with fish.

Rustridge Vineyards, 1986 Napa Valley

 $9.75

Brilliant. Light gold color. Quite intense floral and appley aromas, with smoky tones. Medium bodied. Medium-intense appley fruit on the palate, with a woody dimension. Finishes slightly bitter. Will improve for several years. Try with well-seasoned poultry dishes.

Rutherford Hill Special Cuvée, 1986 Napa Valley, Rutherford Knoll

 $11.00

Light gold color. Medium-intense appley aromas, with lemony scents, and ample spicy oak in support. Medium-full bodied. Rather thin appley/lemony fruit flavors on the palate. The finish is short and somewhat bitter. Best with well-seasoned fish dishes.

Rutherford Hill Winery, 1986 Napa Valley, Jaeger Vineyards

 $12.00

Forward toasty oak and citrusy fruit in the nose. Medium-full bodied. Moderately intense young fruit flavors on the palate, enriched by sweet oak. Slightly coarse finish. Will improve for several years. Best with rich seafood dishes.

Rutherford Hill Winery, 1985 Napa Valley, Jaeger Vineyards

 $11.00

Medium-intense appley fruit in the nose, with ample oak in support. Medium-full bodied. Moderately deep appley fruit on the palate, with a good oak/acid dimension, in a firm structure. Crisp finish. Will improve for several years. Enjoy with well-seasoned fish dishes or white meats.

St. Clement Vineyards, 1986 Napa Valley

 $15.00

Medium-intense tart fruit and mild oak in the nose. Medium bodied. Clean and lively on the palate, with the moderate fruit flavors in balance with nice oak, in a good structure. Slightly bitter finish. Try as an accompaniment to grilled salmon with mustard sauce.

St. Clement Vineyards, 1985 Napa Valley

 $14.50

Nice floral impression in the nose, with appley, lemony, spicy, and oaky scents. Medium-full bodied. Pronounced lemony fruit flavors on the palate, with oak in balance, in a firm structure. Try this fine wine with roast chicken, salmon, or swordfish.

 **St. Francis Winery, 1986 California, 53% Sonoma Valley, 47% Napa Valley**  **$9.00**

Light golden color. Medium-intense appley and herbal aromas. Medium bodied. Round and smooth in the mouth, with the fruit and acid in balance, in a clean presentation. Will go well with a wide range of fish dishes.

 Ste. Chapelle, 1986 Idaho **$10.00**

Pale straw color. Appealing floral fruit in the nose, joined by a touch of toasty oak. Medium bodied. Moderately intense fruit in the mouth, with good acid. Clean, crisp finish. A fine wine for early consumption with moderately seasoned fish dishes or as an apéritif.

 Ste. Chapelle Canyon Chardonnay, 1985 Idaho **$6.00**

Appealing aromas of fresh apples. Medium bodied. Nice appley fruit on the palate, with banana and cinnamon nuances, with good acid. Clean and crisp. Just enjoy. Excellent value.

 Ste. Chapelle Reserve, 1986 Idaho, Symms Family Vineyard **$15.00**

Appealing caramel and creamy oak in the nose. Medium bodied. Refined appley fruit in the mouth, with a nice toasty element, in a clean presentation. Try this fine wine with baked sea bass.

 Saintsbury, 1987 Carneros **$13.00**

Very attractive aromas of apples, pears, lemons and toasty oak. Medium-full bodied. Lots of juicy fruit on the palate, enriched by sweet oak, in a clean presentation. An excellent wine that will improve for a few years. Try with cracked crab or lobster with lemon.

 Saintsbury, 1986 Carneros **$12.00**

Nice floral impression in the nose, with hints of melons, butterscotch, lemons, and spice, and sweet oak throughout. Medium-full bodied. Lush fruit on the palate combines nicely with creamy oak and a touch of citrus. Tart finish. Fine with sautéed scallops, sea bass, or cracked crab.

 Sanford Winery, 1987 Santa Barbara County  **$15.00**

Nice tropical fruit aromas, with lemony and nutty scents, laced in toasty oak. Medium-full bodied. Mouth-filling ripe peach fruit, lemon, and oak flavors, in a good structure. Oaky finish. Try with spicy seafood or poultry dishes.

★★ ½ **Sanford Winery, 1986 Santa Barbara County**   **$14.00**

Intense pineappley and lemony fruit aromas, with earthy scents, and nice toasty oak in support. Medium-full bodied. Viscous and fleshy on the palate, with rich buttery flavors and ample oak, in a tasty combination. This is a substantial Chardonnay, and will hold up to well-seasoned fowl or veal dishes.

★★ ½ **Sanford Winery, 1985 Santa Barbara County**   **$12.00**

Light golden yellow color. Forward honey and butterscotch aromas, with nice toasty oak in support. Medium-full bodied. Fleshy ripe fruit flavors on the palate, with ample acid, in a firm structure. Best with savory seafood dishes.

★★ **Santa Barbara Winery, 1986 Santa Ynez Valley**   **$8.50**

Light golden color. Appealing, medium-intense apple like fruit aromas, with earthy scents, and oaky tones. Medium-full bodied. The lemony fruit is reasonably deep and firm on the palate, with ample oak, in a good structure. Tart finish. Best with rich seafood or fowl dishes.

★★ ½ **Santa Barbara Winery Reserve, 1986 Santa Ynez Valley**   **$14.00**

Loads of toasty oak and ripe apple aromas, with spicy and earthy tones. Medium-full bodied. Lush and full on the palate, with the buttery and lemony fruit flavors nicely balanced with acid. Pronounced fruity finish. Best with rich poultry or fish dishes.

★★★ **Sarah's Vineyard, 1985 Monterey County, Ventana Vineyard** **$17.00**

Attractive appley and floral aromas, with lemon and butterscotch scents. Medium-full bodied. Juicy, lush buttery fruit flavors fill the mouth, with a nice citric dimension. Crisp finish. Enjoy this excellent wine with cracked crab or lobster with lemon.

★★ **Sbarboro Winery, 1985 Alexander Valley, Gauer Ranch** **$8.50**

Light golden color. Nicely focused varietal fruit aromas, with undercurrents of mint, fennel, and oak. Medium bodied. Medium fruit flavors on the palate, with acid in balance, in a clean presentation. Try with Rex sole or sand dabs.

***Sea Ridge Winery, 1985 Sonoma County,
Mill Station Vineyard*** 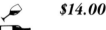 **$12.75**

Bright. Nice golden color. Intense, ripe tropical fruit in the nose, with banana and smoky vanilla tones. Medium-full bodied. Very mature appley and pineappley fruit flavors, with ample oak and tannins. Somewhat woody aftertaste. Best with highly seasoned shellfish and poultry.

 ***Sequoia Grove Vineyards, 1986 Carneros—
Napa Valley***   **$13.00**

Appealing, nicely focused melony fruit in the nose, with ample oak in support. Medium-full bodied. Moderately intense lemony fruit flavors in the mouth, with a full dimension of oak, in a firm structure. Slightly hot finish. Will improve for a couple of years. Try with baked sea bass or turkey with apple-sage dressing.

 ***Sequoia Grove Vineyards, 1985 Carneros—
Napa Valley***   **$12.00**

Forward oaky aromas, joined by floral and appley tones. Medium-full bodied. This is a big mouth-filling wine, with oak dominant throughout. Finishes slightly hot. Try as an accompaniment to roast pork with mustard-sage sauce or veal with rosemary.

 ***Sequoia Grove Vineyards, 1985 Napa Valley,
Allen Family Vineyard***   **$14.00**

Beautiful Chardonnay fruit and toasty oak in the nose. Medium-full bodied. Deep fruit impression on the palate, with the rich fruit and oak flavors in perfect balance. Smooth, lingering finish. This wine will improve for another five years. Try this superior wine with well-seasoned pork, veal, or poultry dishes.

 ***Sequoia Grove Vineyards, Estate Bottled,
1986 Napa Valley***   **$15.00**

Medium intense herbal fruit aromas, with earthy scents, and oaky overtones. Medium-full bodied. Moderate fruit flavors on the palate, with dominant oak throughout, in a firm structure. Harsh finish. Fine with rich seafood or fowl dishes.

 Shafer Vineyards, 1986 Napa Valley  **$12.00**

Medium-intense, fresh appley fruit in the nose, with hints of nectarines. Medium bodied. Moderately deep lemony fruit on the palate, with nice toasty oak, in a firm structure. Pleasant, lingering aftertaste. Fine with a wide range of fish dishes.

Silverado Vineyards, 1987 Napa Valley **$12.50**

Attractive floral and ripe tropical fruit in the nose, with citrusy and toasty oak tones. Medium-full bodied. Soft and supple on entry, with generous apple and pear flavors on the palate, and a butterscotch element, in a clean presentation. This is an easy-drinking wine. Enjoy.

 Silverado Vineyards, 1986 Napa Valley **$12.00**

Rich, ripe, buttery tropical fruit aromas, with a nice dimension of oak. Medium bodied. Generous pineapple and lemony fruit flavors fill the mouth, with oak and acid in perfect balance. Try as an accompaniment to grilled salmon with mustard sauce or chicken with pistachio sauce. Good value.

 Simi Winery, 1986 Mendocino/Sonoma **$11.00**

Appealing, clean, medium-intense aromas of apples and vanillin oak. Medium bodied. Round feel in the mouth, with the green apple fruit and sweet oak in balance in a firm presentation. Crispy finish. This is a fine wine for early consumption with Rex sole, sand dabs, or red snapper.

 Smith-Madrone, 1985 Napa Valley **$12.50**

Forward aroma of ripe apples, with floral, herbal, and lemony scents laced in oak. Medium-full bodied. Moderate fruit in the mouth, with a fair dimension of oak and acid. Hard finish. Best with rich seafoods or fowl.

 Sonoma-Cutrer, 1986 Russian River Valley, Russian River Ranches **$12.00**

Appealing and spicy aromas, with herbal tones, nicely supported by sweet oak. Medium-deep apple and oak flavors on the palate, with a nice lemony dimension, in a good structure. The hallmark here is consistency over the years. Enjoy this excellent wine with soft-shelled crab, poached salmon, or shad roe. Good value.

 Sonoma-Cutrer, 1985 Russian River Valley, Russian River Ranches **$11.75**

Nice golden yellow color. Medium-intense aromas of blossomy fruit, with buttery scents, and a nice touch of toasty oak. Medium-full bodied. The lively fruit is deep and firm on the palate, with citric nuances, and an attractive oaky dimension. Pleasant lingering finish. Try as an accompaniment to grilled salmon with mustard sauce, cracked crab with lemons, or sea bass with ginger and lemon. Good value.

Sonoma-Cutrer, 1986 Sonoma Coast, Cutrer Vineyard

$16.00

Golden yellow color. Pleasant, tight, medium-intense lemony fruit in the nose, with a full dimension of toasty oak in support. Medium-full bodied. Moderate green apple and citric fruit flavors on the palate, in a tight structure. Clean, tart finish. Enjoy with oysters on the half-shell or caviar.

Sonoma-Cutrer, 1985 Russian River Valley, Cutrer Vineyard

$15.00

Attractive, round, ripe appley fruit aromas, with floral tones, joined by lively oak. Medium-full bodied. The wine is broad and fruity on entry, later firmed with good oak and acid. Clean finish. Consistency is the hallmark here. Enjoy this excellent wine with grilled salmon, turkey with sage dressing, or veal roast with rosemary.

Sonoma-Cutrer, 1986 Sonoma Valley, Les Pierres Vineyard

$19.50

Intense appley, pearlike, and lemony aromas, with nice toasty oak in support. Medium-full bodied. Generous lemony fruit on the palate, with nice buttery and oaky elements, in a firm structure. Crisp, tart finish. Good potential for further improvement. Try as an accompaniment to grilled salmon with mustard sauce or Cornish rock hen with an apple-sage dressing.

Sonoma-Cutrer, 1985 Sonoma Valley, Les Pierres Vineyard

$17.50

Another winner! Top-of-the-line consistency over the years. Beautiful appley and toasty oak aromas, with nice honey and floral scents. Medium-full bodied. Broad fruit flavors in the mouth, nicely balanced with oak, in a firm structure. Tasty, lingering finish. Look for further development for at least five additional years. Enjoy.

Spring Mountain Vineyards, 1984 Napa Valley

$15.00

Light golden color. Brilliant. Moderately intense appley fruit, with slight buttery scents, and ample toasty oak. Medium-bodied. The apple and oak flavors come through in the mouth, in a firm structure. Fine with rich shellfish dishes.

Stag's Leap Wine Cellars, 1987 Napa Valley

$18.00

Appealing, fresh appley and lemony fruit in the nose. Medium-full bodied. Attractive, delicate peach, honey, and citrusy fruit flavors on the palate, nicely balanced in a silky texture. Very long, crispy finish. Will improve for several years. Enjoy with grilled salmon or sea bass.

Stag's Leap Wine Cellars, 1986 Napa Valley $17.00

Very appealing floral, buttery, spicy, and toasty oak aromas. Medium-full bodied. Delicate and elegant on the palate, with the butterscotch, pear, and spice flavors perfectly balanced with acid, in a clean presentation. A superior wine. Just enjoy.

Stag's Leap Wine Cellars, 1985 Napa Valley $13.50

Light golden color. Moderately intense toasty Chardonnay aromas, with butterscotch and creamy oak overtones. Medium-bodied. Fresh appley fruit flavors, with nice oak, and pleasant, crisp acidity. Finishes tart. Fine as an accompaniment to grilled salmon with mustard sauce or chicken with pistachio sauce.

Stag's Leap Wine Cellars Reserve, 1986 Napa Valley $26.00

Very intense buttery and lemony aromas, with ample toasty oak in support. Full bodied. Loads of fleshy, ripe lemony fruit on the palate, with a full dimension oak, in a firm structure. Long, brisk finish. A big wine that is not ponderous. Try with lobster Newburg, cold roast goose, or veal roast.

Stag's Leap Wine Cellars Reserve, 1985 Napa Valley $20.00

Appealing aromas of ripe apples, with citrusy and oaky scents. Medium-full bodied. Flavorful fruit on the palate, with the floral, buttery, and lemony elements in nice balance with the oak. Slightly coarse finish. Try with veal or pork with rosemary.

David S. Stare Reserve, 1985 Dry Creek Valley $15.00

Produced by Dry Creek Vineyard. Intense tropical fruit and toasty oak aromas. Medium bodied. Nice balance of exotic fruit and oak on the palate, with a fair dimension of acid. Sharp finish. Best with highly seasoned fish dishes.

Sterling Vineyards, 1986 Carneros—Napa Valley, Winery Lake $20.00

Most attractive, intense ripe apply and toasty/smokey oak aromas, with lemony scents. Medium-full bodied. Loads of ripe varietal fruit on the palate, with a lemony element, and ample spicy oak, in a clean presentation. Pleasant complex finish. This elegant wine will improve for several years. Just enjoy!

Sterling Vineyards, 1985 Napa Valley $14.00

Medium-intense, fresh, clean aromas of apples, pears, and flowers, with hints of butterscotch. Medium bodied. Tightly structured fruit flavors on the palate, with tangy acid, and a touch of oak. Try this very fine wine with grilled salmon or chicken in a light sauce.

☆☆ ½ **Sterling Vineyards, 1985 Napa Valley, Diamond Mountain Ranch**　$15.00

Rich and appealing aromas of apples, lemons, and sweet oak. Medium bodied. Loads of young fruit on the palate, with a nice citric dimension, and sweet oak in balance, in a firm structure. Long, citrusy finish. Try with Rex sole or sand dabs.

☆ **Stevenot Grand Reserve, 1985 Calaveras County**　$9.00

Pleasant tropical fruit aromas, with pronounced oaky overtones. Medium-full bodied. Moderately intense lemony fruit flavors, enriched by an oaky dimension. Finishes a bit coarse. Fine with well-seasoned fish dishes.

☆☆ **Stevenot Winery, 1985 California**　$6.00

Light yellow color. Medium intense herbal Chardonnay aromas, with a touch of creamy oak. Medium-bodied. The wine is supple on the palate, with nice oak flavors and a citric dimension. Excellent with moderately seasoned fish dishes. Good value.

☆☆ ½ **Stonegate Winery, 1986 Napa Valley**　$13.00

Forward appley and buttery aromas. Medium bodied. Full-flavored on the palate, with the buttery pear flavors and toasty elements in perfect balance. Lingering aftertaste. Try as an accompaniment to sautéed chicken breast with a cream sauce.

☆☆ ½ **Stratford, 1985 California**　$9.00

Appealing appley aromas with citric, spicy, and herbal scents. Medium-full bodied. The wine enters the mouth smooth and supple, with the fresh varietal fruit flavors nicely balanced with a long lemony dimension. This is a very fine wine that can be enjoyed with a wide range of fish dishes. Good value.

☆☆ **Taft Street, 1986 Russian River Valley**　$10.00

Pleasant, medium-intense lemony fruit in the nose. Medium bodied. Appealing young fruit on the palate, with a touch of oak, in a delicate presentation. A well-made wine that can be enjoyed with light luncheon dishes.

☆☆ **Taft Street, 1987 Sonoma County**　$7.50

Appealing appley and citrusy fruit aromas. Medium bodied. Nice balance of tropical fruit and lemony flavors on the palate, in a clean presentation. This is an easygoing, well-balanced wine that will do well with moderately seasoned fish dishes or on its own. Good value.

☆☆½ *Trefethen Vineyards, 1985 Napa Valley* $15.25

Appealing, medium-intense green apple, spicy and floral aromas. Medium-full bodied. Round on the palate, with the generous appley/lemony fruit flavors in nice balance with spicy oak. Try as an accompaniment to sautéed breast of chicken with cream.

☆☆½ *Tualatin Private Reserve, 1985 Willamette Valley* $13.00

Rich honey, toast, and spice in the nose, with ample oak in support. Medium-full bodied. Abundant honeylike fruit fills the mouth, with a full dimension of oak through the finish. This is a relatively big wine that will hold for a few years. Best with fowl or light meats.

☆☆½ *Veritas Vineyard, 1986 Oregon* $15.00

Bright. Light gold color. Appealing apple, honey, butterscotch and vanillin oak in the nose. Medium-full bodied. Generous apple and tropical fruit flavors on the palate, with ample acid. Good structure. Fine with grilled salmon, swordfish, or veal piccata.

☆☆ *Veritas Vineyard, 1985 Oregon* $13.00

Very attractive buttery and toasty oak aromas, joined by appley fruit flavors on the palate, with ample oak. Slightly hot finish. Try as an accompaniment to veal or pork roast with rosemary.

☆☆☆ *Viansa Cellars, 1986 Sonoma/Napa* $12.50

Attractive, medium-intense appley, floral, lemony and spicy oak aromas. Medium-full bodied. Smooth and creamy on the palate, with the pearlike fruit flavors nicely balanced with acid, in a clean presentation. Crisp and fruity in the finish. This is the first effort in a new venture by Sam and Vicki Sebastiani, and it is a winner. Just enjoy!

☆☆☆ *Vichon Winery, 1986 Napa Valley* $15.00

Beautiful pearlike aromas, with spicy scents, and nice toasty oak in support. Medium-full bodied. Loads of nicely defined, juicy fruit fills the mouth, with the flavor elements of honey, lemon, and vanilla in perfect harmony. This superior wine will improve for several years. Try with shellfish or veal de la Limone.

☆☆☆ *Vichon Winery, 1985 Napa Valley* $15.00

Very appealing appley fruit in the nose, with floral, pineappley, and citrusy tones, and nice toasty oak in the background. Medium bodied. Deep fruit impression on the palate, with the apple, citrus, and tropical fruit flavors nicely balanced with soft oak, in a firm structure. All the essentials are in the right proportion. Enjoy.

Vina Vista Winery, 1985 Alexander Valley $8.75

Medium-intense citrusy fruit aromas, with floral hints, and ample oak in support. Medium bodied. Enters the mouth smooth and round, with nice lemony fruit flavors and ample acid. Finishes tart. Fine with well-seasoned fish dishes.

Waterbrook Winery, 1985 Washington $10.00

Very attractive peach and lemon aromas, with nice toasty oak scents. Medium bodied. The wine enters the mouth smooth and clean, with the moderately intense fruit and oak flavors in good balance. Finishes slightly hot. Enjoy this fine wine with well-seasoned fish dishes or chicken in a light sauce. Good value.

Wente Bros., 1985 Arroyo Seco $8.50

Attractive light yellow color. Pleasant green apple aromas, with scents of oranges and lemons, and a touch of tasty oak. Medium bodied. Moderately deep young juicy fruit on the palate, with citric nuances. This is the perfect wine with a wide range of fish dishes or moderately seasoned poultry. Good value.

Wente Bros., 1985 California $7.50

Moderate floral and citrusy aromas. Medium bodied. A rounded feel in the mouth, with the medium-low intensity fruit flavors, oak, and acid in nice balance. A pleasant, clean wine that will go well with moderately seasoned fish dishes.

Wente Bros. Reserve, 1986 Livermore Valley, Herman Wente Vineyard $11.00

Attractive ripe tropical fruit aromas, with floral and apricoty scents, and moderate toasty oak in support. Medium bodied. Generous juicy fruit in the mouth, with lemony nuances, and a nice touch of oak. Fruity finish. An excellent wine for current consumption with moderately seasoned chicken or fish dishes.

Wm. Wheeler Vineyards, 1986 Sonoma County $11.50

Medium-intense green apple aromas, with pineapple scents, and a nice touch of creamy oak. Medium bodied. Appealing lemony fruit flavors, with moderate oak. Crispy finish. Try with sautéed orange roughy filet.

Wm. Wheeler Winery, 1985 Sonoma County $11.00

Brilliant. Attractive floral and appley aromas, with herbal scents, and toasty oak overtones. Medium-bodied. Nice fresh fruit impression on the palate, with citric and oak nuances, in a firm presentation. Enjoy this fine wine with baked sea bass or salmon.

White Oak Vineyards, 1986 Sonoma County

 $10.00

Appealing, medium-intense aromas of pears and apples, with floral and citrusy scents, and a touch of oak. Medium-full bodied. Generous appley/lemony fruit flavors on the palate, with moderate oak. Crispy finish. Fine with well-seasoned fish dishes. Good value.

White Oak Vineyards, 1985 Sonoma County

 $10.00

Moderately intense appley aromas, with butterscotch and oak in support. Medium-bodied. The wine enters the mouth firmly structured, with modest varietal characteristics. Finishes tart. Fine with fish dishes.

White Oak Vineyards, Meyers Limited Reserve, 1985 Alexander Valley

 **$14.50**

Brilliant. Light golden color. Very appealing clean, rich buttery, toasty, and floral aromas. Medium-bodied. Deep impression of bright appley and lemony fruit flavors on the palate, with oak and acid in nice balance. This fine wine will hold for several years. Try as an accompaniment to sea bass with ginger and lemon, sautéed chicken breast with cream, or shad roe.

Wild Horse Cellars, 1986 San Luis Obispo, Wild Horse Vineyards

 $9.00

Appealing, medium-intense aromas of apples, spice and toasty oak. Medium bodied. Generous rich appley/lemony fruit flavors are in nice balance with oak and acid. Clean, crisp finish. Try with oysters on the half-shell. Good value.

Wilson Ranch, 1986 Sonoma Valley, Estate Bottled

$15.00

Produced by Sebastiani Vineyards. Forward ripe apples, honey, and sweet oak in the nose. Medium-full bodied. Nicely focused varietal fruit flavors on the palate, with an ample oak dimension throughout. Finishes a bit coarse. Fine with well-seasoned shellfish or poultry.

Winter Creek Winery, 1986 Napa Valley, Takahashi Vineyard

$11.00

Brilliant. Light gold color. Forward aromas of apples and honey, with nice vanillin oak in support. Medium-full bodied. Appealing pineappley fruit flavors on the palate, with nutty nuances, good acid, and a nice oaky dimension. Long finish. Try with well-seasoned shellfish or roast turkey.

Witter Cellars, 1986 California **$8.00**

Attractive ripe Chardonnay fruit in the nose, with floral scents, and nice oaky tones. Medium bodied. Clean, well-ripened fruit in the mouth, with citric nuances. Fruity and crispy in the finish. Enjoy with a wide range of fish dishes. Good value.

 ### Witter Cellars, 1985 California **$7.00**

Appealing apple and citric aromas, with floral scents and a touch of oak. Medium-bodied. Generous fresh fruit flavors in the mouth, with acid in balance. Slightly tart finish. Enjoy with a wide range of fish dishes. Good value.

 ### Zaca Mesa American Reserve, 1984 Santa Barbara **$12.75**

Appealing buttery and toasty aromas. Medium-full bodied. The wine enters the mouth full and round, with the appley and lemony flavors nicely balanced with sweet oak. Crispy, lingering finish. This very fine wine will hold for several years. Best with rich seafood or fowl dishes.

 ### ZD, 1987 California **$18.50**

Assertive tropical fruit aromas, with lemony and spicy tones, laced in rich oak. Medium-full bodied. Rich and lush on the palate, with the apple and tropical fruit flavors balanced nicely with ample oak. Another great bottling from this winery. Just enjoy.

 ### ZD, 1986 California **$18.00**

Very appealing, complex aromas of spice and apples, with pineappley and lemony overtones. Medium-full bodied. Rich melony fruit on the palate, with nuances of tropical fruit and clove, and nice creamy oak, in a balanced presentation. Consistency is the hallmark here. Enjoy this superior wine with stuffed lobster, roast pork with yams, or turkey with sage dressing.

 ### ZD, 1985 California  **$16.00**

I do not know how these people do it, but here is another winner, equal to their 1984 bottling. Complex aromas of ripe apples, herbs, lemons, and apricots, with a nice dimension of toasty oak. Medium-full bodied. Loads of lush tropical fruit fill the mouth, with sufficient acid to give a nice tartness. This superior wine will improve for several years. Enjoy with cold roast goose, stuffed lobster, veal piccata, or baked turkey.

☆

Stephen Zellerbach Winery, 1987 California

    $7.00

Moderately intense sweet appley fruit aromas, with herbal and oaky overtones. Medium bodied. Somewhat sweet varietal fruit on the palate, with spicy nuances, and good acid, in a clean presentation. Try with light luncheon dishes.

☆☆ ½

Stephen Zellerbach Winery, 1986 Sonoma County, Second Bottling

    $7.00

Very attractive, forward appley and toasty oak aromas. Medium-full bodied. The appley/lemony fruit is medium-deep, and nicely focused on the palate. Clean and well structured. Try this fine wine with sautéed chicken breasts or grilled salmon.
Good value.

SAUVIGNON BLANC

Adler Fels Fumé Blanc, 1986 Sonoma County $8.75

Forward ripe varietal fruit aromas, with loads of sweet oak in
support. Medium-full bodied. The wine is supple in the mouth,
with the rich fruit and ample oak in balance, and a nice acid
dimension for structure. Try as an accompaniment to curried
chicken with rice or pork roast with an herbal sauce.

Beaulieu Vineyard, 1987 Napa Valley $8.50

Very appealing floral fruit in the nose, with clean grassy
overtones. Medium bodied. Nicely focused fruit on the palate,
with grassy nuances, in a clean presentation. Crispy finish.
Fine with a wide range of moderately seasoned fish dishes.

Benziger Fumé Blanc, 1987 Sonoma County $8.00

Produced by Glen Ellen Winery. Light yellow color. Forward,
ripe pineapple and floral aromas with oaky overtones. Medium-
full bodied. Generous sweetish fruit on the palate with herbal
elements, through the finish. Best with rich seafood or
fowl dishes.

Beringer Vineyards, 1986 Knights Valley $8.50

Medium-intense figgy and melony aromas, with nice spicy oak in
support. Medium-full bodied. Rich lemony fruit flavors on the
palate, with ample vanillin oak through the finish. Best with rich
seafood dishes.

Buena Vista Winery, 1987 Lake County $7.50

Appealing melony, appley, and floral aromas, with strong grassy
overtones. Medium-bodied. Generous grassy fruit on the palate,
with a lemony element, and a nice touch of residual sugar.
Try with roast chicken. Good value.

Buena Vista Winery, 1986 Lake County $7.00

Medium-intense lemony, floral, and grassy aromas. Medium
bodied. Smooth and soft on the palate, with the slightly sweet
lemony/pineappley fruit flavors nicely balanced with acid. Enjoy
with chicken or white meats in light sauces. Good value.

Davis Bynum Fumé Reserve, 1987 Sonoma County $7.50

Intense varietal fruit and herbaceous aromas. Medium bodied.
The flavors follow the aromas through the finish. The wine is
clean and well balanced. Best with highly seasoned fish dishes.

Byron Vineyard, 1987 Santa Barbara County $7.00

Appealing medium-intense floral fruit and oak in the nose, with herbal overtones. Soft and round on the palate, with the generous fruit in nice balance with the acid, in a good structure. Try with moderately seasoned fish or chicken dishes. Good value.

Cakebread Cellars, 1987 Napa Valley $11.00

Intense sweet fruit and oak in the nose, with strong weedy scents throughout. Medium-full bodied. Wonderful rich fruit fills the mouth, with an intense grassy dimension, in a good structure. This is a superior Sauvignon Blanc made in a grassy style. Try with smoked oysters, duck pâté, stuffed lobster, or snapper in parchment with soy and ginger.

Cakebread Cellars, 1986 Napa Valley $10.00

Brilliant. Light straw color. Restrained, clean fruit in the nose, with grassy scents. Medium bodied. Moderate fruit flavors in the mouth, with ample acid through the finish. Try as an accompaniment to snapper in parchment with light herbs.

J. Carey Cellars, 1986 Santa Ynez Valley $7.50

Medium-intense figgy and oaky aromas. Medium bodied. Concentrated fruit flavors on the palate, with ample oak, in a good structure. Crispy finish. This is a flavorful wine that will go well with moderately seasoned poultry dishes.

Carmenet Vineyard, 1985 Sonoma Valley $8.75

Deep, ripe herbal/grassy fruit aromas, with ample sweet toasty oak. Medium bodied. Generous figgy fruit flavors fill the mouth, nicely supported with creamy oak. Smooth finish. Try with sautéed chicken breast with a cream sauce or sea bass with lemon and ginger.

Caymus Vineyards, 1987 Napa Valley $8.00

Appealing aromas of melons and pears in the nose, with a touch of sweet oak. Medium-full bodied. Melony and lemony fruit on the palate, with a grassy element, and a touch of sweetness through the finish. Soft and easy to drink. Try at lunch with chicken salad.

Caymus Vineyards, 1986 Napa Valley $7.50

Rich melony fruit aromas, with tropical fruit scents, and spicy oak in support. Medium bodied. The wine enters the mouth round, with ripe fruit flavors and ample oak. Finishes slightly harsh. Best with well-seasoned fish dishes.

☆☆   ### *Chalk Hill Winery, 1986, Sonoma County*   *$6.00*

Light yellow color. Medium-intense green olive aromas, with flinty and weedy tones. Medium-full bodied. Intense herbal fruit flavors on the palate, with earthy nuances, in a firm structure. Try with well-seasoned fish dishes. Good value.

☆☆   ### *Chateau Potelle, 1986 Napa Valley*   *$8.75*

Medium-intense floral, figgy, and citrusy aromas, with a full dimension of grassy tones throughout. Medium bodied. Moderately intense grassy fruit and acid in nice balance. Best with moderately seasoned light fish dishes.

☆☆ ½   ### *Chateau St. Jean, Fumé Blanc, 1986 Sonoma County*   *$8.00*

Appealing, persistent grassy fruit aromas. Medium bodied. Generous citric and herbal fruit flavors in the mouth, with ample acid. Tart finish. Try with oysters or cracked crab. Good value.

☆   ### *Christophe Vineyards, 1987 California*   *$4.00*

Medium-intense sweetish melony and appley aromas, with herbal tones, medium bodied. The flavors follow the aromas, with acid in balance. Nice as an apéritif or with light luncheon foods. Good value.

☆☆   ### *Christophe Vineyards, 1986 California*   *$6.00*

Appealing, medium-intense floral and herbal aromas. Medium bodied. Attractive, moderately intense fruit flavors, with good acid. Clean finish. Fine with mildly seasoned fish dishes. Good value.

☆☆ ½   ### *Clos du Bois, 1987 Alexander Valley*   *$8.00*

Appealing, clean lemony fruit in the nose. Medium bodied. Nice tangy grapefruit flavors on the palate, in a refined presentation. Crispy finish. Try with a wide range of moderately seasoned fish dishes. Good value.

☆☆   ### *Clos du Bois, 1986 Alexander Valley*   *$7.50*

Medium-intense grassy fruit aromas, with a touch of oak. Medium bodied. Rounded entry, with narrow grapefruit flavors. Acidic finish. Fine with clams or oysters on the half-shell.

☆☆   ### *Columbia Crest Vineyards, 1986 Columbia Valley, Washington*   *$7.00*

Appealing floral, spicy apple, and honeylike aromas. Medium bodied. Generous, slightly sweet, citrusy fruit flavors in the mouth, with a touch of grass. Clean finish. Fine with chicken or crab salad.

★★   **_Conn Creek Barrel Selected, 1986 Napa Valley_**   _$10.50_

Medium-intense lemony fruit aromas, with grassy overtones. Medium bodied. Moderately deep citric fruit on the palate, with a grassy element, and nice oak through the finish. Try with moderately seasoned chicken dishes.

★★½   **_De Loach Vineyards, Fumé Blanc, 1987 Russian River Valley_**   _$9.00_

Appealing aromas of apples, spice, and toasty oak, with scents of tropical fruit and juniper berry. Medium-full bodied. Very fruity on the palate, with a touch of residual sugar, and sufficient acid for structure. Try with shellfish or shad roe.

★★   **_Domaine Laurier, 1986 Sonoma County_**   _$9.50_

Appealing fresh fruit aromas, with light grassy scents, and nice oak. Medium bodied. Generous lively fruit on the palate, with citric nuances, and a touch of oak. Crisp finish. Fine with a wide range of fish dishes.

★★½   **_Dry Creek Vineyard, Fumé Blanc, 1987 Sonoma County_**   _$8.75_

Attractive, assertive grassy, herbal, and citrusy aromas. Medium bodied. Intense grassy varietal fruit flavors on the palate, with good acid and a touch of oak, in a good structure. Consistency is the hallmark here. An excellent wine that is best with well-seasoned fish dishes.

★★½   **_Dry Creek Vineyard, Fumé Blanc, 1986 Sonoma County_**   _$8.75_

Forward ripe fruit aromas, with floral scents, and ample weedy overtones. Medium bodied. Generous sweet fruit flavors, with herbal/grassy elements throughout. Finishes slightly tart. Best with well-seasoned fish dishes.

★★★   **_Duckhorn Vineyards, 1987 Napa Valley_**   _$9.50_

Appealing melony fruit aromas, with floral and spicy scents. Medium bodied. Nice melon and pear flavors on the palate, with spicy nuances, in a smooth presentation. Good balance. Try with seafood quiche or pasta with shellfish.

★★½   **_Gary Farrell, 1986 Russian River Valley_**   _$8.50_

Assertive grassy aromas, with lemony scents. Medium bodied. Generous, rich, grassy fruit on the palate, with citrusy nuances, in a firm structure. Crisp finish. Fine with rich seafood or fowl dishes.

☆☆½ Ferrari-Carano, Fumé Blanc, 1986 Alexander Valley $9.00

Light yellow color. Medium-intense melony fruit in the nose, with grassy overtones. Medium bodied. Creamy on the palate, with well-focused grassy fruit flavors and acid combined in a firm structure. This is the first bottling from this new winery. Quite impressive for openers. Best with well-seasoned fish dishes.

☆☆½ Ferrari-Carano, Fumé Blanc, 1987 Sonoma County $9.00

Attractive, medium-intense grassy fruit in the nose, with herbal and floral scents. Clean. Medium bodied. Generous young fruit flavors on the palate, in a tight structure. Crispy finish. Try this excellent wine with fish in a cream sauce or sautéed scallops.

☆ Fetzer Valley Oaks, Fumé, 1986 California $6.50

Medium-intense figgy, herbal, and grassy aromas. Medium bodied. Soft in the mouth, with the moderate citrusy fruit flavors and acid in nice balance. This is an appealing wine that will go well with moderately seasoned fish dishes.

☆ Fetzer Valley Oaks, Fumé Blanc, 1987 California $6.00

Moderately intense, herbal fruit in the nose, with earthy scents. Medium bodied. The herbal fruit follows on the palate, soft and clean. Fine with moderately seasoned fish dishes.

☆☆ The Firestone Vineyard, 1986 Santa Ynez Valley $7.50

Moderately intense figgy, grassy, and toasty aromas. Medium bodied. Round on entry, with generous figlike fruit flavors, and herbal nuances, enhanced by a touch of residual sugar. Try with chicken in a cream sauce.

☆☆☆ Flora Springs, 1986 Napa Valley $8.50

Very intense aromas of grassy varietal fruit and earthiness, with scents of figs and alfalfa, framed in rich oak. Medium-full bodied. Powerful deep fruit and oak flavors on the palate, in a good structure. Slightly coarse finish. Try this superior wine with spicy fish dishes. Excellent value.

☆☆ Fritz Cellars, 1987 Dry Creek Valley $7.00

Appealing grassy varietal fruit in the nose, with floral overtones. Medium bodied. Generous spicy fruit in the mouth, with a slight spritz, in a firm structure. Finishes a bit astringent. Try as an accompaniment to pasta with shellfish or fried smelt.

Fritz Cellars, Fumé Blanc, 1986 Dry Creek Valley $7.00

Very appealing figgy fruit in the nose, with nice sweet oak in support, and grassiness in the background. Medium bodied. Round on entry, with the tasty fruit and oak in balance, in a clean presentation. Fine with rich seafood dishes or sautéed chicken with a creamy sauce. Good value.

Fritz Cellars, Fumé Blanc, 1985 Dry Creek Valley $6.00

Medium-intense figlike fruit aromas, with oaky and grassy scents. Medium bodied. Appealing, delicate fruit on the palate, with sufficient acid for structure. Try with moderately seasoned fish dishes. Good value.

Frog's Leap, 1986 Napa Valley $9.00

Moderate figgy fruit aromas, with weedy scents and oaky overtones. Medium bodied. Narrow citric fruit flavors, with ample oak and acid. Tart finish. Fine with well-seasoned fish dishes.

Ernest & Julio Gallo Reserve, 1986 California $3.50

Appealing citric and herbal aromas, with a touch of grass. Medium bodied. Nice flavors of melons and green pears on the palate, with grapefruity nuances, in a clean presentation. Crisp finish. Try as an accompaniment to pasta with shellfish. Super value.

Geyser Peak, 1987 Sonoma County $5.00

Produced by Trione Vineyards. Fresh melony fruit aromas, with grassy overtones. Medium bodied. Moderately intense sweet tropical fruit flavors on the palate, in a soft presentation. Nice as an apéritif or with light luncheon foods.

Geyser Peak, 1986 Sonoma County $5.00

Produced by Trione Vineyards. Medium-light melony and herbal aromas. Medium bodied. Soft, somewhat sweet fruit in the mouth, with grassy nuances, and sufficient acid for structure. Best with moderately seasoned fish dishes. Good value.

Geyser Peak, Fumé Blanc, 1986 Alexander Valley $6.00

Produced by Trione Vineyards. Medium-intense grassy fruit aromas, with floral and oaky scents. Medium bodied. The wine is supple in the mouth, with the slightly sweetish fruit, oak, and herbal elements in nice balance. Appealing and easygoing. Best with light luncheon foods.

Glen Ellen Proprietor's Reserve, 1986 California $4.00

Appealing, delicate aromas of lemony fruit, with grassy scents. Medium bodied. Slightly sweet juicy fruit on the palate, with acid in balance. An easygoing wine. Try with chicken and avocado salad with a creamy citrus dressing. Good value.

☆

Glen Ellen Winery, Fumé Blanc, 1986 Sonoma County

$7.00

Intense grassy aromas, joined by citrusy fruit scents. Medium bodied. Moderate fruit flavors, with a fair acidic dimension. Sharp finish. Best with well-seasoned fish dishes.

☆☆ ½

Grand Cru Vineyards, 1987 Sonoma County

$9.00

Very appealing floral and grassy fruit aromas, with piney and herbal scents. Medium bodied. Generous ripe melony fruit on the palate, with citric nuances, enhanced by a touch of residual sugar, in a clean presentation. A very tasty wine! Try with seafood quiche or sautéed scallops.

☆☆ ½

Grand Cru Vineyards, 1986 Sonoma County

$9.00

Moderately intense, clean citric fruit in the nose, with grassy tones. Medium balance. Slightly viscous and smooth on the palate, with the tasty fruit and acid in balance, in a good structure. Enjoy with seafood quiche and morel mushrooms.

☆☆☆

Grgich Hills Cellar, Fumé Blanc, 1986 Napa Valley

$10.00

Beautiful aromas of grassy varietal fruit and oak, nicely supported by figgy and pineappley scents. Medium-full bodied. Plenty of rich fruit flavors on the palate, with herbal elements, and a fair dimension of spicy oak. Try this superior wine with well-seasoned fish or poultry dishes. Good value.

☆☆ ½

Groth Vineyards, 1986 Napa Valley

$7.00

Appealing, medium-intense pearlike aromas, with vanillin and grassy overtones. Medium-full bodied. Nice melon and peach flavors on the palate, with a subtle weediness, in a clean presentation. Crispy finish. This excellent wine will go well with a wide range of fish dishes. Good value.

☆☆ ½

Guenoc Winery, 1986 Lake/Napa, 55% Lake County, 45% Napa County

$6.75

Very attractive melony and figgy aromas, with herbal and oaky scents. Medium-full bodied. Nicely balanced with a good sense of varietal fruit, and a touch of oak and acid through the finish. Try as an accomplishment to pasta with shellfish. Good value.

☆☆

Hacienda Winery, 1986 Sonoma County

$8.00

Assertive grassy fruit aromas, with herbal scents. Medium-full bodied. Moderately deep herbal fruit flavors on the palate, with ample acid. Tart, crisp finish. Best with well-seasoned fish dishes.

Handley Cellars, 1986 Dry Creek Valley $8.00

Brilliant. Light straw color. Forward floral, honey, and pineappley nose, with ample oak in support. Medium-full bodied. Lots of ripe apple flavors on the palate, with a nice grassy dimension, and ample oak and acid. Broad flavors throughout. Nice finish. Try as an accompaniment to baked chicken with an herbal sauce. Good value.

Hanna Winery, 1987 Sonoma County $8.75

Assertive, nicely focused grassy fruit and herbal aromas, with oaky overtones. Medium bodied. The wine is sharp and tight, with the melony fruit flavors in good balance with oak and acid. Try as an accompaniment to pasta with shellfish.

Hanna Winery, 1986 Sonoma County $8.75

Forward grassy fruit and floral aromas, with sweet oak overtones. Medium-full bodied. Generous fleshy fruit in the mouth, nicely balanced with rich oak and acid. Try this very fine wine as an accompaniment to roast chicken with rosemary and pepper.

Haywood Winery, Fumé Blanc, 1986 Sonoma Valley $8.50

Aggressive grassy fruit in the nose. Medium bodied. Generous lemony fruit flavors on the palate, with a pungent weedy element. Good depth. This is a well-made wine that will go best with rich seafood dishes.

Hogue Cellars, Fumé Blanc, 1987 Washington $8.00

Wonderful perfumed aromas of melons, pears, herbs, and vanilla. The ripe, complex fruit flavors are intense on the palate, with a nice lemony dimension, in a clean presentation. A very tasty superior wine. Fine as an apéritif or with rich seafood dishes. Excellent value.

Hogue Cellars, Fumé Blanc, 1986 Washington $7.50

Very attractive, moderately intense floral and herbal aromas, with oaky tones. Medium bodied. Well-balanced flavors fill the mouth, in a clean presentation. Crisp finish. Enjoy this fine wine with steamed clams, fresh oysters, or cracked crab.

Louis Honig Cellars, 1986 Napa Valley $8.25

Appealing, medium-intense fresh fruit aromas. Medium bodied. Attractive peachlike fruit flavors on the palate, with oak and acid in perfect balance. Fruity, crispy finish. Fine with shellfish.

Husch, 1987 Mendocino, La Ribera Ranch   *$7.50*

Very appealing varietal fruit aromas, with floral and oaky overtones. Medium bodied. Generous citrusy fruit flavors on the palate, with a weedy dimension throughout, in a good structure. best with rich seafood dishes. Good value.

 ### Husch, 1986 Mendocino, La Ribera Vineyards   *$7.50*

Attractive aromas of ripe melons and sweet oak, with nice grassy tones. Medium-full bodied. Rich fruit flavors fill the mouth, with ample oak, in a good structure. This is a big wine that will go best with rich seafood or fowl dishes. Excellent value.

 ### Iron Horse Vineyards, Fumé Blanc, Barrel Fermented, 1987 Alexander Valley   *$10.00*

Subdued grassy fruit aromas, with floral scents. Opens up with airing. Medium bodied. Smooth on entry, with nicely focused fruit flavors, and ample oak that carries throughout. Fruity and slightly astringent in the finish. This is a well-made Sauvignon Blanc that will go best with rich seafood dishes.

 ### Iron Horse Vineyards, Fumé Blanc, Barrel Fermented, 1986 Alexander Valley   *$9.25*

Attractive floral, figgy, and melony aromas, with oaky overtones. Medium bodied. Deep, citric fruit on the palate, with oak and acid in balance, in a firm presentation. Tart finish. Best with well-seasoned fish dishes.

 ### Jepson Vineyards, 1986 Mendocino   *$7.50*

Appealing, medium-intense grassy fruit aromas, with flavorful overtones. Medium bodied. Appealing flavors of melon, figs, nutmeg, and sweet oak, nicely balanced with acid. Fruity, crispy finish. Try with well-seasoned fish dishes or poultry.

 ### Kendall-Jackson Vineyards, 1987 Clear Lake   *$8.00*

Medium-intense grassy and herbal aromas, with hints of tropical fruit and flowers. Medium bodied. Rich tropical fruit flavors on the palate, with herbal nuances, and a touch of residual sugar, in a soft presentation. Fine as an apéritif or with light luncheon dishes.

 ### Kenwood Vineyards, 1987 Sonoma County   *$9.00*

Here we go again—another winner! Beautifully focused grassy and herbal varietal fruit aromas, with scents of pineapples, lemons, grapefruit, and green peppers. Medium-full bodied. Loads of flavorful, complex fruit flavors fill the mouth, enhanced with rich oak, in a good structure. Finishes fruity and crisp. I have tasted this wine many times. It is great. Good availability. Enjoy. Excellent value.

☆☆☆☆ **Kenwood Vineyards, 1986 Sonoma County** $8.75

Another winner from this winery! Intense figgy fruit aromas, fully supported by grassy and oaky tones. Medium bodied. Layers of attractive flavors on the palate, with the citric fruit, oak, and herbs carrying through the aftertaste. A superior wine as in prior bottlings. Just enjoy! Excellent value.

☆ **Charles Krug Winery, 1986 Napa Valley** $7.00

Fresh, delicate varietal fruit aromas, with grassy scents. Medium bodied. Moderate fruit flavors on the palate, with acid in balance. Crisp finish. This wine will go very well with lighter foods.

☆☆ ½ **Lakespring Winery, 1986 Napa Valley** $7.50

Intense weedy and earthy aromas with lemongrass overtones. Medium-full bodied. Deep herbal fruit impression on the palate, with ample oak, in a good structure. This is a herbaceous wine that will go well with highly seasoned fish dishes. Good value.

☆☆ **Lolonis Winery, Fumé Blanc, 1985 Mendocino County, Lolonis Vineyards** $8.00

Attractive light gold color. Nice citric and honeysuckle aromas. Medium bodied. Generous citric fruit flavors on the palate, in nice balance with sweet oak, in a clean presentation. Try with cracked crab or chicken breasts in a cream sauce.

☆☆ **Lyeth White, 1985 Alexander Valley** $10.00

Attractive floral and citrusy aromas, with herbal and oaky tones. Medium bodied. Nice pear and citric fruit flavors on the palate, with oak and acid in balance. Pleasant, lingering aftertaste. Try with pasta and shellfish.

☆☆☆ **Matanzas Creek Winery, 1986 Sonoma County** $11.00

Continues the string of outstanding Sauvignon Blancs from this winery. Intense aroma of ripe figs, herbs, and oak. Medium-full bodied. The fruit is fresh and attractive on the palate, with ample oak, in a firm structure. Pleasant, lingering finish. Try this excellent wine with highly seasoned seafood or white meats.

☆☆☆☆ **Matanzas Creek Winery, 1985 Sonoma County** $10.50

Same quality as the prior bottling—great! Attractive floral, citrusy, and spicy aromas, with a nice herbal dimension in the background. Medium-full bodied. Generous well-ripened fruit on the palate, with ample acid for structure. This is a superior wine by any standard, and can best be enjoyed with highly seasoned seafood or white meats.

Melim, 1986 Alexander Valley $8.00

Brilliant. Yellow straw color. Medium-intense honey and appley aromas, with lemony and grassy scents. Medium-full bodied. Generous tangy fruit on the palate, with oak in balance. Pleasant, lingering finish. Fine with moderately seasoned fish or poultry dishes. Good value.

Robert Mondavi Winery, Fumé Blanc, 1986 Napa Valley $9.50

Medium-intense oak and spice in the nose, with appley overtones. Medium-full bodied. Weighty oak and buttery flavors on the palate, joined by apple and pear elements. A rather big wine that finishes a bit coarse. Try with fowl or veal dishes.

Monticello Cellars, 1986 Napa Valley $7.50

Intense weediness in the nose, with herbal overtones. Medium-full bodied. Loads of rich, asparaguslike fruit flavors on the palate, with a full dimension of herbaceousness, in a good structure. Fresh, crisp finish. Best with rich seafood dishes.

Monticello Cellars, 1985 Napa Valley $7.50

Forward herbal and weedy aromas. Medium bodied. Pronounced herbal fruit on the palate, which carries throughout. This is a well-made herbaceous Sauvignon Blanc. Will do well with fowl or light meats.

Morgan Winery, 1987 Alexander Valley $8.50

Appealing melony fruit and sweet oak in the nose, with grassy and floral overtones. Medium bodied. Lots of juicy fruit flavors on the palate, with ample acid, in a firm structure. Crisp and clean finish. Try with shellfish or sautéed scallops.

Murphy-Goode, Fumé Blanc, 1986 Alexander Valley $7.00

Appealing melony fruit aromas, with herbal and grassy tones. Medium bodied. Deep, rich fruit flavors on the palate, with nice acid for structure. Tart finish. Try as an accompaniment to grilled salmon with mustard sauce or snapper with soy and ginger. Good value.

Obester Winery, 1987 Mendocino County $8.00

Appealing blossomy fruit in the nose. Medium-full bodied. Attractive melon/orange flavors on the palate, enhanced by a touch of residual sugar. Pleasant, lingering aftertaste. Excellent as an apéritif or with light luncheon dishes such as chicken salad.

Parducci Wine Cellars, 1986 Mendocino County   *$6.00*

Moderate floral and herbal aromas, with citric and apricot tones. Medium bodied. Sweet appley fruit on the palate, with citric nuances, in a good structure. Try with moderately seasoned white meats.

Robert Pecota Winery, Barrel Fermented, 1987 Napa Valley   *$9.25*

Assertive varietal fruit in the nose, with floral tones, and oak in the background. Medium-full bodied. Rounded and somewhat creamy in the mouth, with ripe, slightly sweet grassy fruit and ample oak, in a firm structure. Pleasant, lingering oaky finish. This is a substantial Sauvignon Blanc that will go well with fowl or rich seafood dishes.

Robert Pecota Winery, Barrel Fermented, 1986 Napa Valley   *$9.25*

Forward herbal, spicy, and oaky aromas, with floral scents. Medium-full bodied. The wine enters the mouth round and full, with herbal and oaky flavors in balance with acid, in a good structure. Fine with smoked salmon, shad roe, stuffed clams, or frogs' legs.

J. Pedroncelli Fumé Blanc, 1986 Sonoma County   *$6.00*

Appealing citrusy and figgy fruit aromas, with grassy and spicy scents. Medium bodied. Somewhat viscous and fleshy on the palate, with a nice figgy and herbal dimension throughout. Try with pasta and shellfish or curried chicken with rice. Good value.

Robert Pepi Winery, 1986 Napa Valley   *$8.50*

Most appealing melon and fig aromas with floral and oaky tones. Medium-full bodied. Moderately deep citruslike fruit on the palate, with herbal nuances and rich oak, in a good structure. Tart, lingering finish. Try as an accompaniment to snapper in parchment with soy and ginger.

Robert Pepi Winery, 1985 Napa Valley   *$8.50*

Pleasant figlike fruit in the nose, with grassy and vanillin scents. Medium bodied. Moderately deep figgy and lemony fruit on the palate, with oaky and grassy nuances, and ample acid, in a well-structured presentation. Tart finish. Best with rich seafood dishes.

Joseph Phelps Vineyards, 1986 Napa Valley   *$9.00*

Forward herbal aromas, joined by ripe fruit scents. Medium bodied. Slightly sweet juicy fruit on the palate, with an ample herbal dimension. Somewhat bitter finish. Best with well-seasoned fish dishes.

Plam Vineyards, 1986 Napa Valley, Sacrashe Vineyard

 $8.00

Medium-intense pearlike aromas, with hints of grassiness and oak. Medium-full bodied. Generous herbal fruit flavors on the palate, with citric nuances, in a firm structure. Crisp finish. Excellent with cracked crab.

Preston Cellars, Fumé Blanc, 1985 Washington

 $7.00

Very appealing buttery, citrusy and oaky aromas, with weedy overtones. Medium-full bodied. Big depth of melony/citrusy fruit on the palate with ample acid. Crisp finish. Best with rich seafood dishes. Good value.

Preston Cuvée de Fumé, 1987 Dry Creek Valley

 *$7.25*

Assertive spicy fruit and herbal aromas, with melony and piney tones. Medium bodied. Fresh, clean appley and herbal flavors on the palate, in a firm structure. Try with broiled salmon or pasta with shellfish. Good value.

Preston Cuvée de Fumé, 1986 Dry Creek Valley

 $7.00

Pleasant aromas of melons and apricots, with grassy scents. Medium bodied. Moderate melon and grapefruit flavors on the palate, with grassy nuances, and ample acid. Tart finish. Best with a wide range of fish dishes.

Preston Estate Reserve, 1987 Dry Creek Valley

 $9.50

Medium-intense sweetish varietal fruit aromas, with weedy and sweet oak tones. Medium-full bodied. The fruit flavors are moderately deep on the palate, enhanced by a nice dimension of creamy oak, with ample acid, in a good structure. Slightly coarse finish. Has aging potential of several years. Try with shad roe, stuffed clams, or snapper in parchment with soy and ginger. Good value.

Preston Estate Reserve, 1986 Dry Creek Valley

 $9.50

Attractive figgy and melony fruit aromas, with floral and grassy scents, and creamy oak overtones. Medium-full bodied. Deep, rich fruit flavors fill the mouth, with oak and acid in perfect balance. Crisp, lingering finish. A big wine. This is *one* Sauvignon Blanc that will improve for at least five years. Just enjoy. Good value.

Quivira Vineyards, 1987 Dry Creek Valley

 $8.50

Forward pineappley, floral and herbal aromas, with figgy, minty, and oaky overtones. Medium bodied. The fruit flavors are expansive on the palate, with ample acid and a touch of oak. Slightly tart finish. Try with roast chicken or pasta with shellfish.

Quivira Vineyards, 1986 Dry Creek Valley $8.00

Forward oaky aromas, joined by ripe fruit and grassy scents. Medium bodied. Generous figgy fruit on the palate, with weedy nuances, and ample oak. Finishes a bit hot. Try with chicken breasts in spicy tomato compote.

Raymond Vineyard, 1987 Napa Valley $8.00

Medium-intense aromas of figs and oak, with grassy scents. Medium bodied. Moderate, somewhat fleshy fruit at entry, narrowing at the finish. Fine with a wide range of fish dishes.

Richard Michaels, 1986 Sonoma County $7.00

Brilliant. Light gold color. Pleasant appley and figgy aromas, with grassy scents. Medium bodied. Generous ripe fruit on the palate, with acid in balance. Slightly sharp finish. Try with fried smelt or broiled sea bass. Good value.

J. Rochioli Vineyards, 1986 Russian River Valley $8.50

Assertive grassy/herbal aromas, joined by grapefruit scents. Medium-full bodied. Deep, herbal fruit impression on the palate, with citric nuances. Crisp finish. Fine with well-seasoned fish dishes.

Rustridge Vineyards, 1987 Napa Valley $7.50

Bright. Light straw color. Intense melony, pineappley, and figgy aromas, with a touch of oak. Dry. Medium bodied. Moderately deep pineappley fruit in the palate, with citric nuances, and mild oak, in a clean presentation. Pleasant, fruity finish. Try with broiled scallops or chicken breasts with a cream sauce. Good value.

Rutherford Hill Winery, 1986 Napa Valley $7.00

Intense grassiness in the nose, joined by a fair dimension of oak. Medium-full bodied. Lots of lively herbal fruit flavors on the palate, with ample acid. Tart finish. Best with highly seasoned fish dishes.

St. Clement Vineyards, 1986 Napa Valley $9.50

Subdued appley fruit aromas, joined by grassy and oaky scents. Medium bodied. The appley fruit is deep and tight on the palate, nicely enhanced by a citric element and rich oak, in a firm structure. Will improve for several years. Try with shad roe, stuffed clams, or snapper in parchment with soy and ginger.

St. Vrain, 1986 Alexander Valley $8.00

(Another label from Morgan Winery.) Attractive floral and figgy fruit aromas, with grassy and floral scents. Medium bodied. Nicely focused fruit in the mouth, with moderate grassy nuances. Pleasant, lingering finish. Fine with well-seasoned fish dishes. Good value.

Simi Winery, 1986 Sonoma County $9.00

Moderate melony and figgy aromas, with herbaceous scents, and a touch of oak. Medium-full bodied. Somewhat narrow fruit flavors. Clean, tart finish. Fine with a wide range of moderately seasoned fish dishes.

Simi Winery, 1985 Sonoma County $10.00

Pretty sweet oak and floral aromas, joined by melony fruit and grassy scents. Medium-full bodied. Deep, sweet melony fruit on the palate, with creamy oak, grass and acid combined in a firm structure. A lovely wine. Try as an accompaniment to halibut with ginger and lemon or with veal piccata.

Spottswoode Winery, 1987 Napa Valley $10.00

Attractive, moderately intense aromas of ripe melons, with herbal scents, and a touch of oak. Medium-full bodied. Loads of ripe varietal fruit flavors, with weedy and citrusy nuances, enriched by sweet oak, in a good structure. Slightly harsh finish. Good potential for several years aging. Try with rich seafood dishes.

Spottswoode Winery, 1986 Napa Valley $10.00

Intense, complex aromas of figs, flowers, lemons, and sweet oak, with scents of fennel and green apples. Medium-full bodied. The wine is fat and round on entry, with the deep fruit flavors balanced with ample acid, in a firm structure. This is a superior wine that will go well with rich seafood or poultry dishes. Good value.

Sterling Vineyards, 1987 Napa Valley $10.00

Appealing, medium-intense floral aromas, with grassy tones. Medium bodied. Moderately intense grassy/citrusy fruit flavors on the palate, balanced with acid and oak, in a firm structure. Crisp finish. Try with delicately seasoned fish dishes.

Sterling Vineyards, 1986 Napa Valley $8.75

Moderately assertive fruit aromas, with earthy scents. Medium bodied. Somewhat restrained fruit flavors on the palate, with good acid, in a firm structure. Tart finish. Enjoy with shellfish.

Stonegate Winery, 1986 Napa Valley $8.50

Light-intensity figgy and weedy aromas. Medium bodied.
Moderate fruit flavors on the palate, in a firm structure.
Crisp finish. Fine with fish.

Streblow Vineyards, 1986 Napa Valley, $7.50
Rancho Otranto

Brilliant. Light straw/gold color. Pleasant, forward, appley, figgy,
nutty nose. Medium bodied. Moderately intense spicy fruit in
the mouth, with grassy nuances, and an ample oak dimension.
Finishes a bit sharp. Fine with well-seasoned fish dishes.

Taft Street, 1987 Napa Valley $6.00

Intense grassy and herbal aromas. Medium bodied. Generous,
sweetish fruit flavors on the palate, with citric nuances, in a firm
structure. Nice with chicken and herbs. Good value.

Viansa Cellars, 1986 Napa/Sonoma $8.50

Forward, grassy varietal fruit, with weedy scents. Medium
bodied. The grassy/weedy character follows into the mouth,
joined by ample fruit, in a good structure. Try this fine wine as
an accompaniment to pasta with shellfish, garlic, and tomatoes.

Vichon Chevrignon, 1986 Napa Valley $9.50

Medium-intense citrusy fruit and toasty oak in the nose. Medium
bodied. Soft on the palate, with the figlike fruit and oak in balance, in a good structure. Tart finish. Fine with a wide range of
fish dishes.

Wente Special Selection, 1986 Chalk Hill, $9.00
Fortney Stark Vineyard

Attractive melony and figgy fruit aromas, with floral and spicy
scents, framed in sweet oak. Medium bodied. Fairly rich sweet
fruit on the palate that continues through the aftertaste. Try as
an accompaniment to roast chicken with rosemary.

Wm. Wheeler Winery, 1986 Sonoma County $8.00

Medium-intense aromas of flowers and figs, with grassy scents.
Medium bodied. Appealing fresh fruit on the palate, with herbal
nuances, and acid in balance. Crisp finish. Fine with petrale of
sole or soft-shelled crab. Good value.

White Oak Vineyards, 1986 Sonoma County $7.00

Appealing aromas of melons and figs, with grassy and oaky
tones. Medium-full bodied. Nicely focused fruit on the palate,
with ample acid, in a good structure. Slightly tart finish.
Best with well-seasoned fish dishes.

Winter Creek Winery, 1986 Napa Valley, Takahashi Vineyard

 $7.00

Brilliant. Light straw/gold color. Pleasant, soft, melony fruit aromas, with spicy and grassy scents. Medium-full bodied. Attractive, somewhat rich fruit flavors in the mouth, with nice acid, and a touch of oak. Long finish. Enjoy with well-seasoned fish dishes or with chicken in a light sauce. Good value.

GEWÜRZTRAMINER

Adler Fels, 1987 Sonoma County $7.00

Somewhat sweet. Very attractive, intense, complex aromas of apples, almonds, cloves, and honey. Medium-full bodied. Rich, ripe fruit on the palate, with spicy and nutty elements throughout. This is a powerful Gewürz. Try with Oriental spicy chicken salad and with sausages. Excellent value.

Adler Fels, 1986 Sonoma County $7.00

Slightly sweet (1.4% residual sugar). Appealing, forward floral, honey, and spicy aromas. Medium-full bodied. Soft at entry, with nice melony and spicy flavors on the palate, with ample acid. Slightly tart in the finish. Fine with curried chicken or roast pork. Good value.

Alexander Valley Vineyards, 1986 Alexander Valley $6.50

Somewhat sweet (1.5% residual sugar). Attractive aromas of apples, apricots, and spices. Medium bodied. Nice, spicy fruit on the palate, with a touch of spritz. Slightly short finish. Enjoy with well-seasoned chicken dishes.

Bargetto Winery, 1987 Santa Maria Valley $7.00

Somewhat sweet (1.5% residual sugar). Nice peach and honeysuckle aromas. Medium bodied. Attractive, spicy fruit flavors on the palate, with floral nuances, and ample acid. Crisp finish. Try this excellent wine with Oriental spicy chicken salad and toasted almonds. Fine value.

Bargetto Winery, Dry, 1987 Santa Maria Valley $7.00

Dry. Appealing peach, honey, and spicy aromas. Medium bodied. Soft and round at entry, with a heavy fruit impression on the palate, and ample spice throughout. Slightly bitter finish. Try with pork roast or sausages

Beringer Vineyards, 1987 Napa Valley $6.00

Slightly sweet (1.3% residual sugar). Appealing floral and honey aromas. Medium bodied. Generous peach fruit flavors on the palate, with a touch of spice, in a clean presentation. Fine at lunch with chicken salad or as an apéritif. Good value.

Beringer Vineyards, 1986 Napa Valley, Gamble Ranch $6.00

Slightly sweet. Nice spice in the nose, joined by floral scents. Medium bodied. Supple on entry, with the spicy fruit and a citric element joined in a tasty combination. Fine with a wide range of light luncheon dishes. Good value.

Buena Vista Winery, 1986 Sonoma Valley—Carneros $7.00

Slightly sweet. Appealing, delicate fruit aromas, with flowery and spicy scents. Medium bodied. Crisp and clean on the palate, with the gentle fruit and spice in perfect balance. Try with trout or baked snapper. Good value.

Davis Bynum Reserve Bottling, 1987 Russian River Valley, Mc Ilroy Vineyard $7.00

Dry (0.45% residual sugar). Beautiful aromas of rose petals, grapefruit, and spice. Medium bodied. Moderately intense, clean varietal fruit on the palate, with attractive lemony and spicy elements in perfect balance. Crisp finish. Fine with trout or red snapper. Excellent value.

Chateau St. Jean, 1987 Sonoma County $9.50

Slightly sweet (0.65% residual sugar). Medium-intense spicy fruit in the nose. Medium bodied. Moderate fruit and spice on the palate. Short finish. Try with moderately seasoned chicken dishes.

Clos du Bois Early Harvest, 1987 Alexander Valley $8.00

Somewhat sweet (1.6% residual sugar). Appealing, medium-intense floral and pineappley aromas. Medium bodied. Soft on entry, with the citrus fruit flavors and mild spice in nice balance. Fruity finish. Fine with picnic luncheons or as an apéritif. Good value.

Clos du Bois Early Harvest, 1986 Alexander Valley $7.50

Slightly sweet (1.48% residual sugar). Pleasant, delicate aromas of spicy apples. Medium bodied. Loads of clean fruit on the palate, with a moderately spicy dimension. Fruity finish. Fine with light luncheon dishes such as chicken salad or as an apéritif. Good value.

Columbia Crest Vineyards, 1986 Columbia Valley, Washington $6.00

Slightly sweet. Light gold color. Clean, grapefruit rind aromas, with spicy tones. Medium bodied. Pleasant peachlike flavors on the palate, with citric and spicy nuances. Clean finish. Try with light luncheon dishes.

De Loach Vineyards Early Harvest, 1987 Russian River Valley $7.00

Slightly sweet (1.2% residual sugar). Attractive aromas of rose petal and nutmeglike spice. Medium bodied. Soft and delicate on the palate, with the fresh fruit flavors and spice in nice balance. Enjoy this fine wine with moderately seasoned chicken dishes. Good value.

De Loach Vineyards Early Harvest, 1986 Russian River Valley

$7.50

Slightly sweet (1.2% residual sugar). Delicate aromas of melons and cinnamon. Medium bodied. Moderate peachlike fruit flavors on the palate, with spicy nuances, in a clean presentation. Crisp finish. Try with moderately seasoned dishes.

Fetzer Vineyards, 1987 California

$6.00

Sweet (3.5% residual sugar). Medium-intense apricot and honeysuckle aromas. Medium bodied. Very attractive, sweetish apricot fruit on the palate, with a nice ginger dimension, in a well-balanced presentation. Excellent as an apéritif. Good value.

Field Stone Winery, 1986 Alexander Valley

$7.00

Slightly sweet (1.47% residual sugar). Medium-intense spicy fruit aromas, with herbal tones. Medium bodied. Generous spicy fruit on the palate, with ample acid in a firm structure. Best with moderately seasoned light meats.

Thomas Fogarty Winery, 1987 Santa Cruz Mountains, Spring Ridge Vineyard

$8.00

Slightly sweet. Fresh apricot fruit in the nose, with orange-peel and spicy scents. Medium bodied. The fruit is clean and bright on the palate, joined by a mild spicy dimension through the finish. Perfect balance. Try as an accompaniment to roast chicken with rosemary or pork loin with dried apricots and walnuts. Excellent value.

Ernest and Julio Gallo, 1986 California

$3.50

Somewhat sweet. Pleasant floral and honey aromas. Medium bodied. Appealing, sweetish fruit on the palate, with a touch of spice in a smooth presentation. Fruity finish. Fine with light fish dishes or as an apéritif. Good value.

Geyser Peak, 1986 Sonoma County

$5.50

Somewhat sweet. Appealing, clean, candied fruit aromas. Medium bodied. Moderately intense fruit on the palate, in a soft structure. Fine as an apéritif.

Grand Cru Vineyards, 1987 Alexander Valley

$8.00

Somewhat sweet (2% residual sugar). Brilliant. Light gold color. Appealing apricoty fruit aromas, with spicy nuances. Medium bodied. Generous sweetish spicy fruit flavors on the palate, with ample acid, in a good structure. Try with Hawaiian chicken or country-style hams. Good value.

☆☆ ½ **Grand Cru Vineyards, Select Late Harvest, 1986 Sonoma Valley** $8.50 375 ml.

Sweet (9.5% residual sugar). Brilliant. Nice golden color. Forward aromas of flowers, apricot and melons. Loads of apricoty, melony and figgy flavors in the mouth with acid in balance. An excellent dessert wine. Just enjoy.

☆ **Gundlach-Bundschu Winery, 1986 Sonoma Valley, Rhinefarm Vineyards** $7.00

Dry (0.4% residual sugar). Medium-intense floral aromas, with spicy and appley scents. Medium bodied. Moderately intense, clean fruit on the palate, with a touch of spice. Try with moderately seasoned chicken dishes.

☆☆ **Hacienda Wine Cellars, Dry, 1987 Sonoma County** $7.00

Slightly sweet (0.9% residual sugar). Attractive varietal fruit in the nose, with clovelike spice in support. Medium bodied. Moderately intense. Nicely focused on the palate, with ample acid. Sharp finish. Fine with baked chicken.

☆ **Haywood Winery, 1986 Sonoma Valley** $8.00

Somewhat sweet (1.8% residual sugar). Moderately intense aromas of peaches and spice. Medium bodied. Well-balanced, sweetish fruit in the mouth, finishing slightly sharp. Try with moderately seasoned chicken dishes.

☆ **Hop Kiln Winery, 1986 Russian River Valley** $7.50

Slight sweet (0.69% residual sugar). Medium-intense fruit in the nose, with yeasty and earthy scents. Medium bodied. Tight grapefruit and spice flavors on the palate. Tart finish. Best with well-seasoned fish dishes.

☆☆ ½ **Husch, 1987 Anderson Valley** $6.25

Slightly sweet (0.86% residual sugar). Beautiful aromas of rose petals and grapefruit, with honey scents. Medium-full bodied. Lush in the mouth, with tasty flavors of apples, grapefruit, melons, and honey, balanced with ample acid. Try as an accompaniment to roast turkey with dried fruit and nut dressing.

☆☆ **Husch, 1986 Anderson Valley** $6.25

Slightly sweet (1.2% residual sugar). Appealing aromas of lilacs and honeysuckle, with spearmint scents. Generous fresh fruit flavors on the palate, with a fair acidic dimension. Tart finish. Try as an accompaniment to sautéed shrimp with ginger.

Mill Creek Vineyards, 1986 Sonoma County $6.00

Slightly sweet (1.1% residual sugar). Fragrant spicy fruit aromas, with citrusy scents. Medium bodied. Soft on entry, with the varietal fruit and moderate spices in good balance. Try with Oriental spicy chicken salad and toasted almonds. Good value.

Mirassou Vineyards, 1987 Monterey County $7.00

Somewhat sweet. Moderately intense floral and citric aromas. Medium bodied. Moderately intense sweetish fruit on the palate, in a soft structure. Sharp finish. Best with light luncheon dishes.

Mirassou Vineyards, 1986 Monterey County $7.00

Somewhat sweet. Moderate floral aromas, with pine and eucalyptus scents. Medium bodied. Full and round on the palate, with nice sweet fruit through the finish. Fine with moderately seasoned chicken dishes.

Monticello Cellars, 1986 Napa Valley $7.50

Slightly sweet (0.7% residual). Intense aromas of rose petals and spice. The varietal fruit is rich and deep on the palate, with an ample, spicy dimension through the finish. Try this excellent wine with Oriental spicy chicken or pork loin filled with dry apricots and walnuts. Fine value.

Obester Winery, 1987 Anderson Valley $7.50

Somewhat sweet (2.1% residual sugar). Medium-intense fresh varietal fruit in the nose, with herbal scents. Medium bodied. Generous, sweetish fruit on the palate, with grassy nuances. Slightly tart finish. Try with moderately seasoned chicken dishes.

Obester Winery, 1986 Anderson Valley $7.00

Somewhat sweet (2.2% residual sugar). Very appealing, complex floral, spicy, and citrusy aromas. Medium bodied. Lush feel on entry with loads of spicy fruit throughout. Try this excellent wine with curried chicken or pork chops with applesauce. Fine value.

Parducci Wine Cellars, 1986 Mendocino County $6.25

Somewhat sweet. Medium-intense peach and orange peel aromas, with earthy overtones. Medium bodied. Generous crispy fruit on the palate, in a firm structure. Slightly bitter finish. Will go well with sweet and sour pork.

J. Pedroncelli Winery, 1986 Napa Valley $5.50

Slightly sweet (1.32% residual sugar). Forward aromas of ripe fruit and flowers, with grassy tones. Medium bodied. Generous fruit and acid in the mouth, which fades in the finish. Best with moderately seasoned chicken dishes.

Joseph Phelps Vineyards, 1986 Napa Valley — $8.00

Slightly sweet (0.9% residual sugar). Forward aromas of ripe apples and butter. Medium bodied. Mature fruit on the palate, with ample spice. Finishes slightly bitter. Enjoy this wine with sausages or roast pork with apples.

Preston Wine Cellars, 1987 Washington, Preston Vineyard — $5.75

Somewhat sweet. Pale straw color. Low intensity rose petal aromas, with spicy tones. Medium bodied. Generous green apple fruit flavors on the palate, with citric nuances. Clean, short finish. Fine with light luncheon dishes.

J. Rochioli Vineyards, 1986 Russian River Valley — $6.00

Slightly sweet (1.0% residual sugar). Medium-intense varietal fruit in the nose, with herbal scents. Medium-light bodied. Moderate fruit on the palate, with spicy and weedy nuances, in a soft structure. Try with moderately seasoned chicken dishes.

Round Hill Vineyards, 1986 Napa Valley — $4.75

Slightly sweet (1.3% residual sugar). Intense rose petal aromas, with orange blossom and spicy scents. Medium bodied. Generous honeyed fruit flavors on the palate, with nice spice in perfect balance. Try this excellent wine with Oriental spicy chicken salad or roast pork with apples. Super value.

Rutherford Hill Winery, Dry, 1986 Napa Valley — $6.75

Slightly sweet (0.6% residual sugar). Low-intensity honeysuckle aromas, with spicy and smoky scents. Medium-light bodied. Moderately intense finish on the palate, with a fair acidic dimension. Slight buttery finish. Best with light meats.

St. Francis Winery, 1986 Sonoma County — $7.00

Somewhat sweet (2.01% residual sugar). Restrained honeysuckle and citrus in the nose. Medium-full bodied. Generous, sweetish fruit in the mouth, with a fair citric dimension. Sharp finish. Try with well-seasoned chicken dishes.

Ste. Chapelle, 1986 Idaho — $6.00

Somewhat sweet (2.3% residual sugar). Appealing aromas of ripe melons with perfumy and nutty scents. Medium bodied. The fruit is clean and light on the palate, with a nice tropical dimension through the finish. Try with chicken and avocado salad or as an apéritif. Good value.

Wente Bros., 1986 Arroyo Seco — $7.50

Slightly sweet (0.6% residual sugar). Moderately intense melony fruit in the nose, with flowery and spicy scents. Medium bodied. Moderately intense fruit on the palate, with ample acid. Crisp finish. Fine with light meats.

JOHANNISBERG RIESLING

☆☆   *Alexander Valley Vineyards, 1986 Alexander Valley*   🍷   **$6.00**

Slightly sweet (1.6% residual sugar). Appealing floral, pineappley and lemony aromas. Supple on entry, with generous apricot flavors and good acidity. Long, pleasant finish. Try as an accompaniment to chicken and avocado salad. Good value.

☆☆½   *Amity Vineyards, Dry, 1987 Oregon*   🍷   **$7.50**

Dry (0.6% residual sugar). Intense floral, spicy, and green pear aromas. Lots of spicy fruit in the mouth, in a good structure. Long, crispy finish. Try as an accompaniment to smoked trout with a horseradish cream sauce. Good value.

☆☆☆   *Arbor Crest Select Late Harvest, 1986 Washington*   🍷   **$9.50**
    🍾   **375 ml.**

Sweet (8.9% residual sugar). Intense apricot and honey aromas, with smoky tones. Luscious on the palate. Intense peach and melon flavors. Very long finish. Will improve for several years. Extraordinary quality. Enjoy.

☆   *Bargetto Winery White Riesling,*
1985 Santa Maria Valley, Tepusquet Vineyards   🍷   **$7.00**

Somewhat sweet (1.8% residual sugar). Moderately intense candied fruit in the nose. Fruit flavors are clean and crisp in the mouth. Well balanced. Try with light luncheon foods.

☆☆   *Boeger Estate Bottled, 1987 El Dorado*   🍷   **$7.00**

Slightly sweet. Delicate appley and rose petal aromas. Intense floral and spicy flavors on the palate, in nice balance. Long, pleasant finish. Fine as an apéritif or with light meats.

☆☆   *Buena Vista Winery, 1986 Carneros Estate*   🍷   **$7.25**

Slightly sweet. Pretty Riesling fruit in the nose. Concentrated green apple flavors on the palate, with spicy nuances. Crispy and fruity in the finish. Try with smoked trout.

☆   *Callaway White Riesling, 1987 California*   🍷   **$5.50**

Slightly sweet. Appealing varietal fruit in the nose. Smooth and soft in the mouth, with the citric and peach flavors in nice balance with the acid. Has a touch of sweetness. Fine as an apéritif or with light foods.

☆☆   *Chateau St. Jean, 1987 Sonoma County*   🍷   **$9.00**

Somewhat sweet (1.6 residual sugar). Distinct aromatic nose of rose petals and peaches. Lots of spicy fruit on the palate carries through the long finish. Try as an accompaniment to Oriental spicy chicken with toasted almonds.

Chateau St. Jean Special Select Late Harvest, 1986 Alexander Valley

$23.00
375 ml.

Very sweet (30.5% residual sugar). Light gold color. Intense aromas of pineapple, melon, and honey. Very deep honeylike fruit impression on the palate. Flavor persists through a long finish. Another great late harvest from this winery. Just enjoy.

Chateau Ste. Michelle, 1987 Washington

$6.50

Dry. Moderately intense peach, banana, and honeydew melon aromas, with floral scents. Supple, and delicately flavored on the palate. Long, fruity finish. Fine with light luncheon foods.

Chateau Ste. Michelle Reserve, Late Harvest White Riesling, Hand-Selected Clusters, 1985 Yakima Valley, Washington

$14.00

Sweet (12.0% residual sugar). Medium-intense apple and honey aromas. Generous fruit on the palate, in a good structure. Slightly crisp, in a long, pleasant finish. A nice wine. Enjoy.

The Christian Brothers, 1985 Napa Valley

$6.50

Slightly sweet. Light gold color. Appealing aromas of pears and peaches, with a touch of botrytised ripe fruit. Nice apricoty flavors on the palate, with good acidity. Long, full finish. Try with chicken and pecan salad. Good value.

Clos du Bois Early Harvest, 1987 Alexander Valley

$8.00

Somewhat sweet. Appealing aromas of apples and peaches, with spicy scents. Medium bodied. Clean appley fruit flavors on the palate, with acid in balance. Fine with sautéed chicken or as an apéritif.

Columbia Cellarmaster's Reserve, 1987 Washington

$7.00

Somewhat sweet, appealing peach and floral and spicy aromas. Nice honeyed apple and peach flavors on the palate, with good acid balance. Fine with Cantonese chicken and almond dish. Good value.

Congress Springs Vineyards, 1987 Santa Clara County, San Ysidro Vineyard

$7.50

Slightly sweet. Medium-intense appley and pineappley aromas. Medium-light bodied. Moderately intense clean fruit flavors on the palate. Crisp finish. Enjoy with light meats.

½

Covey Run, Botrytis Affected White Riesling, 1986 Yakima Valley, Mahre Vineyards, Washington $7.00

Sweet (7.8% residual sugar). Intense peach, pineapple, and honey aromas. Quite intense peach and honey flavors on the palate, with smoky nuances. Long, pleasant finish. Super value.

Estrella River Estate Bottled, 1987 Paso Robles $5.50

Slightly sweet. Medium-intense pear and melon aromas. Supple on entry, with generous fruit in a good structure. Finishes slightly coarse. Try as an accompaniment to pasta salad or smoked turkey.

The Firestone Vineyard, 1987 Santa Ynez Valley $6.50

Slightly sweet. Moderately intense apricot and citrus aromas. Supple at entry, with medium rich fruit on the palate, in a good structure. Finishes slightly coarse. Fine with light luncheon dishes.

The Firestone Vineyard Selected Harvest, 1986 Santa Ynez Valley, The Ambassador's Vineyard $9.50 / 375 ml.

Very sweet (17.6% residual sugar). Medium-intense aromas of apricots and honey, with scents of dill. Soft and richly flavored on the palate. The finish is slightly sharp, long, and pleasant. Enjoy.

Franciscan Vineyards Select Late Harvest, 1983 Napa Valley $10.00 / 375 ml.

Very sweet (20% residual sugar). Most attractive, intense peach and honey aromas. Heavily concentrated peach, pineapple, and honey flavors on the palate. Luscious. Unusually long finish. An outstanding dessert wine that will improve for several years. Just enjoy.

The Gainey Vineyard, 1987 Santa Barbara County $7.00

Somewhat sweet (2.0% residual sugar). Intense apricot and tropical fruit aromas, with floral and spice scents. Deep spicy fruit impression on the palate, with lively acidity. Try as an accompaniment to pasta salad or smoked turkey and almonds.

Ernest & Julio Gallo Limited Release Reserve, 1986 California $3.50

Slightly sweet, appealing, clean fruit in the nose. Light bodied. Soft, delicate fruit flavors in the mouth. Finishes crisp and fruity. Enjoy as an apéritif or with light luncheon foods. Good value.

★★½ Hogue Cellars, 1987 Yakima Valley, Washington $5.50

Slightly sweet. Light straw color, with a bit of spritz. Intense
floral, peach, and tropical fruit aromas. Medium-full bodied.
Supple and rich on the palate. Long finish. Try this fine wine
with chicken and avocado salad. Excellent value.

★★½ Hogue Cellars Late Harvest Riesling, Estate Bottled, 1986 Yakima Valley, Markin Vineyard, Washington $7.50

Sweet (4.2% residual sugar). Appealing honey, peach, and lemon
aromas, with smoky scents. Warm and viscous in the mouth.
Generous honey, apple, and pineapple flavors on the palate,
with herbal nuances. Crisp finish. Allow this wine two more
years of development, then enjoy. Good value.

★★½ Inglenook Vineyards, 1985 Napa Valley $6.50

Slightly sweet, appealing honey and apple aromas and flavors.
Velvety texture. Long, smooth finish. An excellent wine for early
consumption. Just enjoy. Good value.

★★½ Kenwood Vineyards, 1987 Sonoma Valley $7.50

Slightly sweet (1.3% residual sugar). Wonderful floral and peach
aromas. Generous fruit on the palate, in a delicate structure.
A delicious wine. Just enjoy. Good value.

★★ J. Lohr, 1987 Monterey County, Greenfield Vineyards $6.00

Somewhat sweet (2.4% residual sugar). Intense aromas of lilacs,
honey, and tropical fruit. Rich fruit flavors in the mouth. Long
finish. Charming style. Enjoy this fine wine as an apéritif or with
chicken salad. Good value.

★★ Mirassou Harvest Reserve, 1986 Monterey County $9.00

Sweet (9.2% residual sugar). Appealing floral and honeylike
aromas. Generous sweet fruit on the palate, with good acid.
Long, pleasant finish. Consume in the next three years for
optimum enjoyment.

★ Mirassou Vineyards, 1987 Monterey County $6.00

Slightly sweet. Floral spiciness in the nose, with grapefruitlike
tones. Medium bodied. Attractive appley fruit flavors, with good
acid. Long, pleasant finish. Try with moderately seasoned
chicken dishes.

★★ The Monterey Vineyard, 1987 Monterey County $6.00

Slightly sweet. Appealing appley and citric aromas, with floral
spiciness in support. Generous fruit on the palate, with good
acid. Long, crisp finish. Try with Oriental spicy chicken.

Navarro White Riesling, 1986 Anderson Valley, Mendocino
$7.00

Somewhat sweet. Appealing apricoty and citrusy aromas. Nice green apple and grapefruit flavors on the palate, with a touch of sweetness, in a firm structure. Very long, pleasant finish. Try this excellent wine with smoked trout. Good value.

Rodney Strong, 1985 Russian River Valley, Claus Vineyard
$7.00

Slightly sweet. Most attractive honey and melon aromas, with pine and smoky tones. Medium-full bodied. Supple on the palate, with loads of rich, complex fruit flavors. Very long finish. This is a wonderful wine. Try as an accompaniment to grilled chicken with an orange-ginger sauce. Super value.

Rodney Strong Late Harvest, 1985 Russian River Valley, Le Baron Vineyard
$9.00
375 ml.

Very sweet (12.1% residual sugar). Nice gold color, with an amber tinge. Very attractive, complex aromas of apricots, honey, and mint, with a touch of botrytis. Luscious rich fruit on the palate through a long finish. A superior wine for optimum enjoyment during the next three or four years.

Ste. Chapelle, 1987 Idaho
$6.00

Sweet (3.2% residual sugar). Ripe apricot and tropical fruit aromas. Soft and lush on the palate. Peach and green apple flavors, with crisp acidity. Long, pleasant finish. Perfect on its own. Good value.

Ste. Chapelle, Botrytis, 1986 Late Harvest Johannisberg Riesling, Symms Family Vineyards, Idaho
$15.00

Very sweet (10.6% residual sugar). Medium-intense floral, apricoty, and appley aromas. Supple on entry, with attractive peach, honey, and spice flavors throughout. Pleasant finish. A fine wine for consumption during the next three years or so.

Sea Ridge Winery, 1987 Sonoma Coast, Hirsch Vineyard
$7.00

Somewhat sweet (1.5% residual sugar). Bright. Light straw color. Nice floral and tropical fruit aromas. Medium bodied. Generous sweetish fruit on the palate, with ample acid for good structure. Lingering, pineappley aftertaste. Fine for afternoon sipping or with light lunches.

Sokol Blosser White Riesling, 1986 Yamhill County $6.50

Slightly sweet. Appealing peach aromas, with lemony and honey scents. Light bodied. Sweet peach flavors on the palate, with good acid. Crisp finish. Try as an accompaniment to chicken and avocado salad with a creamy citrus dressing.

Trefethen White Riesling, 1986 Napa Valley $7.00

Slightly sweet (0.6% residual sugar). Brilliant. Light yellow color. Nice varietal fruit aromas, with pronounced floral tones. Attractive apple and apricot flavors on the palate, with piny nuances, in a firm structure. This is a pleasant Riesling that can accompany light meats.

Ventana Vineyards White Riesling, 1987 Monterey $6.50

Slightly sweet. Beautiful floral and spicy fruit in the nose. Intense ripe fruit on the palate, in a good structure. Persistent finish. Try this excellent wine as an accompaniment to pork loin filled with dried apricots and walnuts. Good value.

Zaca Mesa Winery, 1986 Santa Barbara County $5.50

Slightly sweet. Forward apricoty fruit in the nose, joined by piny tones. Generous ripe varietal fruit in the mouth, with lemony nuances. Crisp finish. Try as an accompaniment to chicken and avocado salad. Good value.

Zaca Mesa Winery, 1985 Santa Barbara County $7.00

Somewhat sweet (1.9% residual sugar). Medium-intense floral nose. Moderate peach flavors in the mouth, with a touch of sweetness in a clean composition. Slightly sharp finish. Fine with cold chicken salad.

WHITE ZINFANDEL

Aciero Estate Bottled, 1987 Paso Robles $5.00

Medium sweet. Ripe melony and pineappley fruit in the nose.
Medium bodied. Intense sweetish fruit flavors on the palate,
with just a touch of tannin in the finish. Nice aftertaste.
Try with moderately seasoned white meats.

Amador Foothill Winery, 1987 Amador County $5.25

Slightly sweet. Appealing plumlike fruit aromas. Medium-light
bodied. Moderate fruit on the palate, with a citric dimension.
Crisp finish. Fine with light meats.

The Christian Brothers, 1987 Napa Valley $5.50

Moderately intense aromas of raspberries and melons. Fresh and
lively on the palate, with the fruit and acid in perfect balance.
Long, crispy finish. Delicate and refined. Enjoy this excellent
wine as an apéritif or with light luncheon dishes. Good value.

Corbett Canyon Coastal Classic, 1987 California $6.00
1.5 ltr.

Somewhat sweet. Medium-intense berry and melon aromas.
Supple and full at entry. The fruit has some depth on the palate,
with a touch of tannin in the finish. Fine with light luncheon
dishes. Good value.

De Loach Vineyards, 1987 Russian River Valley $6.00

Slightly sweet. Light pink color. Appealing berrylike fruit aromas,
with spicy tones. Lively fruit on the palate, with acid in perfect
balance. Enjoy with Cantonese chicken and almond dish or as an
all-occasion festive wine. Good value.

Estrella River Estate Bottled, 1987 Paso Robles $5.00

Intense floral and spicy nose, with pineappley scents. Medium
bodied. Rich fruit flavors in the mouth, with spicy nuances.
Long finish. Enjoy with light meals or as an apéritif.

Grand Cru Vineyards, 1987 California $5.00

Somewhat sweet (2.3% residual sugar). Attractive pink salmon
color. Medium-intense floral and strawberry nose. Medium-light
bodied. Generous strawberry fruit flavors on the palate, with
acid in balance. Crisp finish. Nice as an apéritif or with chicken
salad. Good value.

Hop Kiln Winery, 1987 Russian River Valley $5.50

Somewhat sweet. Intense plummy and pineappley aromas. Medium-full bodied. Generous ripe fruit flavors in the mouth. Finishes somewhat coarse. Try with Oriental spicy chicken salad.

Mirassou, 1987 California $3.00

Somewhat sweet. Nice cassislike fruit aromas. Moderate sweetish fruit on the palate, with mild acidity. Pleasant finish. A fine wine for afternoon sipping. Good value.

The Monterey Vineyard, 1987 Monterey County $4.50

Medium sweet. Appealing floral, apricot, and watermelon aromas. Supple on entry, with sweetish apricot-tinged fruit flavors through the long finish. Enjoy with light foods or as an apéritif.

Mt. Madonna Estate Bottled, 1987 Santa Clara Valley $4.50

Most attractive, rich spicy fruit in the nose. Medium-full bodied. Very flavorful, spicy fruit in the mouth, in a good structure. The finish is medium-long and somewhat tart. Try this fine wine with Cantonese chicken and almond dish. Excellent value.

Parducci Wine Cellars, 1986 North Coast $4.75

Sweet. Moderate peachlike fruit aromas. Quite lush on entry, with moderate berrylike fruit flavors on the palate. Finishes slightly sharp. Nice as an apéritif.

J. Pedroncelli Winery 1987 Sonoma County $5.00

Intense pineapple fruit aromas. Off dry. Medium bodied. Supple at entry, with nice pineappley fruit flavors throughout. Finishes slightly coarse. Fine with chicken salad.

R. H. Phillips Vineyard, 1987 California $4.25

Appealing, medium-intense aromas of cherries and pineapples. Medium-light bodied. Moderately intense sweetish fruit on the palate, in good balance. Pleasant fruity finish. Fine as an apéritif or with light luncheon foods. Good value.

Santa Barbara Winery, 1987 Central Coast $6.00

Somewhat sweet. Appealing ripe berry fruit in the nose. Medium bodied. Generous, fresh melony and berry fruit flavors on the palate. Crisp finish. Fine with chicken and pecan salad.

Santa Barbara Winery, 1986 Santa Ynez Valley $5.50

Somewhat sweet (1.5% residual sugar). Very appealing, young raspberry nose. A touch of spritz at entry adds liveliness and freshness in the mouth. Nice cherry nuances. Clean finish. Fine as an apéritif or with light luncheon foods.

Santino White Harvest, 1987 Amador County $5.25

Medium sweet. Moderately intense raspberry and watermelon aromas. Medium-light bodied. Generous sweet fruit in the mouth, with ample acid to balance. Pleasant finish. Fine with chicken and pecan salad.

Sebastiani Vineyards, 1987 Sonoma County $4.00

Somewhat sweet. Medium-intense floral and melony aromas. Moderately sweet fruit on the palate, with a citric dimension. Pleasant finish. Fine as an apéritif.

Seghesio Winery, 1986 Northern Sonoma $3.50

Somewhat sweet. Fresh, pretty, and sweetish varietal fruit in the nose, with berry and tropical fruit tones. Fairly deep fruit impression on the palate, with the berry and melon flavors in nice balance with the acid. Slightly sharp finish. Try with chicken and pecan salad. Excellent value.

Sutter Home, 1987 California $4.50

Nice plummy fruit in the nose. Supple at entry, with good fruit. Nice balance. Best as an apéritif.

Weibel, 1987 Mendocino County $4.50

Nice watermelonlike aromas, with floral scents off dry. Medium-full bodied. Rich fruit on the palate, in a good structure. Long, tart finish. Fine with chicken salad. Good value.

Wm. Wheeler Young Vines, 1987 Sonoma County $5.00

Somewhat sweet. Appealing aromas of fresh raspberries and melons. Medium-light bodied. Flavorful sweet fruit on the palate. Nice balance. Sweet, long finish. An excellent wine. Just enjoy. Fine value.

Almaden Blush, NV California
Bulk Process $5.00

Nice fresh fruit aromas. Good bubble activity. Generous sweet grape flavors on the palate. Pleasant, lingering finish. Fine quaffing wine.

S. Anderson Blanc de Noirs, 1985 Napa Valley
Méthode Champenoise $16.00

Appealing, fresh fruit and yeast in the nose. An abundance of frothy mousse that persists. Beautifully focused citric fruit flavors, with minimal sweetness, and ample acid, in a clean, refreshing combination. Tart and yeasty at the finish. A great wine with cracked crab or caviar.

S. Anderson Blanc de Noirs, 1984 Napa Valley
Méthode Champenoise $16.00

Attractive salmon color. Pineappley and toasty aromas, overlaid by effusive mousse. Medium rich and toasty on the palate, fully dry, long finish. Superior as an apéritif, and has enough going for it to be matched with fresh lobster.

S. Anderson Brut, 1984 Napa Valley
Méthode Champenoise $18.00

Moderately intense pearlike fruit in the nose, with toasty scents, overlaid by persistent mousse. Fruity and round on the palate, with ample acid. Finishes slightly tart. Fine with moderately seasoned white meats.

S. Anderson Brut, 1983 Napa Valley
Méthode Champenoise $16.00

Loads of nice fruit in the nose, joined by a fair dimension of toasty yeast. Persistent beads on the palate, with ample fruit and acid in perfect balance. Enjoy with cracked crab or oysters on the half-shell.

Andre Brut, NV California
Bulk Process $3.15

Light golden color. Clean, young grape aromas. Generous fruit flavors on the palate, with low acid. A touch of sweetness in the short finish. Fine as an apéritif. Good value.

Ballatore Spumante, NV California
Bulk Process $5.00

Moderately intense sweetish fruit aromas. Nice bubbles, with some persistence. Fruity flavors throughout. Short, clean finish. Fine as an apéritif or with light luncheon foods.

Beaulieu Champagne de Chardonnay, 1982 Napa Valley
Méthode Champenoise

$14.00

Abundant toasty yeast and mature fruit in the nose. Somewhat austere on the palate, with nutty nuances, and pleasant yeasty dimension throughout. Fine for early consumption with moderately seasoned chicken dishes.

Chandon Blanc de Noirs, NV Napa Valley
Méthode Champenoise

$14.00

Wonderful aromas of toasty yeast and ripe cherries. Persistent, tiny bubbles. Generous fruit on the palate and a touch of sugar, in a vigorous presentation. Finishes toasty and slightly austere. A great wine on its own, and can stand up to fresh lobster or salmon roe.

Chandon Brut, NV Napa Valley
Méthode Champenoise

$13.00

Youthful fruit in the nose, within a toasty yeast framework. The fruit is round and supple on the palate, with medium-length flavor persistence. An excellent apéritif, and will also go well with cracked crab.

Chandon Reserve, NV Napa Valley
Méthode Champenoise

$19.00

Beautiful, intense toasty yeast aromas. Powerful mousse of tiny beads that persist. Rich and creamy on the palate, with mature apple and honey flavors. This is a great sparkling wine. Just enjoy!

Chateau St. Jean Blanc de Blancs, 1984 Sonoma County
Méthode Champenoise

$10.50

Appealing toasty yeast in the nose, with citric scents. Soft and somewhat sweet on the palate, with nice fruit and creamy yeast throughout. Pleasant lemony finish. Try with chicken in a cream sauce or sautéed scallops. Good value.

Chateau St. Jean Brut, 1985 Sonoma County
Méthode Champenoise

$11.00

Intense yeasty aromas, joined by nice fresh fruit scents. Vibrant mousse. Lots of yeastiness and fresh, citric fruit in the mouth. Tasty. Tart finish. Fine with shellfish.

Chateau St. Jean Brut, 1984 Sonoma County
Méthode Champenoise

$10.50

Medium-intense yeasty aromas, with appley and lemony scents. Generous fruit on the palate, with foamy yeast throughout. Finishes tart. Enjoy with chicken in a cream sauce.

The Christian Brothers Brut, NV California
Bulk Process

$4.50

Pleasant, clean fruit in the nose. Moderate bubble activity. Pleasant fruit flavors on the palate, and through the finish. A fine wine to be considered for festive occasions or as an apéritif.

Cook's, NV American Blanc de Noir
Bulk Process

$5.00

Very attractive aromas of strawberries and kiwi, with mushroomy scents. Nice bubble activity, with some persistence. Somewhat complex fruit flavors on the palate, with acid in good balance. Try with chicken in a cream sauce or sautéed scallops. Excellent value.

Cook's, NV Extra Dry
Bulk Process

$4.00

Moderately intense young fruit and yeast in the nose. Lively bubbles. Clean and fruity on the palate. Finishes slightly bitter. Can be enjoyed with light meats. Good value.

Cribari Extra Dry, NV California
Bulk Process

$2.25

Appealing fresh floral fruit in the nose. Nice bubble activity, with some persistence. Generous floral fruitiness in the mouth, with an ample acidic dimension. Well made. Crisp finish. Fine as an apéritif or with light luncheon foods. Super value.

Culbertson Blanc de Noir, 1986 California
Méthode Champenoise

$11.50

100% Pinot Noir. Heavy toasty aromas, with some earthy scents. Lots of sweetish fruit and toasty oak on the palate, in a soft structure. Toasty finish. Try with chicken in a light sauce.

Domaine Mumm Cuvée Napa, NV Napa Valley
Méthode Champenoise

$14.00

Appealing zesty fruit in the nose, with nice toasty yeast in support. Fine beads persist. Stylish fruit is the hallmark here. A fine wine for receptions.

Domaine Mumm Cuvée Napa Brut Prestige, NV Napa Valley
Méthode Champenoise $15.00

Powerful yeasty and fruity aromas. Generous creamy mousse. Very fruity on the palate, with ample toasty yeast and acid in nice balance. Fruity and crisp in the finish. Try this excellent wine with quail pâté, sautéed scallops, or on its own.

Domaine Mumm Cuvée Napa Vintage Reserve Brut, 1985 NapaValley
Méthode Champenoise $21.00

Intense toasty yeast in the nose, joined by a fair fruit dimension. Loads of tiny beads that persist. Smooth and creamy in the mouth, with the strong yeasty element and moderate fruit nicely balanced with acid. Crisp, yeasty finish. This is a superior sparkling wine. Just enjoy.

Gloria Ferrer Brut, NV Sonoma County
Méthode Champenoise $13.00

Abundant cherrylike fruit in the nose, with nice yeast throughout. Persistent mousse. Clean fruit flavors on the palate, with spicy nuances, and firming acid. A refreshing sparkler that will do well on its own or with light luncheon dishes.

Gloria Ferrer Brut, Royal Cuvée, 1985 Sonoma County
Méthode Champenoise $16.00

72% Pinot Noir; 28% Chardonnay. Appealing, medium-intense, fresh fruit and yeasty aromas. Nice fine bubbles. Generous fruit on the palate, with moderate yeasty elements, and ample acid. Fruity and crispy finish. Try with sautéed scallops or chicken in a cream sauce.

Gloria Ferrer Brut, Royal Cuvée, 1984 Sonoma County
Méthode Champenoise $15.00

Moderately intense toasty yeast in the nose. Fresh and lively on the palate, with the yeasty fruit nicely balanced with crispy acids. A very appealing, delicate wine that will do well as an apéritif.

Geyser Peak Blanc de Noirs, 1984 Sonoma County
Méthode Champenoise $10.00

Produced by Trione Vineyards. Appealing cherrylike fruit and yeasty aromas. Generous fruit on entry, with nice yeast. Fades a bit as it crosses the palate. Slightly bitter finish. Fine with light meats.

Handley Cellars Brut, 1984 Anderson Valley
Méthode Champenoise

$15.00

Appealing toasty, yeasty, and nutty aromas. Lots of tiny bubbles. Clean, well balanced. Tart finish. Enjoy with moderately seasoned white meats.

Handley Cellars Rosé, 1984 Anderson Valley
Méthode Champenoise

$16.75

Nice pink salmon color. Restrained cherry fruit and yeast in the nose. Frothy mousse. Moderate fruit and toasty yeast on the palate, in a clean presentation. Slightly sharp finish. Try with chicken in a light sauce.

Robert Hunter Blanc de Noirs, 1983 Sonoma Valley
Méthode Champenoise

$15.00

Juicy cherry and peach aromas, with toasty bread scents, and mild yeast in the background. Softly textured in the mouth. Sweet fruit in the mouth, with insistent bubbles. Try this easy-to-drink wine as an apéritif or with moderately seasoned chicken dishes.

Robert Hunter Brut de Noirs, 1984 Sonoma Valley
Méthode Champenoise

$15.00

Medium-intense cherry fruit in the nose, with butterscotch tones, and nice overall yeastiness. Lots of foam. Full and round on the palate, with the cherry, pear, and plum flavors nicely stiffened with ample acid. Fine with moderately seasoned chicken dishes.

Iron Horse Blanc de Blancs, 1984 Sonoma— Green Valley
Méthode Champenoise

$19.00

Appealing, medium-intense lemony fruit and toasty aromas. Lots of mousse that persists. Generous clean fruit on the palate, with an ample toasty element, in a well-balanced combination. Crisp finish. Try with fresh lobster, smoked salmon, or hors d'oeuvres.

Iron Horse Blanc de Noirs, Wedding Cuvée, 1985 Sonoma County—Green Valley
Méthode Champenoise

$17.00

Very attractive Pinot Noir fruit in the nose, nicely framed in toasty yeast. Ample fruit in the mouth, with considerable acid through the finish. A bit harsh. Enjoy with shellfish.

Iron Horse Brut, 1985 Sonoma County— Green Valley
Méthode Champenoise

🍷 **$17.50**

Very attractive, clean fruit and nice yeast in the nose. The effervescence of fine beads persists. Generous flavorful fruit on the palate, with ample yeast and acid, in a clean, well-balanced presentation. Crisp finish. Try this excellent wine with quail pâté, caviar, or on its own.

Iron Horse Brut, 1984 Sonoma County— Green Valley
Méthode Champenoise

🍷 **$16.50**

Very attractive, complex, fruity, yeasty, toasty bread dough aromas. The wine sits firmly in the mouth, with nice froth and intense fruit. The finish is long, tart, and clean. All elements are in perfect proportion. Enjoy this excellent wine with cracked crab, smoked salmon, or caviar.

Iron Horse Brut Rosé, 1985 Sonoma County— Green Valley
Méthode Champenoise

🍷 **$20.00**

Forward sweetish fruit in the nose, with yeasty overtones. Nice mousse. Lots of sweet fruit flavors in the mouth, with ample acid for structure. Fruity finish. Try with cold smoked chicken breasts or baked ham.

Jepson Brut, 1985 Mendocino County
Méthode Champenoise

🍷 **$14.00**

Moderate yeasty aromas. Vigorous effervescence. Nice lemony fruit on the palate, with good acid. Crisp finish. Try with cracked crab or oysters on the half-shell.

Korbel Blanc de Blancs, NV California
Méthode Champenoise

🍷 **$12.75**

100% Chardonnay. Appealing toasty yeast and floral aromas. Vigorous mousse. Moderately intense fruit in the mouth, with sufficient acid in balance. Slightly sweet. Enjoy as an apéritif or with chicken in a light sauce.

Korbel Blanc de Noirs, NV California
Méthode Champenoise

🍷 **$12.75**

100% Pinot Noir. Intense toastiness in the nose, with nutty overtones. Generous ripe fruit in the mouth, with ample acid. The finish is a bit tart. Try with chicken in a cream sauce or pasta in a light pesto sauce.

☆☆

Korbel Brut, NV California
Méthode Champenoise   🍷   **$8.00**

Straw color. Clean fruit in the nose, with floral scents. Strong effervescence that starts slowly and continues. Slightly sweet fruit on the palate, with sufficient acid, in a clean presentation. This very popular wine can be enjoyed as an apéritif or at most meals with light meats. Good value.

☆☆ ½

Korbel Brut Rosé, NV California
Méthode Champenoise   🍷   **$10.00**

Light cherry color. Appealing raspberry and cherry aromas, nicely framed in creamy yeast. Intense, slightly sweet cherrylike fruit flavors on the palate, joined by yeast and acid, in a good structure. Crispy and fruity on the finish. Try with baked ham, seafood quiches, or cold smoked chicken breasts. Good value.

☆☆ ½

Korbel Natural, NV California
Méthode Champenoise   🍷   **$12.50**

Attractive figgy fruit in the nose, with floral and yeasty tones. Tiny beads that persist. Quite creamy on the palate, with good fruit and acid. Tart finish. Try with shellfish croquettes, quail pâté, or caviar.

☆☆

Hanns Kornell Brut, NV California
Méthode Champenoise   🍷   **$11.00**

Light straw color, with green hue. Moderately intense fruit in the nose, with nice yeast. Tiny beads persist. Appley and lemony flavors, with good acid. Clean and tart in the finish. Fine with cracked crab.

☆☆ ½

Maison Deutz Brut Cuvée, NV Santa Barbara County
Méthode Champenoise   🍷   **$15.00**

Medium-intense toasty, smoky aromas, framed in mature yeasty character. Beautiful creamy mousse that persists, with nice acidity. Crisp finish. Fine with shellfish croquettes or caviar.

☆☆

Mark West Blanc de Noirs, 1984 Russian River Valley
Méthode Champenoise   🍷   **$16.50**

Appealing fresh fruit and yeasty aromas. Plenty of fine bubbles that persist. Nicely focused fruit and creamy yeast are combined in a clean presentation. Very tasty. Pleasant, lingering finish. Enjoy with moderately seasoned chicken dishes.

☆☆ **Paul Masson Blanc de Noirs, 1984 Monterey County, Centennial Cuvée**
Méthode Champenoise   *$9.00*

Medium-intense, clean fruit in the nose, with yeasty scents. Moderate fruit flavors in the mouth, with lively effervescence, in a clean presentation. Crispy finish. Fine as an apéritif or with moderately seasoned chicken dishes.

☆☆ **Paul Masson Brut, 1984 California**
Transfer Method   *$8.00*

Appealing fresh fruit in the nose, with slight yeasty scents. Active bubbles that persist. The fruit is clean and fresh in the mouth, with a nice tart dimension. Enjoy as an apéritif or with light foods.

☆☆ **Paul Masson Extra Dry, 1984 California**
Transfer Method   *$8.00*

Clean and delicate fruit aromas, with a touch of yeast. Nice bubble activity. Sweetish fruit on the palate throughout. Enjoy as an apéritif or on festive occasions.

☆☆½ **Mirassou Brut, 1983 Monterey County**
Méthode Champenoise   *$9.00*

Moderately intense yeasty and buttery aromas. Nice mousse. Generous, slightly sweet cherry fruit flavors on the palate, joined by creamy yeast, in a soft presentation. A touch of lemon in the finish. A very fine wine that can be enjoyed as an apéritif or at most meals with light meats. Good value.

☆ **Monterey Vineyard Brut, 1985 Monterey County**
Méthode Champenoise   *$10.00*

Somewhat sweet pineappley fruit aromas, with yeasty scents. Sweetish fruit flavors on the palate. Short finish. Best as an apéritif.

☆ **Monterey Vineyard Brut, 1984 Monterey County**
Méthode Champenoise   *$10.00*

Lively appley, toasty, and yeasty aromas. The fruit is thin in the mouth, with moderate effervescence and a slightly bitter aftertaste. Best with light meats.

☆☆½ **Parsons Creek Brut Reserve, NV Mendocino County**
Méthode Champenoise   *$13.50*

Very attractive, clean aromas of citric fruit and moderate yeast. Fine mousse. Quite dry, with the somewhat narrow fruit flavors in delicate balance with the acid. Clean and refreshing. Excellent as an apéritif.

☆☆☆   ***Piper Sonoma Blanc de Noirs, 1986 Sonoma County***   🍷   ***$13.00***
Méthode Champenoise

100% Pinot Noir. Beautiful aromas of refined fruit and toast. Loads of tiny bubbles that persist. Lots of lively fruit on the palate, with ample acid, in a fine-tuned combination. Try this superior sparkler with cracked crab, fresh lobster, or caviar.

☆☆☆   ***Piper Sonoma Blanc de Noirs, 1985 Sonoma County***   🍷   ***$13.00***
Méthode Champenoise

100% Pinot Noir. Appealing, nicely focused fruit and yeast in the nose. Good mousse. Nice cherry fruit and yeasty flavors in the mouth, with sufficient acid for structure. The finish is fruity, crisp, and long. A refined wine. Try with salmon mousse, fresh lobster, quail pâté, or caviar.

☆☆½   ***Piper Sonoma Blanc de Noirs, 1984 Sonoma County***   🍷   ***$15.00***
Méthode Champenoise

Generous fruit and yeasty aromas. Loads of beads that persist. Nice yeasty character throughout, with citric fruit flavors. Well balanced. Crispy. Enjoy with cracked crab or fresh lobster.

☆☆½   ***Piper Sonoma Brut, 1986 Sonoma County***   🍷   ***$14.00***
Méthode Champenoise

Medium-intense yeasty aromas, joined by clean fruity scents, in an overall elegant framework. Lots of foamy mousse. Moderately intense citrusy fruit on the palate, with a nice yeasty dimension, and ample acid, in a firm structure. Finishes dry. Enjoy with oysters on the half-shell or cracked crab.

☆☆½   ***Piper Sonoma Brut, 1984 Sonoma County***   🍷   ***$14.00***
Méthode Champenoise

Forward fresh appley fruit, with vanilla scents, and a nice yeasty dimension. Attractive juicy fruit on the palate with ample acid, and creamy yeast flavors. Nice frothy mousse. Good balance. Enjoy with baked sea bass or cold chicken breasts.

☆☆☆   ***Piper Sonoma Brut Reserve, 1983 Sonoma County***   🍷   ***$20.00***
Méthode Champenoise

Intense, rich pineappley and toasty aromas, with a nice dimension of aged yeasts. The fruit is bright and fresh on the palate, with substantial acids pushing through. Brisk. Try with shellfish croquettes, caviar, or oysters on the half-shell.

☆☆☆ ***Roederer Estate Brut, NV Anderson Valley*** 🍷 ***$15.75***
Méthode Champenoise

Most attractive, medium-intense fruity and toasty aromas in perfect balance. An abundance of creamy mousse. Generous refined yeast on the palate, joined by subtle fruit. Clean and elegant. This is a first offering. A superior sparkling wine. Enjoy!

☆☆ ***Scharffenberger Blanc de Blancs,*** 🍷 ***$18.00***
1985 Mendocino County
Méthode Champenoise

Low-intensity fruity and yeasty aromas. Lots of tiny bubbles that keep coming. Moderate fruit and yeast, with good acid. Well balanced. Crisp finish. Fine with mild shellfish preparations.

☆☆ ***Scharffenberger Brut, NV Mendocino County*** 🍷 ***$14.00***
Méthode Champenoise

Appealing sweet cherries and butterscotch in the nose. Generous froth. Soft, honeyed fruit flavor on the palate, with mild acids. An easy-drinking wine for enjoyment as an apéritif.

☆☆ ***Scharffenberger Brut Rosé, NV Mendocino County*** 🍷 ***$16.00***
Méthode Champenoise

Appealing, medium-intense, sweetish fruit and yeast in the nose. Nice froth. Somewhat candied fruit, nicely balanced with acid, in a clean presentation. A very fine wine for quaffing or with light lunches.

☆☆ ***Scharffenberger Cellars Brut,*** 🍷 ***$13.50***
1984 Mendocino County
Méthode Champenoise

Fresh, moderately intense, blossomy fruit in the nose, with nice yeast in support. The fruit is light and clean on the palate, balanced with light toastiness. Good bubbles and firmness throughout. Fine as an apéritif or with light foods.

☆☆ ***Schramsberg Blanc de Blancs, 1985 Napa Valley*** 🍷 ***$19.00***
Méthode Champenoise

Forward toasty/yeasty aromas. Nice mousse. Lots of yeasty flavors, joined by mature fruit, in a good structure. Pleasant yeasty, long finish. Fine with moderately seasoned white meats or poultry.

☆☆½ ***Schramsberg Blanc de Blancs, 1984 Napa Valley*** 🍷 ***$18.00***
Méthode Champenoise

Aggressive appley and lemony aromas, with nice toasty, yeasty scents. Slightly sweet fruit flavors on the palate, with a full dimension of lively mousse. Well balanced. Fruity finish. Fine with baked sea bass or chicken.

☆☆☆☆ **Schramsberg Blanc de Noirs, 1983 Napa Valley**   🍷   *$21.00*
Méthode Champenoise

Expansive rich fruit and yeastiness in the nose. A long dimension
of refined mousse. Complex flavors of fruit and yeast on the
palate, nicely balanced with acids, in an elegant presentation.
Creamy and toasty through a long finish. A top-notch
sparkling wine. Enjoy.

☆☆ **Sebastiani Blanc de Noirs, NV Sonoma County**   🍷   *$10.00*
Méthode Champenoise

Appealing cherry fruit aromas, with orange peel scents, and nice
yeast in support. Fresh and lively on the palate. Long finish.
Excellent as an apéritif.

☆☆ ½ **Shadow Creek Blanc de Blanc, 1984 California**   🍷   *$14.50*
Méthode Champenoise

Attractive, forward, buttery fruit aromas, with a full dimension
of toasty yeast. Generous, mouth-filling foamy mousse, with
lemon components. Crisp, clean finish. Enjoy this fine wine
with cracked crab, caviar, or smoked salmon.

☆☆☆ **Shadow Creek Blanc de Noir, 1984 California**   🍷   *$12.50*
Méthode Champenoise

Intense, fresh appley fruit in the nose, with scents of toast, bread
dough, and aged yeast. Generous rich fruit on the palate, with
an abundance of lively mousse throughout, in a well-structured
presentation. An elegant reception wine, and will also go well
with steak tartaré or sautéed scallops.

☆☆ **Shadow Creek Brut, NV California**   🍷   *$11.50*
Méthode Champenoise

Nice cherry fruit and yeast in the nose, with herbal scents. Beads
of creamy bubbles in the mouth, with a nice fruity dimension
throughout. Crispy finish. Excellent as an apéritif.

☆☆ **M. Tribaut Blanc de Noirs, 1985 Monterey County**   🍷   *$13.00*
Méthode Champenoise

100% Pinot Noir. Nice cherrylike fruit aromas, with yeasty tones.
Lively mousse. Attractive young fruit flavors on the palate, with
a touch of sweetness, and good acid, in a clean presentation.
Slightly tart finish. Try with chicken in a cream sauce.

☆☆☆ **M. Tribaut Brut, 1985 Monterey County**   🍷   *$13.00*
Méthode Champenoise

75% Pinot Noir; 25% Chardonnay. Medium-intense fruity and
toasty aromas. Nice frothy mousse. Deep flavors on the palate,
with the fruit and toasty elements in good balance, in a soft
structure. Excellent as an apéritif or with light luncheon dishes.

☆☆½ M. Tribaut Brut, 1984 Monterey County — $12.00
Méthode Champenoise

Forward toasty, smoky aromas, joined by restrained fruit scents, in a nice yeasty framework. Fine beads that persist. Good fruit and acid in balance, in a clean, crisp presentation. Fine on its own or with baked sea bass or chicken.

☆☆ M. Tribaut Brut, NV Monterey County — $13.00
Méthode Champenoise

Medium-intense aromas of mature fruit and yeast, with buttery and herbal scents. Lots of tiny beads that persist. Generous ripe fruit on the palate, with a nice toasty dimension. Tasty. Fine with lightly seasoned white meats.

☆☆½ M. Tribaut Rosé, 1984 Monterey County — $12.00
Méthode Champenoise

Intense, fresh, cherrylike fruit in the nose, with toasty scents. Slightly sweet, concentrated cherry fruit flavors on the palate, with ample acid, lending an overall crispy impression. Clean, fruity finish. Fine as an apéritif or with light lunches such as chicken salad.

☆☆ Wente Bros. Brut, 1983 Arroyo Seco — $10.00
Méthode Champenoise

Medium-intense toasty yeast aromas, with appley and citrusy scents. Lively, tiny bubbles. The fruit is firm on the palate, with a nice yeasty dimension. Slightly sharp finish. Try with cracked crab.

OTHER WHITE WINES

☆   ***Ahlgren Vineyard, Semillon,***   🍷   ***$6.00***
1986 Santa Cruz Mountains, St. Charles Vineyard

Dry. Medium-intense melony fruit in the nose, with buttery and
oaky tones. Medium-full bodied. Rich fruit on the palate, with
ample oak. Finishes slightly hot. Best with lightly seasoned
poultry dishes.

☆☆½   ***Alderbrook Winery, Semillon, 1986 Dry Creek Valley***   🍷   ***$7.00***

Dry. Appealing fresh floral fruit in the nose, with weedy tones.
Medium bodied. Very attractive, clean fruit on the palate, in a
firm structure. Lingering finish. Try with red snapper or
Rex sole. Good value.

☆☆   ***Alexander Valley Vineyards, Dry Chenin Blanc,***   🍷   ***$6.50***
1986 California

Brilliant. Straw color. Dry (.05% residual sugar). Appealing,
medium-intense floral and melony aromas, with a touch of oak.
Medium bodied. The moderately intense fruit flavors on the palate are nicely balanced with acid. Clean finish. Fine with light
luncheon dishes such as chicken or tuna salad.

☆☆½   ***Bogle Vineyards, Semillon, 1987 Clarksburg***   🍷   ***$6.00***

Dry. Very appealing, intense melony, figgy, and floral aromas.
Medium-full bodied. Lush, somewhat sweet fruit on the palate
carries through the finish. Nice balance. Fine with light
luncheon dishes. Good value.

☆   ***Chateau Ste. Michelle, Semillon, 1986 Washington***   🍷   ***$6.00***

Dry. Appealing, medium-intense floral fruit in the nose, with
hints of oak. Medium bodied. Moderately intense fruit flavors on
the palate, in a firm presentation. Best with lightly seasoned
fish dishes.

☆☆   ***Chateau Ste. Michelle, Semillon Blanc,***   🍷   ***$5.50***
1986 Washington

Somewhat sweet. Fresh aromas of pears and melons, with
vanillin scents. Medium bodied. Moderately intense sweet fruit
flavors on the palate, with sufficient acid for good structure.
Crisp finish. Fine with cracked crab and lemon. Good value.

☆☆   ***Clos du Val, Semillon, 1986 California***   🍷   ***$8.50***

Dry. Nice figgy aromas, with herbal tones. Medium bodied.
Round and smooth in the mouth, with the figgy flavors and
herbal nuances nicely supported by the acid, in a firm structure.
Try with poached salmon.

Columbia Crest Vineyards, Semillon, 1986 Columbia Valley, Washington **$5.00**

Dry. Appealing, medium-intense honeylike fruit and floral aromas. Medium bodied. Attractive clean pearlike fruit on the palate, with floral nuances. A fine wine for early consumption with light luncheon foods. Good value.

 Grand Cru Vineyards, Dry Chenin Blanc, 1987 Clarksburg **$6.50**

Slightly sweet (1.16% residual sugar). Very attractive floral, honey, melony, and figgy aromas. Medium bodied. Nice melony and tropical fruit flavors on the palate, with nutty nuances, and good acid. Crisp finish. Continues the string of fine Chenins from this winery. Fine with spicy chicken dishes.

 Grand Cru Vineyards, Dry Chenin Blanc, 1986 Clarksburg **$6.00**

Slightly sweet (0.92% residual sugar). Brilliant. Pronounced melony fruit in the nose. Medium bodied. Intense melony fruit flavors on the palate, with ample acid. Pleasant, tangy finish. Fine with poultry or fish in a cream sauce. Good value.

 Inglenook Gravion, 1986 Napa Valley, 51% Semillon, 49% Sauvignon Blanc **$9.50**

Dry. Beautiful aromas of figs and flowers. Medium bodied. Moderately intense fruit flavors on the palate, with grassy nuances, in a firm structure. Can accompany a wide range of moderately seasoned fish dishes.

 Monticello Chevrier Blanc, 1986 Napa Valley, 80% Semillon, 20% Sauvignon Blanc **$7.50**

Dry. Forward aromas of flowers and figs, with a touch of oak. Medium bodied. Nice figgy fruit flavors on the palate, with weedy nuances, in a good structure. Fruity finish. Try as an accompaniment to pasta with shellfish.

 Andrew Quady Essensia, Orange Muscat, 1987 California **$11.00**

Very sweet (12% residual sugar). Very attractive ripe apricot aromas, joined by pronounced orange blossom fragrances. Intense sweet apricoty fruit fills the mouth, with a nice citric element, in a good structure. The finish is clean, long, and smooth. A specialty of this winery—and a great wine. Enjoy with fresh fruit tarts. Good value.

Wente Bros., Semillon, 1986 Livermore Valley, Louis Mel Vineyard, 18% Sauvignon Blanc

$7.00

Dry. Attractive, medium intense varietal fruit in the nose, with spicy scents, and rich oak in support. Medium bodied. Generous floral fruit in the mouth, with ample oak and acid, in a firm structure. Long, crisp finish. Try with well-seasoned fish or light poultry dishes. Good value.

RED WINES

CABERNET SAUVIGNON

☆☆½ **Alexander Valley Vineyards, 1986 Alexander Valley**  **$11.00**

Deep ruby color. Appealing ripe fruit fruit in the nose, with bell pepper and mint scents in full support. Medium-full bodied. Full and round in the mouth, with the ripe cherry, plum, and anise flavors balanced with mild tannins. Pleasant, lingering finish. Try as an accompaniment to duck breast with an olive sauce.

☆☆½ **Beaulieu Private Reserve, 1984 Napa Valley** 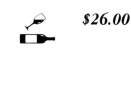 **$26.00**

Moderately intense ripe fruit in the nose, with spicy and perfuming scents, in an oaky framework. Medium-full bodied. Full on entry, with some plummy richness, and a full dimension of spicy oak, in a good structure. Enjoyable now, and will improve for several years. Try with braised lamb or breast of veal.

☆☆½ **Beaulieu Private Reserve, 1983 Napa Valley**  **$24.00**

Medium-intense, ripe curranty fruit aromas, with spicy and minty scents, framed in abundant vanillin oak. Medium-full bodied. Moderate curranty fruit on the palate, with a full dimension of oak. Not quite up to prior bottlings, but still, a fine wine. Enjoy with broiled steaks or rack of lamb.

☆☆☆ **Beaulieu Private Reserve, 1982 Napa Valley** 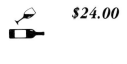 **$24.00**

Dark ruby color. Generous ripe fruit in the nose, with spicy and toasty oak overtones. Medium-full bodied. Rich and flavorful fruit on the palate, nicely balanced with oak and tannin. The wine will improve for a number of years. Enjoy with beef ribs, braised lamb, veal scallops, or roast quail.

☆☆ **Beaulieu Vineyard Beau Tour, 1986 Napa Valley**  **$7.00**

Moderately intense herbal-scented fruit, with minty overtones. Medium bodied. Attractive raspberry flavors on the palate, with a touch of spice, and soft tannins, in a harmonious combination. Enjoy with moderately seasoned red meats. Good value.

☆☆½ **Beaulieu Vineyard Rutherford, 1985 Napa Valley** **$9.50**

Attractive dark ruby color. Medium-intense cherry fruit aromas, with herbal and dusty scents, and oaky tones. Medium bodied. Smooth and velvety on the palate with the moderate fruit flavors and tannin in perfect balance. An excellent wine for current consumption and for several more years. Appropriate for a wide range of meat dishes. Good value.

Bell Ranch, 1985 Sonoma Valley, Estate Bottled

 $14.00

Produced by Sebastiani Vineyards. Appealing cassis and sweet oak aromas. Medium bodied. Generous fruit on the palate, with ample oak and tannins. Astringent finish. Give this wine several more years of development, then enjoy with well-seasoned meat dishes.

Bellerose Vineyard, Cuvée Bellerose, 1985 Sonoma County

 $16.00

Pleasant, medium-intense aromas of ripe cherries and oak, with herbal and briary overtones. Medium-full bodied. Loads of ripe, concentrated fruit flavors on the palate, with ample oak, and abundant tannins. Harsh finish. This wine needs at least five more years of development. Best with well-seasoned meat dishes.

Belvedere Winery, 1984 Napa Valley, Robert Young Vineyards

 $13.00

Forward blackberry fruit aromas, with chocolaty and earthy scents. Medium-full bodied. Generous cherry fruit flavors on the palate, with minty nuances, and ample vanillin oak. Good structure. Accessible now, and will improve for several years. Fine as an accompaniment to rack of lamb with Cabernet sauce.

Beringer Private Reserve, 1983 Napa Valley

 $19.00

Intense currant and black pepper aromas, with ample sweet oak in support. Medium-full bodied. Intensely concentrated fruit flavors fill the mouth, with a full dimension of tannin through the finish. This superior wine will improve for at least five more years. Enjoy with beef Wellington, veal Orloff, or roasted game.

Beringer Vineyards, 1984 Knights Valley

 $12.00

Medium-intense cherry fruit aromas, with herbal scents. Medium bodied. Generous herbal fruit flavors on the palate, with oak and tannin in balance. A fine wine for early consumption with a wide range of moderately seasoned meat dishes.

Boeger Winery, 1984 El Dorado

 $10.50

Dark ruby color. Attractive ripe currant aromas, with minty, chocolaty, and spicy scents. Medium-full bodied. Smooth and fleshy in the mouth, with the rich fruit and vanillin oak flavors in nice balance. Medium tannins. Best with highly spiced meat dishes.

Brutocao, 1982 Mendocino County $9.00

Very appealing cassis and cedar in the nose, with chocolaty overtones. Medium-full bodied. The generous berry fruit flavors, sweet oak, and tannins are in perfect harmony in an elegant style. Very enjoyable now, and will improve for several years. Try as an accompaniment to grilled quail with Cabernet jelly. Good value.

Buehler Vineyards, 1985 Napa Valley $14.00

Dark ruby color. Intense aromas of ripe currants and cassis, with vanilla scents. Medium-full bodied. Loads of rich, fleshy fruit on the palate, with substantial tannins. Harsh finish. Give this wine several years to smooth out, then enjoy for years to come with highly seasoned meat dishes.

Buehler Vineyards, 1984 Napa Valley $11.00

Dark ruby color. Rich, ripe fruit and sweet oak aromas, with overtones of ripe currants and cassis. Medium-full bodied. The wine enters the mouth soft and supple, with the fleshy fruit and oak in nice balance. A bit of tannic roughness in the finish does not detract. Enjoy this fine wine with standing rib of beef or braised lamb.

Buena Vista Private Reserve, 1983 Carneros— Sonoma Valley $14.50

Dark ruby color. Intense briary, herbal, minty, and earthy aromas, joined by a nice dimension of sweet cherry fruit. Medium-full bodied. Rich, fleshy cherry fruit on the palate, with considerable tannin. Coarse finish. This wine needs time to smooth out. Wait until 1992, then enjoy with well-seasoned meat dishes.

Buena Vista Winery, 1984 Carneros $9.50

Pleasant, medium-intense herbal-scented blackberry fruit aromas, with earthy overtones. Medium bodied. The wine is soft on the palate, with herbal fruit flavors and medium tannins. This is a good wine for current consumption with moderately seasoned beef or lamb dishes.

Burgess Vintage Selection, 1984 Napa Valley $17.00

Intense aromas of ripe fruit, herbs, and briar, with olive and spice scents, and a full dimension of oak in support. Full bodied. Concentrated fruit flavors and ample oak, with a sizeable tannic dimension. This is a big Cabernet—rich and wonderful— that needs several years to smooth out. Try it in 1992 at that special dinner.

Burgess Vintage Selection, 1983 Napa Valley *$16.00*

Attractive ripe berry and earthy aromas, with chocolaty scents, and a touch of oak. Medium-full bodied. Rich, ripe blackberry fruit flavors on the palate, with moderate tannins. Tart finish. This wine is accessible now, and will improve for a number of years. Enjoy with well-seasoned meats.

 Cain Cellars, 1984 Napa Valley *$14.00*

Subdued ripe currant fruit in the nose, with spicy scents, and nice oak in support. Medium-full bodied. Deeply extracted fruit flavors on the palate, with ample tannin, in a firm structure. Astringent finish. Give this wine a couple of years to smooth out, then enjoy with well-seasoned meat dishes.

 Cain Cellars, 1983 Napa Valley *$14.00*

Dark ruby color. Medium-intense aromas of ripe curranty fruit, herbs, and sweet oak. Medium-full bodied. Rich, briary, ripe fruit flavors in the mouth, with ample oak, and considerable tannins. Harsh finish. Needs time to smooth out; say, four years or so. Enjoy with savory dishes.

 Cakebread Cellars, 1985 Napa Valley *$17.00*

Most attractive, generous ripe cherry and sweet oak in the nose. Medium-full bodied. Loads of rich fruit flavors on the palate, with oak and tannin in balance, in an elegant presentation. Accessible now, with good aging potential. Try this superior wine with beef Wellington, rack of lamb, or roast quail.

 Cakebread Cellars, 1984 Napa Valley *$16.00*

Appealing black currant aromas, nicely supported with spicy, herbal, and vanillin oak scents. Medium bodied. The wine is firm in the mouth, with the fruit and oak in good balance. Some tannin in the finish. This is a refined wine with excellent potential for aging. Enjoy with braised lamb, veal scallops, or saddle of hare.

 Carmenet Vineyard, 1985 Sonoma Valley, 8% Merlot; 5% Cabernet Franc *$18.50*

Intense, complex aromas of ripe berries, cedar, and spice. Medium-full bodied. Loads of black cherry, currants, and spice on the palate, with woody nuances, and ample tannins. Harsh finish. This is a muscular wine of superior quality that needs time to smooth out. Start consuming in 1995 for optimum enjoyment.

Carmenet Vineyard, 1984 Sonoma Valley, 10% Merlot, 5% Cabernet Franc $16.00

Rich and plummy ripe fruit aromas, with herbal and creamy oak scents. Medium-full bodied. Broad fruit flavors in the mouth are nicely balanced with oak and young tannins. Very fine now, and bodes even better for the future. Best with savory meat dishes.

Caymus Napa Cuvée, 1985 Napa Valley $12.00

Appealing spicy Cabernet fruit in the nose, with earthy and green olive scents. Medium bodied. Moderately intense tasty fruit on the palate, with medium tannins, and a rich oak dimension. A fine wine for consumption in the next few years with beef or lamb dishes.

Caymus Napa Cuvée, 1984 Napa Valley $12.00

Forward cherrylike nose, with herbal and oak overtones. Medium bodied. Rich and supple in the mouth, with ripe fruit, oak, and tannins in nice balance. This wine is accessible now, and will improve for several years. Try as an accompaniment to rolled leg of lamb with rosemary or roast beef au jus.

Caymus Special Selection, 1983 Napa Valley $35.00

Another superior bottling, consistent with prior years. Intense aromas of ripe currants, cassis, and spice, with lots of rich oak throughout. Medium-full bodied. Wonderful ripe fruit flavors fill the mouth, joined by an abundance of sweet oak, in a good structure. This is an elegantly styled Cabernet that is accessible now, but better to wait a few years for further development, then enjoy.

Caymus Special Selection, 1982 Napa Valley $35.00

Another great bottling. Consistent over the years. Beautiful, complex aromas of ripe currants, spice, violets, and sweet oak. Medium-full bodied. Supple on entry, with the richly textured fruit in perfect balance with oak and tannins. Accessible now, and will improve for at least another ten years. Enjoy with braised lamb, small game, broiled steaks, or stuffed breast of veal.

Caymus Vineyards, 1985 Napa Valley $18.00

Attractive, moderately intense cassis and spicy oak in the nose, with hints of mint, herbs, and tobacco. Medium-full bodied. Deep and firm in the mouth, with the herbal Cabernet fruit flavors and oak in nice balance, in a good structure. Slightly rough finish. Good aging potential. Enjoy this superior wine with braised lamb or broiled steaks.

☆☆☆   ***Caymus Vineyards, Estate Bottled, 1984 Napa Valley***   *$16.00*

Dark ruby color. Attractive, rich, ripe curranty fruit aromas, with green olive, spicy, and cedary overtones. Medium-full bodied. Loads of mature berry fruit flavors, with ample oak and moderate tannins. The wine is drinkable now, but best to wait a few years for the wine to reach its potential, then enjoy.

☆☆☆   ***Chalk Hill Winery, 1984 Sonoma County***   *$10.00*

Forward ripe black currants and cassis in the nose, with smoky oak tones in support. Medium-full bodied. Deep, fleshy fruit impression on the palate, with the cherry, oak, and herbal flavors combined in a firm structure. Although enjoyable now, best to wait a couple of years for further improvement. Try with well-seasoned beef dishes. Excellent value.

☆☆½   ***Chappellet Vineyard, 1984 Napa Valley***   *$18.00*

Dark ruby color. Plummy, ripe fruit aromas, with earthy and herbal scents, and ample sweet oak in the background. Medium-full bodied. Supple feel in the mouth, with the rich blackberry fruit flavors in nice balance with the tannins. This is a somewhat heavy wine that will go well with highly seasoned foods.

☆☆   ***Chappellet Vineyard, 1983 Napa Valley***   *$12.00*

Moderate aromas of currants and spice, with some toasty oak in the background. Medium-full bodied. The fruit, oak, and tannin are in nice balance. The wine is fine for early consumption with beef or lamb dishes.

☆☆☆   ***Chateau Montelena, 1984 Napa Valley***   *$20.00*

Strong cassislike fruit in the nose, with tarry, herbal, and cedary scents. Medium-full bodied. Heavily extracted ripe fruit on the palate, balanced with strong tannins. Astringent finish. This is a wine of the future; I suggest a wait of five years. Then enjoy with hearty dishes.

☆☆½   ***Chateau Montelena, 1983 Napa Valley***   *$18.00*

Attractive cedary, briary, and cigar box aromas, joined by plummy fruit and oaky overtones. Medium-full bodied. Concentrated berry fruit on the palate, with a full tannic dimension. Harsh finish. Needs time to smooth out. Wait until 1992, then enjoy with highly spiced meat dishes.

☆☆½   ***Chateau Potelle, 1984 Alexander Valley***   *$13.00*

Medium-intense cherry fruit, spice, and herbs in the nose, nicely supported by creamy oak. Medium-full bodied. Very ripe fruit flavors on the palate, with tarry nuances, and oak in balance. Soft tannins. Try as an accompaniment to duck breast with olive sauce.

Chateau St. Jean, 1985 Alexander Valley
$19.00

Appealing, intense ripe herbal fruit in the nose, with spicy overtones. Medium-full bodied. Supple on entry, with the ripe berry fruit, herbs, and oak balanced in a good structure. Slightly bitter finish. Try with grilled New York steak.

Chateau Ste. Michelle, 1983 Washington
$11.00

Deep ruby color. Attractive aromas of cherries, currants, flowers, mint, and sweet oak. Medium-full bodied. Velvety smooth texture, with the deep fruit flavors, tarry/minty nuances, mild oak, and tannins, in perfect balance for early enjoyment. Fine with a wide range of moderately seasoned meat dishes.

Chateau Souverain, 1984 Sonoma County
$8.00

Moderately intense cherry fruit aromas, with herbal scents, and a touch of oak. Medium bodied. Tasty fruit on the palate, with oak and tannin in balance. A pleasant wine that will go well with a wide range of meat dishes.

Cherryblock, 1985 Sonoma Valley, Estate Bottled
$17.50

Produced by Sebastiani Vineyards. Very appealing aromas of ripe cherries and sweet oak. Medium-full bodied. Supple on entry, with the fruit and oak nicely balanced in a good structure. Should improve for at least five more years. Try as an accompaniment to duck breast with cherry-peppercorn sauce.

Chimney Rock Wine Cellars, 1985 Napa Valley
$15.00

Beautiful rich oak and cassislike fruit in the nose. Medium-full bodied. Generous young fruit on the palate, with nice creamy oak, and ample tannins, in a firm structure. Slightly astringent finish. Try this excellent wine with Beef Wellington or rolled leg of lamb with rosemary.

Chimney Rock Wine Cellars, 1984 Napa Valley
$15.00

Ripe cherry fruit aromas, with herbal, floral, and cedary scents. Medium-full bodied. Fleshy fruit on the palate, which fades a bit as it counteracts the noticeable tannins. Lean finish. Fine with beef or lamb dishes.

The Christian Brothers, 1984 Napa Valley
$7.00

Sweet cherry fruit aromas, with herbal and cedary overtones. Medium-bodied. Supple fruit in the mouth, with modest tannins. This is a fine wine for early consumption, and will hold for a number of years. Excellent value.

The Christian Brothers, 1985 Napa Valley, Oakville Ranch *$8.00*

Medium-intense cherry fruit aromas, with herbal and spicy tones. Medium bodied. Moderate fruit on the palate, with oak and tannins in balance, in a smooth presentation. Enjoy with moderately seasoned meat dishes. Good value.

 Clos du Bois, 1985 Alexander Valley *$10.00*

Beautiful cherry fruit in the nose, with chocolaty, minty, and cedary scents. Medium-full bodied. Soft and velvety smooth in the mouth, with the sweet fruit, oak, and mild tannins in perfect balance. I am particularly attracted to this wine. You do not have to wait for this one, just enjoy. Good value.

 Clos du Bois, 1984 Alexander Valley  *$9.00*

Attractive herbal-scented Cabernet fruit, with hints of dill and olives, enriched by sweet oak. Medium-full bodied. The rich cherry and currant flavors, with herbal nuances and sweet oak, are perfectly proportioned in a firm presentation. The wine is great now, and will improve for at least five years. Just enjoy! Super value.

 Clos du Bois Briarcrest, 1984 Alexander Valley *$16.00*

Beautiful cherry fruit aromas, with herbal and sweet oak accents. Medium bodied. The wine is supple in the mouth, with generous ripe fruit and sweet oak flavors, and moderate tannins. Smooth, fruity finish. Will improve for a few years. Fine with rack of lamb or grilled quail with currant jelly.

 Clos du Bois Briarcrest, 1983 Alexander Valley *$14.00*

Medium-intense sweetish fruit in the nose, with floral, cedary, and herbal scents. Medium-full bodied. Ripe, plummy fruit flavors on the palate, which fall off a bit in the slightly harsh finish. Best with well-seasoned meat dishes.

 Clos du Bois Marlstone, 1984 Alexander Valley, 37% Merlot, 12% Cabernet Franc, 3% Malbec *$20.00*

Very attractive, medium-intense aromas of cherry fruit, herbs, and flowers, with spicy and smoky scents. Medium-full bodied. Rich and supple on the palate, with very pleasing flavors through the finish. This wine has finesse and elegance. It tastes great now, and will improve for at least five more years. Enjoy!

 Clos du Bois Marlstone, 1983 Alexander Valley *$18.00*

Pleasant aromas of spice, herbs, bell peppers, and berry fruit. Medium bodied. The wine is supple in the mouth, with moderately intense juicy fruit and soft tannins. Drinkable now and for the next few years. Try with duck breast or veal scallops.

Clos du Bois Proprietor's Reserve, 1982 Dry Creek Valley **$19.00**

Appealing cherry and currant aromas, with herbal tones, and a nice dimension of sweet oak in support. Medium-full bodied. Smooth on the palate, with the ripe cherry flavors in balance with oak and tannins. This is an enjoyable wine to drink now. Best with braised lamb, standing rib of beef, or stuffed breast of veal.

 Clos du Val, 1984 Napa Valley **$15.50**

Appealing curranty fruit aromas, with chocolaty and herbal scents, and nice creamy oak tones. Medium bodied. Medium-deep flavors of ripe fruit on the palate, with modest tannins. Enjoyable now, and will improve for a few years. Best with moderately seasoned meat dishes.

 Clos du Val Reserve, 1982 Napa Valley **$28.00**

Pleasant aromas of curranty fruit and herbs, with some chocolaty tones. Medium-full bodied. Smooth and silky on the palate, with the ripe fruit flavors in perfect balance with soft oak and tannins. Has elegance and finesse. Try with duck breast, rack of lamb, or roast beef au jus.

 B. R. Cohn, 1985 Sonoma Valley, Olive Hill Vineyard **$16.00**

Very attractive, intense black cherry and ripe currant aromas, with coffee and pepper scents, nicely framed in smoky oak. Full bodied. Deep concentration of spicy fruit on the palate, with ample oak and tannin, in a firm structure. This wine was selected as the favorite, against stiff competition, in a series of tastings conducted by a wine society to which I belong. It is clearly a winner. Will improve for at least five more years. Enjoy.

 B. R. Cohn, 1984 Sonoma Valley, Olive Hill Vineyard **$15.00**

Intense rich jammy fruit in the nose, with pronounced spicy and cedary tones. Full bodied. Rich cassis and blackberry flavors on the palate, with tarry nuances, in a good structure. This is a big Cabernet that is enjoyable now; however, I suggest waiting several years for further improvement. Try with beef Wellington, veal Orloff, or leg of lamb.

 Columbia Crest Vineyards, 1984 Columbia Valley, Washington **$7.50**

Very deep ruby color. Restrained black cherry and cassis in the nose, with sweet oak scents. Medium bodied. Moderate cherry flavors on the palate, with firm acidity. Clean finish. Best with moderately seasoned meat dishes.

Concannon Vineyard Reserve, 1985 Livermore Valley

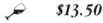 $13.50

Medium intense sweetish fruit and oaky aromas, with herbal and earthy tones. Medium bodied. Generous, very ripe fruit on the palate, with pronounced oaky and herbal elements, in a soft presentation. Fine with fowl or veal dishes.

Conn Creek Barrel Select, 1983 Napa Valley

$15.00

Appealing aromas of ripe currants and sweet oak. Medium-full bodied. Supple on entry, with the mature cherry fruit flavors nicely balanced with oak and mild tannins. Try with roast beef au jus.

Cosentino Cellars, 1985 North Coast

$10.50

Appealing spicy berry fruit in the nose, with minty scents, and oaky overtones. Medium bodied. Nice black currant fruit flavors on the palate, with ample oak and tannins. Somewhat bitter finish. Accessible now, and will improve for several years. Best with well-seasoned meat dishes.

Cuvaison, 1984 Napa Valley

$14.50

Very attractive ripe cherry aromas, with hints of chocolate, and a nice rich oak dimension. Medium-full bodied. The wine enters the mouth round and full, with generous curranty fruit, oak, and moderate tannins in perfect balance. Enjoy this excellent wine with roast beef au jus, grilled quail with currant jelly, or rack of lamb.

De Loach Vineyards, 1984 Sonoma County

$11.00

Attractive smells of ripe fruit, herbs, and rich oak. Medium-full bodied. Abundant rich flavors in the mouth, with a fair tannic dimension for aging. Enjoy this very fine wine as an accompaniment to duck breast with cherry-peppercorn sauce or rolled leg of lamb with rosemary.

De Moor Winery, 1983 Napa Valley

 $14.00

Intense black currants, spice, and piney oak in the nose. Medium-full bodied. Loads of ripe fruit flavors on the palate, a full dimension of spice and oak, and ample tannins. Somewhat harsh finish. Give this wine a few years to smooth out, then enjoy with well-seasoned meat dishes.

Dehlinger Winery, 1984 Russian River Valley

 $12.00

Medium-intense ripe fruit aromas, with earthy and spicy overtones. Medium bodied. Appealing curranty fruit on the palate, with herbal nuances and a fair tannic dimension. Finishes slightly astringent. Give this wine a couple of years to smooth out, then enjoy with well-seasoned meat dishes.

Dehlinger Winery, 1983 Russian River Valley

$11.00

Pleasant cherrylike fruit in the nose, with herbal and cedary tones. Medium-full bodied. Slightly rich herbal fruit flavors in the mouth, nicely balanced with vanillin oak, in a firm presentation. The wine will continue to improve for a number of years. Enjoy this fine wine with roast beef or leg of lamb.

Devlin Wine Cellars, 1984 Sonoma County

$8.00

Dark ruby color. Moderately intense varietal fruit, with scents of herbs, mints, and oak in support. Medium-full bodied. Deep fruit impression on the palate, with ample oak and tannin in balance. Finishes a bit rough. Fine with beef or lamb dishes. Good value.

Diamond Creek Vineyards, 1986 Napa Valley, Gravelly Meadow

$30.00

Intense aromas of ripe fruit and sweet oak. Medium-full bodied. Generous berry fruit on the palate, with chocolaty nuances, and abundant tannins. Astringent finish. This superior wine will improve for at least five more years. Try as an accompaniment to rolled leg of lamb with rosemary.

Diamond Creek Vineyards, 1985 Napa Valley, Gravelly Meadow

$30.00

Very attractive deep cassis aromas, with slightly floral and herbal overtones. Medium-full bodied. Rich berry fruit fills the mouth, with moderate tannins in a firm structure. This is an elegant wine that can be enjoyed now, but best wait for a few years for still further improvement. Then enjoy with roast quail, beef Wellington, rack of lamb, or roasted game.

Diamond Creek Vineyards, 1986 Napa Valley, Red Rock Terrace

 $30.00

Rich cherry fruit in the nose, with earthy nuances, and oaky overtones. Medium-full bodied. Loads of rich fruit on the palate, with earthy elements, and ample oak/tannin, in a good structure. Good aging potential. Try with savory dishes.

Diamond Creek Vineyards, 1985 Napa Valley, Red Rock Terrace

 $30.00

Rich, concentrated ripe curranty, chocolaty, and herbal aromas, with a definite oaky impression. Medium-full bodied. Big and full in the mouth, with deep currant and mint flavors, and considerable tannic. This superior wine will improve for a few years and hold for an additional ten years. Wait until 1992, then enjoy on that special occasion.

Diamond Creek Vineyards, 1986 Napa Valley, Volcanic Hill   **$30.00**

Another great bottling. Beautiful, rich cherry and cassis aromas, with ample creamy oak in support. Medium-full bodied. Loads of concentrated fruit flavors on the palate, with oak and tannins combined in perfect harmony. Long, fruity finish. A superior wine by any standard. Although accessible now, give it five more years to reach a more elegant level. Then enjoy.

 Diamond Creek Vineyards, 1985 Napa Valley, Volcanic Hill  **$30.00**

Dark ruby color. Intense, concentrated, rich blackberry and spice in the nose, with nice oak in support. Medium-full bodied. The wine enters the mouth supple and round, with the rich fruit, ample oak, and tannins in a firm structure. A superior wine that needs time. Try it in five years with that special meal.

 Domaine Laurier, 1985 Sonoma County— Green Valley   **$14.50**

Medium-intense ripe currant and rich oak in the nose. Medium-full bodied. Generous ripe fruit on the palate, with herbal nuances, and ample tannins. A bit rough in the finish. Best with well-seasoned meat dishes.

 Domaine Laurier, 1984 Sonoma County— Green Valley   **$13.00**

Pleasant raspberry fruit, floral, and herbal aromas, with a touch of sweet oak. Medium bodied. Moderate cherry and raspberry flavors in the mouth, with light tannins and oak. A fine wine for early consumption and for the next few years. Best with moderately seasoned meat dishes.

 Domaine Michel, 1984 Sonoma County   **$19.50**

Intense aromas of cassislike fruit, spice, herbs, and a hint of eucalyptus. Medium-full bodied. Generous ripe fruit on the palate, with a nice dimension of sweet oak, and abundant tannins. Needs time to smooth out. Wait until 1992, then enjoy with well-seasoned beef or lamb dishes.

 Dominus Estate, Red Table Wine, 1984 Napa Valley   **$40.00**

Attractive aromas of ripe currants, flowers, and spice, with a full dimension of oak throughout. Medium-full bodied. Loads of ripe cherry/currant fruit on the palate, with briary nuances, and a full measure of oak and tannin. Hard finish. This wine will need at least five years to reach an elegant level. Patience will be rewarded. Start enjoying in 1994.

☆☆

Dry Creek Vineyard, 1985 Sonoma County

$11.00

Medium-intense ripe currant, herbal, and floral aromas, with a touch of oak. Medium bodied. Round on entry, with the generous young fruit nicely balanced with moderate oak and light tannins. Pleasant fruity finish. Enjoy with moderately seasoned meat dishes.

☆☆

Dry Creek Vineyard, 1984 Sonoma County

$10.00

Pleasant berry fruit aromas, with herbal tones. Medium bodied. Moderate herbal fruit flavors on the palate, with oak and olive dimensions. Slightly lingering aftertaste. Enjoy with moderately seasoned red meats.

☆☆☆

Duckhorn Vineyards, 1985 Napa Valley

$17.50

Rich Cabernet fruit in the nose, with herbal and oaky tones. Full bodied. Deeply extracted fruit in the mouth, with earthy nuances, and loads of tannin and sweet oak. This is a big wine of superior quality. Wait until 1994, then start enjoying with savory foods.

☆☆☆

Duckhorn Vineyards, 1984 Napa Valley

$17.00

Forward aromas of black cherries and ripe currants, with cedary scents. Medium-full bodied. Loads of solid fruit on the palate, with ample oak and tannin, in a firm structure. Hold this one for five years, then enjoy.

☆☆☆☆

Dunn Vineyards, 1984 Howell Mountain, Napa Valley

$25.00

Still another great one. Intense curranty and spicy fruit aromas, with a nice dimension of vanillin oak. Medium-full bodied. Loads of curranty fruit flavors in the mouth, with oak and tannin balanced in a tight structure. This wine will improve for at least another ten years. Wait until 1992, then serve on that special occasion with well-seasoned foods.

☆☆☆☆

Dunn Vineyards, 1983 Howell Mountain, Napa Valley

$25.00

The winning streak continues! Dark ruby color. Very intense and attractive rich currantlike fruit in the nose, with spicy oak in support. Medium-full bodied. The fruit is rich and abundant on the palate, with a fair degree of tannin for aging. This is a big wine that needs several years to smooth out, and can be enjoyed for many years thereafter. Wait until 1992, then serve on that special occasion with well-seasoned foods.

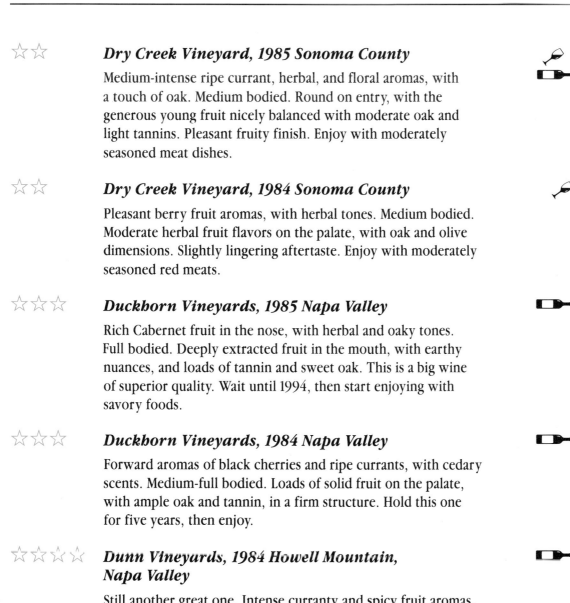

Dunn Vineyards, 1985 Napa Valley
 *$20.00*

Intense, complex aromas of ripe black cherries, cassis, and currants, with cedary and briary tones. Medium-full bodied. Full and fleshy in the mouth, with the nicely focused curranty fruit joined by ample oak, acid, and tannins. This is a substantial wine that will require ten more years of cellaring for optimum enjoyment. Continues the string of superior bottlings from this winery.

Dunn Vineyards, 1984 Napa Valley
 *$16.00*

Another winner here! Beautiful aromas of ripe plums, currants, and orange rind, and a hint of violets, nicely framed in sweet oak. Medium-full bodied. The rich fruit, oak, and tannin come together in perfect harmony. This is a special-occasion wine that can be enjoyed for years to come.

Durney Vineyards, 1983 Carmel Valley
 *$11.00*

Forward ripe curranty fruit in the nose, with smoky and oaky scents. Medium-full bodied. Generous rich fruit flavors on the palate, with ample tannins for structure. Enjoyable now, and will improve for a few years. Try as an accompaniment to filet mignon with herbs.

Estancia, 1985 Alexander Valley
 $6.50

Forward spicy oak and rich cassis aromas, with herbal and green pepper tones. Medium-full bodied. Generous herbal fruit flavors on the palate, with dimensions. Slightly rough in the finish. Best with well-seasoned meat dishes. Good value.

Estancia, 1984 Alexander Valley
$6.50

Appealing, medium-intense aromas of cherries, herbs, sweet oak, and spice. Medium bodied. Soft and round in the mouth, with moderate fruit flavors, rich oak, and mild tannins, in a pleasing presentation. Excellent for early consumption with moderately seasoned meat dishes. Good value.

Far Niente Winery, 1985 Napa Valley
 $25.00

Moderately intense cherry fruit in the nose, with briary and herbal tones, laced in an oaky framework. Medium-full bodied. Fairly dense, with the concentrated fruit flavors in balance with oak and tannins. Slightly harsh finish. Will improve for at least five more years. Best with highly seasoned beef or lamb dishes.

Fenestra Winery, 1984 Monterey County, Smith and Hook Vineyard $11.00

Powerful, deep aromas of very ripe fruit, spice, and rich oak. Full bodied. Very intense ripe fruit flavors on the palate, with briary nuances, considerable oak, and ample tannins. This is a very big wine. Enjoy now and for years to come with highly spiced meat dishes. Good value.

Fetzer Barrel Select, 1985 Mendocino County $9.00

Attractive cherry fruit, spicy, smoky, and cedary aromas, with piney and herbal tones. Medium bodied. The cherry fruit is firm on the palate, with earthy and herbal nuances, and ample tannins. Finishes slightly harsh. Good aging potential. Best with beef or lamb dishes. Good value.

Fetzer Barrel Select, 1984 Mendocino County $9.00

Attractive aromas of plummy cherry fruit, herbs, spice, and oak. Medium bodied. Generous herbal fruit on the palate, with a touch of oak, in a firm structure. This is an enjoyable, well-made wine that goes well with moderately seasoned meats.

Fetzer Vineyards, 1985 Lake County $6.50

Moderately intense herbal fruit aromas, with a touch of oak. Medium bodied. The medium-intense fruit, oak, and tannin come together in a clean presentation. An easy-drinking wine that will go well with fowl or light meats.

Fetzer Vineyards, 1984 Lake County $6.50

Dark ruby color. Moderate cherrylike aromas, with herbal tones. Medium bodied. The wine enters the mouth smooth and clean, with medium-intense fruit flavors nicely balanced with oak and tannins. Enjoy with poultry or light meats.

The Firestone Vineyard, 1984 Santa Ynez Valley $9.50

Medium-intense cherry fruit aromas, with curranty and herbal scents. Medium bodied. Supple in the mouth, with the juicy berry fruit on the palate throughout, in a good structure. Pleasing, long aftertaste. Best with moderately seasoned meat dishes.

The Firestone Vineyard, 1983 Santa Ynez Valley $9.00

Medium-intense cherry fruit aromas, with strong scents of plums, chocolate, and oak. Medium-full bodied. The wine enters the mouth smooth and round, with the black currant flavors, oak, and tannin in nice balance. Will improve for a number of years. Try with duck breast, rack of lamb, or medallions of veal.

Fisher Coach Insignia, 1985 Sonoma County $18.00

Forward, slightly plummy berry fruit in the nose, with spicy and cedary tones. Medium-full bodied. Loads of rich fruit on the palate, nicely balanced with oak and tannins, in a firm structure. Astringent finish. A great wine for aging. Patience will be your reward. Wait until 1994, then enjoy.

Fisher Coach Insignia, 1984 Sonoma County $16.00

Medium-intense ripe cherry fruit aromas, with sweet oak overtones. Medium bodied. The wine is soft and supple on the palate, with the young fruit, spicy oak, and tannins in nice balance. A fine wine for enjoyment over the next few years. Best with moderately seasoned meat dishes.

Flora Springs, 1984 Napa Valley $14.50

Appealing oaky aromas, joined by cassis and minty tones, with a smoky element in the background. Medium-full bodied. Generous fruit on the palate, with ample oak and tannin. Slightly astringent finish. Try with braised lamb, beef roast, or saddle of veal.

Louis J. Foppiano Winery, 1984 Russian River Valley $8.50

Medium-intense ripe cherry fruit aromas. Medium-full bodied. Moderate fruit flavors in the mouth, with oak and tannins in balance. Finishes slightly coarse. Can be enjoyed with a wide range of moderately seasoned meat dishes.

Forman Vineyards, 1985 Napa Valley $17.00

Another great one here. Intense, properly focused aromas of very ripe fruit, spice, and oak. Medium-full bodied. The fruit flavors are deep and concentrated on the palate, with ample vanillin oak, and moderate tannins for structure. This superior wine will improve for many years. Patience will reward you. Wait until 1992, then start to enjoy.

Forman Vineyards, 1984 Napa Valley $17.00

Very appealing curranty aromas, with olive and mint scents, and a full dimension of toasty oak. Medium-full bodied. The wine is smooth on entry, with the deep fruit, ample oak, and tannin harmonized in a firm structure. This superior wine will develop for at least ten years. Should be accessible beginning about 1991.

Fox Mountain Reserve, 1984 Russian River Valley $18.00

Produced by Foppiano Vineyards. Loads of ripe berry fruit and
sweet oak in the nose, with scents of herbs and tea. Medium-full
bodied. Supple on entry, with the ripe curranty fruit, creamy
oak, and spicy flavors nicely balanced with soft tannins.
Fruity finish. Will develop for at least five more years.
A superior wine. Just enjoy.

Franciscan Vineyards, 1984 Napa Valley, Oakville Estate $9.50

Dark ruby color. Attractive, medium-intense blackberry, tarry,
and herbal aromas. Medium-full bodied. Generous ripe fruit in
the mouth, with nice toasty oak, in a smooth presentation.
Enjoy this very fine wine with roast pork, medallions of veal,
or roast rabbit. Good value.

Freemark Abbey Winery, 1984 Napa Valley $12.00

Very appealing ripe berrylike fruit in the nose, with cedary and
chocolaty scents. Medium bodied. Softly textured, with the
rounded fruit and sweet oak balanced with mild tannins, in a
smooth presentation. Try as an accompaniment to duck breast
with an olive sauce.

Freemark Abbey Winery, 1984 Napa Valley, Bosche Vineyard $20.00

Moderately intense aromas of ripe cherries, spice, and herbs,
with earthy scents, and nice oak in support. Medium full bodied.
Supple on entry, with rich, ripe currant flavors in a nice combination with oak and tannin. Lingering aftertaste. Very enjoyable
now, and will improve for several years. Try as an accompaniment to rack of lamb with Cabernet sauce.

Freemark Abbey Winery, 1983 Napa Valley, Bosche Vineyard $18.00

Medium ruby color. Moderately intense curranty fruit in the
nose, with floral, herbal, and oaky scents. Medium bodied.
Firm in the mouth, with the currant-cherry flavors in nice
balance with oak and moderate tannin. The wine will improve
for several years. Enjoy with beef or lamb dishes.

Frog's Leap, 1985 Napa Valley $10.50

Medium-intense aromas of ripe cherries, with peachy scents, and
oaky overtones. Medium-full bodied. Deep and intense fleshy
fruit in the mouth, with the cherry and oak flavors in nice
balance, and sufficient tannin for aging. Slightly astringent
finish. Give this wine two or three years to smooth out, then
enjoy with well-seasoned meat dishes.

Ernest & Julio Gallo Limited Release, 1981 Northern Sonoma

$8.00

Appealing ripe fruit in the nose, with minty and herbal tones. Medium-full bodied. Attractive cherry and spicy flavors on the palate. A tasty wine for current consumption and for the next few years. Try with roast beef au jus or rack of lamb. Fine value.

Geyser Peak, 1984 Alexander Valley

$7.50

Produced by Trione Vineyards. Moderately intense aromas of plummy fruit, with oaky and earthy scents. Medium bodied. Soft on the palate, with ripe herbal fruit flavors dominating in a soft structure. Fine for early consumption with fowl or veal dishes.

Geyser Peak Reserve Alexandre, 1984 Alexander Valley

$18.75

Appealing, moderately intense cherrylike and sweet toasty oak aromas with herbal overtones. Medium bodied. Smooth in the mouth, with generous cherry fruit, and a nice dimension of vanillin oak, in a good structure. A touch of astringency in the finish. Will improve for at least five more years. Try as an accompaniment to duck breast with an olive sauce.

Girard Winery, 1985 Napa Valley

$14.00

Medium-intense aromas of cherries, green olives, and spice. Medium bodied. Moderate cherryish flavors on the palate, with toasty oak, in a firm presentation. Slightly astringent finish. Enjoyable now, and will improve for several years. Best with moderately seasoned meat dishes.

Girard Winery, 1984 Napa Valley

$12.50

Rich, plummy berry fruit aromas, with herbal and earthy scents, laced in oak. Medium bodied. The wine is smooth and supple in the mouth, with deep cherry flavors, oak, and tannin balanced in a firm structure. Accessible now, and will improve for a number of years. Enjoy with well-seasoned foods.

Girard Winery Reserve, 1984 Napa Valley

$25.00

Lots of rich black cherry and currant fruit in the nose, joined by an abundance of creamy oak. Medium-full bodied. Very deep fruit impression on the palate, with ample tannin for aging. With proper storage, this superior wine will improve for at least ten more years. Wait, then enjoy.

Glen Ellen Proprietor's Reserve, 1986 California

$4.00

Nice fresh grape aromas. Medium-light bodied. Refreshing on the palate, with nice cherry fruit flavors, and a black pepper element, in a smooth and clean presentation. Try with moderately seasoned meat dishes. Good value.

Glen Ellen Proprietor's Reserve, 1985 Sonoma County

$5.00

Pleasant, low-intensity cherry and spicy aromas. Medium bodied. Soft and supple in the mouth, with the ripe grapy flavors and moderate tannins in nice balance. Fruity finish. Enjoy with moderately seasoned meats. Good value.

Glen Ellen Winery, 1984 Sonoma Valley, Glen Ellen Estate

$12.00

Pronounced aromas of peppermint and eucalyptus, with herbal and cedary overtones. Medium-full bodied. Lush fruit impression on the palate, with a long minty/cedary dimension, and ample tannin. Astringent finish. This is a well-made wine that will soften in a couple of years. Enjoy with savory meat dishes.

Glen Ellen Winery, 1983 Sonoma Valley, Glen Ellen Estate

$12.00

Pleasant black currant and cherry aromas, with hints of sweet oak and mint. Medium-full bodied. Moderately intense currant fruit flavors in the mouth, with some oak, and a fair tannic dimension for aging. Enjoy with savory meat dishes.

Grace Family Vineyards, 1985 Napa Valley

$50.00

Beautiful aromas of black currants, spice, and sweet oak. Medium-full bodied. Loads of plum, butter, chocolate, and oak flavors fill the mouth, with sufficient tannin for good structure. A big and elegant wine. Very enjoyable now, but better to wait until 1993 or so for further improvement.

Gran Val, 1985 Napa Valley

$8.50

Produced by Clos du Val Wine Company. Pleasant, medium-intense berry fruit in the nose, with herbal and olive scents. Medium bodied. Moderate cherry flavors on the palate, with oak and tannin in balance, in a good structure. Best with moderately seasoned meat dishes.

Gran Val, 1984 Napa Valley

$8.50

Made by Clos du Val. Medium-intense black cherry fruit in the nose, with herbal scents, and oak in support. Medium-full bodied. Supple in the mouth, with the cherry fruit and oak nicely balanced with moderate tannins. A fine wine for near-term drinking, and will improve for a few years. Fine with beef or lamb dishes.

Grand Cru Vineyards, 1984 Sonoma County **$9.00**

Appealing, medium-intense cherrylike fruit in the nose, with earthy scents. Medium bodied. Soft, fleshy, moderate fruit flavors on the palate, with mild tannins, in a clean presentation. This is a fine wine for early consumption and for a number of years to come. Enjoy with fowl, veal, or light meats.

 ### Grgich Hills Cellar, 1983 Napa Valley **$17.00**

Moderately intense aromas of ripe cherries, with briary scents. Medium-full bodied. Generous ripe fruit flavors on the palate, with a full dimension of tannins. Astringent finish. Give this wine several years to smooth out, then enjoy with well-seasoned meat dishes.

 ### Groth Vineyards, 1985 Napa Valley **$16.00**

Forward ripe curranty fruit aromas, with nice scents of herbs, tea, and tobacco, and handsome oak in support. Medium-full bodied. Generous mouth-filling fruit on the palate, with herbal nuances, and ample tannins, in a firm structure. This is an elegant wine that is enjoyable now, and will improve for a number of years. Try with filet mignon, rack of lamb with Cabernet sauce, or duck breast with a cherry-peppercorn sauce.

 ### Groth Vineyards, 1984 Napa Valley **$15.00**

Attractive, very rich curranty fruit in the nose, with earthy, briary, and olivey scents. Medium-full bodied. Lush and supple on entry, with the rich, plummy fruit flavors and herbal nuances, in balance with soft tannins. This excellent wine will improve for at least another five years. Enjoy with beef, lamb, a cheese board, or chocolate dishes and truffles.

 ### Guenoc Winery, 1984 Lake County **$9.00**

Nicely focused varietal fruit in the nose, joined by toasty oak. Medium bodied. Supple and expansive in the mouth, with the ripe fruit and oak in nice balance with moderate tannins. Enjoy in the next few years with beef or lamb dishes.

 ### Guenoc Winery, 1983 Lake County **$8.00**

Medium-intense herbal aromas, joined by cherry and oaky scents. Medium bodied. Soft and round in the mouth, with the moderate sweet cherry fruit, herb, and oak flavors in balance. A nice wine for current consumption with moderately seasoned meat dishes. Good value.

☆☆ ½

Gundlach-Bundschu Winery, 1984 Sonoma Valley, Rhinefarm Vineyards

$12.00

Complex aromas of ripe fruit, spice, and herbs, in an elegant combination. Medium-full bodied. Supple in the mouth, with the rich cassislike fruit and chocolaty elements in nice balance with oak and tannins. The wine is accessible now, and will improve for several years. Best with savory dishes.

☆☆

Hacienda Wine Cellars, 1983 Sonoma Valley

$11.00

Moderately intense aromas of curranty fruit, flowers, spice, and oak. Medium bodied. Medium-intense fruit on the palate, with soft tannins. Pleasant, lingering finish. Fine with moderately seasoned meat dishes.

☆☆ ½

Hagafen Cellars, 1984 Napa Valley

$13.50

Dark ruby color. Attractive, forward currantlike fruit aromas, with spicy and cedary overtones. Medium bodied. The wine enters the mouth rich and supple, with the varietally correct fruit flavors nicely balanced with soft tannins. Fine with braised lamb or roast beef.

☆☆ ½

Hanna Winery, 1985 Sonoma County

$14.50

Appealing aromas of ripe blackberries and oak, fully supported by earthy and peppery tones. Medium-full bodied. Rich concentration of ripe fruit on the palate, with spicy elements, and ample tannins in balance. Lingering aftertaste. Try this very fine wine as an accompaniment to rolled leg of lamb with rosemary or roast beef au jus.

☆

Hawk Crest, 1986 North Coast

$7.50

Made by Stag's Leap Wine Cellars. Appealing young Cabernet Sauvignon aromas, with herbal and oaky tones. Medium bodied. Moderately fruity in the mouth, in a good structure. A very pleasant wine for early consumption with mildly flavored beef or lamb dishes.

☆☆

Haywood Winery, 1984 Sonoma Valley

$14.00

Dark ruby color. Forward oaky aromas, joined by fruity, spicy, and herbal tones. Full bodied. Loads of rich fruit and heavy tannins fill the mouth. Astringent finish. Needs time to smooth out. Wait until 1994, then enjoy with savory dishes.

☆☆ ½

Haywood Winery, 1984 Sonoma Valley, Steiner Vineyard

$9.00

Attractive ripe blackberry aromas, with cedary overtones. Medium bodied. Rich berry fruit on the palate, with a nice dimension of oak, in a firm structure. Pleasant, lingering aftertaste. Enjoy with beef or lamb dishes. Good value.

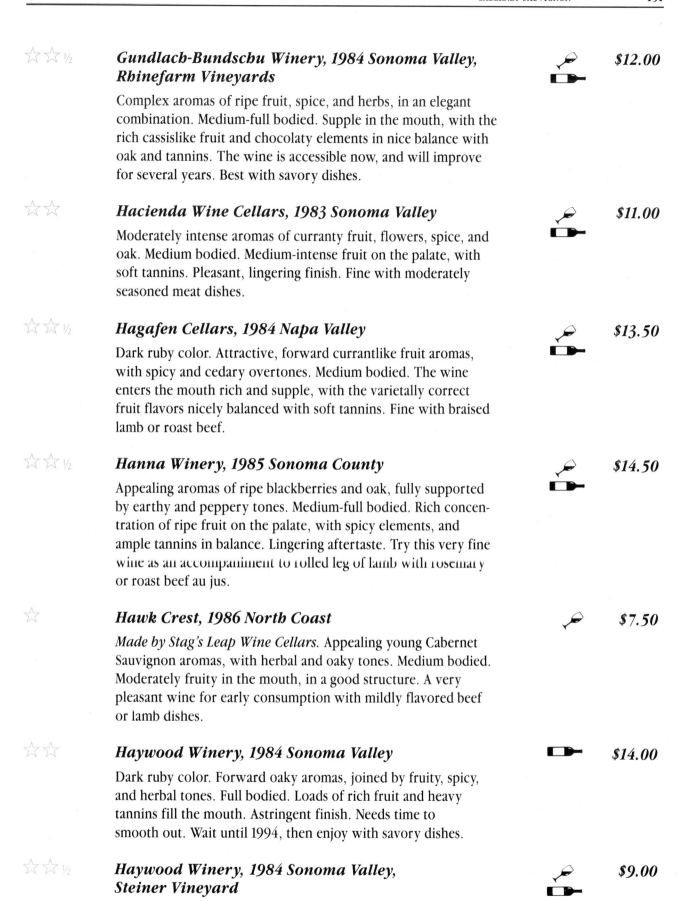

Heitz Cellar, 1983 Napa Valley

$13.00

Pleasant cherry and oaky aromas, with spicy and herbal nuances. Medium bodied. Moderate cherry fruit flavors on the palate, with cedary and herbal nuances, in a good structure. Slightly harsh finish. Best with well-seasoned meat dishes.

Heitz Cellar, 1982 Napa Valley

 $13.25

Medium intense berry fruit aromas, with mushroomy and spicy overtones. Medium-full bodied. Ripe fruit flavors in the mouth and an ample dimension of tannins. Finishes tart. The wine is accessible now, and will improve for a number of years. Enjoy with beef or lamb dishes.

Heitz Cellar, 1983 Napa Valley, Bella Oaks Vineyard

$20.00

Appealing, medium-intense berry fruit in the nose, with floral, spicy, earthy, and oaky scents. Medium-full bodied. Nice herbal fruit on the palate, with oak and tannin in balance. Slightly tart finish. This excellent wine is accessible now, and will improve for a number of years. Trying to project improvement is only a guess! The 1977 vintage is drinking wonderfully right now, and is available at the winery.

Heitz Cellar, 1982 Napa Valley, Bella Oaks Vineyard

 $21.00

Medium ruby color. Forward floral and spicy aromas, with oaky overtones. Medium-full bodied. Moderately rich cherry fruit on the palate, with oak and tannin balanced in a firm structure. Tart finish. Will improve with bottle aging. Enjoy with rack of lamb or beef roast.

Heitz Cellar, 1983 Napa Valley, Martha's Vineyard

$37.50

Attractive, medium-intense aromas of ripe curranty fruit, herbs, spice, and mint. Medium-full bodied. The generous ripe fruit flavors are nicely balanced with oaky and herbal elements, and soft tannins. A wonderful wine for current consumption, and will improve for at least another five years. Try as an accompaniment to rolled leg of lamb with rosemary, veal Orloff, or roast quail.

Heitz Cellar, 1982 Napa Valley, Martha's Vineyard

 $35.00

Very attractive floral and spicy aromas, with minty and cedary scents. Medium-full bodied. Abundant fleshy fruit on the palate, with a hard core and a substantial tannic dimension for aging. Slightly bitter finish. Although accessible now, best to wait a couple of years for further improvement. Then enjoy!

Hess Collection, 1985 Napa Valley **$13.50**

Attractive aromas of black currants, spice, and sweet oak, with herbal, minty, and tealike tones. Medium-full bodied. Lots of ripe Cabernet fruit on the palate, joined by abundant sweet oak and sufficient tanning for aging. A superior wine that will improve for at least five more years. Enjoy.

 ### *Hess Collection Reserve, 1983 Napa Valley* 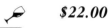 **$22.50**

Very attractive, forward ripe curranty fruit and sweet oak in the nose, with spicy overtones. Medium-full bodied. Loads of concentrated cherry fruit and oak flavors on the palate, with anise nuances, and a full measure of acid and tannins, in a firm structure. This is a wine of the future. Give it five more years, then enjoy.

 ### *William Hill Reserve, 1985 Napa Valley* **$22.00**

Intense black currant and cranberry aromas, with spicy and tarry scents, and toasty oak in support. Medium-full bodied. Young, concentrated ripe cherry and strawberry flavors, in nice balance with oak and tannins, in a tight structure. Astringent finish. An elegant wine that needs time to develop further; however, it can be enjoyed in its youth with savory dishes.

 ### *William Hill Reserve, 1984 Napa Valley* **$18.00**

Powerful aromas of ripe curranty fruit, with minty tones. Medium-full bodied. Loads of ripe blackberry and cassis flavors on the palate, with ample toasty oak and tannins, in a firm structure. This is a wonderful young wine that needs time to reach a level of elegance. Wait five years, then enjoy.

 ### *William Hill Silver Label, 1985 Napa Valley* **$12.00**

Very attractive cherry fruit in the nose, with floral and oaky tones. Medium-full bodied. Loads of ripe cherry and cassis flavors on the palate, with ample oak and tannins, in perfect balance. Flushes with an intense flourish. Accessible now, and will improve for years. Just enjoy. Good value.

Hop Kiln Winery, 1984 Alexander Valley, Stickrod Vineyards **$10.00**

Appealing, medium-intense aromas of blackberry fruit, with earthy scents, and a nice oak dimension. Medium bodied. The wine enters the mouth soft and round, with sweet fruit and oak in an attractive balance. This is an enjoyable wine now and for the next few years. Try with moderately seasoned dishes. Good value.

Hop Kiln Winery, 1985 Dry Creek Valley $10.00

Appealing cherrylike fruit in the nose, with spicy and oaky overtones. Medium bodied. Supple on entry, with rich berry fruit and ample oak nicely balanced with tannins, in a good structure. Slightly astringent finish. Try with rack of lamb in a Cabernet sauce. Good value.

Inglenook Reserve Cask, 1982 Napa Valley $18.50

Moderately intense ripe curranty fruit in the nose, nicely supported with minty, spicy, floral, and oaky scents. Medium-full bodied. Generous, rich, concentrated fruit on the palate, with oak and tannins in perfect balance. This is an excellent wine for early consumption, and will improve for a few years. Enjoy with roast beef au jus or rolled leg of lamb with rosemary.

Inglenook Reunion Reserve Cask, 1984 Napa Valley $34.00

Appealing ripe berry fruit in the nose, with briary and cedary tones. Full bodied. An abundance of cherry fruit on the palate, with the vanillin, briar, and orange rind elements in attractive balance, in a firm structure. Astringent finish. Needs time. Try, beginning in 1992, with roast beef au jus, rolled leg of lamb with rosemary, or veal Oscar.

Inglenook Reunion Reserve Cask, 1983 Napa Valley $30.00

Intense ripe berry fruit aromas, with spicy and herbal tones. Medium-full bodied. Rich fruit in the mouth, with tobacco and cedar nuances, and a full dimension of tannin. Slightly harsh finish. Great potential. Wait a few years to smooth out, then enjoy.

Inglenook Vineyards, 1983 Napa Valley $9.50

Attractive, medium-intense aromas of curranty fruit, spice, cedar, and mint. Medium bodied. Moderate fruit flavors on the palate, nicely balanced with mild tannins and acid. An excellent wine for early consumption and for the next five years. Can be enjoyed with a wide range of moderately seasoned meat dishes. Good value.

Innisfree, 1985 Napa Valley $9.50

Very ripe varietal fruit in the nose, with scents of tobacco and mushrooms, framed in rich oak. Medium-full bodied. Generous curranty fruit on the palate, with ample oak and tannins. Slightly tannic finish. Will improve for at least five more years. Best with well-seasoned meat dishes. Good value.

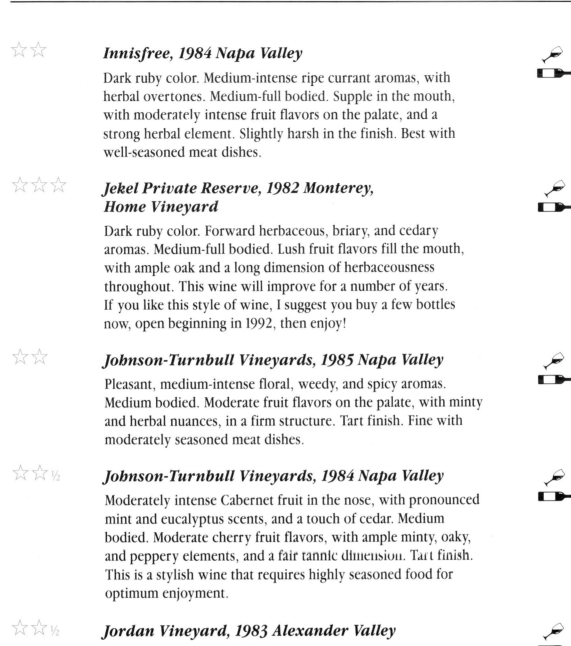

Innisfree, 1984 Napa Valley
☆☆ $9.00

Dark ruby color. Medium-intense ripe currant aromas, with herbal overtones. Medium-full bodied. Supple in the mouth, with moderately intense fruit flavors on the palate, and a strong herbal element. Slightly harsh in the finish. Best with well-seasoned meat dishes.

Jekel Private Reserve, 1982 Monterey, Home Vineyard
☆☆☆ $18.00

Dark ruby color. Forward herbaceous, briary, and cedary aromas. Medium-full bodied. Lush fruit flavors fill the mouth, with ample oak and a long dimension of herbaceousness throughout. This wine will improve for a number of years. If you like this style of wine, I suggest you buy a few bottles now, open beginning in 1992, then enjoy!

Johnson-Turnbull Vineyards, 1985 Napa Valley
☆☆ $14.50

Pleasant, medium-intense floral, weedy, and spicy aromas. Medium bodied. Moderate fruit flavors on the palate, with minty and herbal nuances, in a firm structure. Tart finish. Fine with moderately seasoned meat dishes.

Johnson-Turnbull Vineyards, 1984 Napa Valley
☆☆ ½ $14.50

Moderately intense Cabernet fruit in the nose, with pronounced mint and eucalyptus scents, and a touch of cedar. Medium bodied. Moderate cherry fruit flavors, with ample minty, oaky, and peppery elements, and a fair tannic dimension. Tart finish. This is a stylish wine that requires highly seasoned food for optimum enjoyment.

Jordan Vineyard, 1983 Alexander Valley
☆☆ ½ $18.00

Attractive aromas of herbs, cassis, and oak, with some earthy overtones. Medium-full bodied. Medium intense supple fruit in the mouth, with herbal nuances, and a tannic dimension through the finish. The wine is accessible now, and will improve for a number of years. Fine with leg of lamb or saddle of veal.

Robert Keenan Winery, 1984 Napa Valley
☆☆☆ $13.50

Attractive aromas of ripe currants and sweet oak, with herbal scents. Medium-full bodied. Rich and expansive cherry fruit flavors on the palate, with moderate oak and tannins, in a firm structure. Finishes slightly hot. Good aging potential. Best with highly seasoned foods.

Kendall-Jackson Cardinale, 1984 California

$12.00

Moderately intense aromas of cherry fruit, herbs, green olives, and spice. Medium-full bodied. Supple and round at entry, with the rich herbal fruit and oak in nice balance with mild tannins. A versatile and flavorful wine that may be enjoyed with most lamb, veal, or beef dishes.

Kendall-Jackson Vineyards, 1984 Lake County

$7.50

Forward oaky aromas, joined by ripe fruit and dusty tones. Medium bodied. Moderate fruit on the palate, with a tight center core. Slightly tart finish. Fine for early consumption and for the next couple of years. Try with veal or light meats. Good value.

Kathryn Kennedy Winery, 1985 Santa Cruz Mountains

$25.00

Forward smoky oak and black cherry aromas, with minty and herbal tones. Medium-full bodied. Deep cherry fruit impression on the palate, with a nice touch of oak, and ample tannins, in a firm structure. Accessible now, but better to wait until, say, 1995 for optimum enjoyment.

Kathryn Kennedy Winery, 1984 Santa Cruz Mountains

$18.00

Forward ripe berry aromas, with chocolaty, herbal, and spicy scents, and toasty oak in support. Medium bodied. Ripe, mouth-filling fruit on the palate, with an ample herbal/earthy dimension. Best with savory dishes.

Kathryn Kennedy Winery, 1983 Santa Cruz Mountains

$18.00

Dark ruby color. Rich black cherry aromas, with herbal and spicy scents, laced in substantial oak. Medium-full bodied. Loads of ripe, jammy fruit flavors in the mouth, with smoky nuances, and long tannic dimension. Finishes slightly rough. Best with highly spiced meat dishes.

Kenwood Artist Series, 1984 Sonoma Valley

$30.00

Very attractive aromas of currants, spice, herbs, chocolate, and toasty oak. Medium-full bodied. Loads of young Cabernet fruit fills the mouth, and is challenged by substantial tannins. Harsh finish. This is a great wine that needs time. Be patient and enjoy beginning in 1992 and for years thereafter.

Kenwood Vineyards, 1984 Sonoma Valley $12.00

Very attractive, medium-intense ripe currant fruit and rich oak in the nose, with floral and herbal tones. Medium-full bodied. The curranty fruit is deep and broad on the palate, with ample oak, and a fair tannic dimension, in a good structure. This superior wine is enjoyable now, and will improve for at lease five more years. Good value.

Kenwood Vineyards, 1985 Sonoma Valley, Jack London Vineyard $18.00

Attractive curranty fruit and oak in the nose, supported by vanilla, coffee, and spicy tones. Medium-full bodied. Generous fruit and oak on the palate, with abundant tannins. This is a tough, young wine, with good aging potential. Wait until 1995, then enjoy.

Kenwood Vineyards, 1984 Sonoma Valley, Jack London Vineyard $16.00

Intense aromas of spicy oak, curranty fruit, and herbs. Medium-full bodied. Deep fruit impression on the palate, with chocolate nuances, rich oak, and a fair tannic dimension for aging. Tart finish. Accessible now, due to rich fruit flavors; however, better to wait a few years for the wine to reach an elegant level, then enjoy.

Kenwood Vineyards, 1983 Sonoma Valley, Jack London Vineyard $15.00

Appealing black currant, blackberry, and herbal aromas, with chocolaty and oaky overtones. Medium-full bodied. Deep fruit impression on the palate, with herbal nuances, and young aggressive tannins throughout. Slightly bitter finish. Give the wine a couple of years to smooth out, then enjoy with highly seasoned foods.

Kistler Vineyards, 1985 California, Kistler Vineyard $16.50

Forward, appealing cassislike fruit in the nose, supported by nice oak. Medium-full bodied. Deep fruit impression on the palate, with the generous cassis and oak flavors in balance, and a lengthy tannin dimension for aging. This is a firmly structured wine that needs time for further development. Wait five years, then enjoy.

Kistler Vineyards, 1985 Sonoma Valley $13.50

Forward curranty fruit aromas, with a fair dimension of oak in support. Medium bodied. Deep fruit impression on the palate, with ample oak, and considerable tannins. Astringent finish. Good aging potential. Give this wine five years, then enjoy with well-seasoned beef or lamb dishes.

Charles Krug Winery, 1982 Napa Valley

 $7.00

Dark ruby color. Medium-intense cassis aromas. Medium bodied. The wine enters the mouth round and smooth, with the moderate grape flavors nicely balanced with soft tannins. Fine with most veal, poultry, or light meat dishes. Excellent value.

 ### La Jota Vineyard, 1984 Howell Mountain, Napa Valley

$15.00

Nice cherry fruit in the nose, with scents of olives, spice, and oak. Medium-full bodied. The wine enters the mouth round and full, with attractive spicy fruit and oak flavors, and considerable tannin. Astringent finish. Give this wine at least five years to smooth out, then enjoy with highly spiced meat dishes.

 ### Lakespring Reserve Selection, 1984 Napa Valley

$15.00

Very attractive ripe currant fruit in the nose, joined by earthy, spicy, chocolaty, and olivey scents, and nice sweet oak in support. Loads of flavors follow consistently from the aromas with ample tannins for good structure. Exceptionally fine tasting now, and will improve for a number of years. Just enjoy. Good value.

 ### Lakespring Winery, 1985 Napa Valley

$12.00

Forward herbal and brassy aromas, joined by nice dimension of attractive fruit. Medium-full bodied. Loads of juicy fruit on the palate, with earthy nuances, and ample rich oak. Enjoyable now and for several more years. Try with savory foods.

 ### Lambert Bridge, 1984 Sonoma County

$10.00

Dark ruby color. Attractive ripe fruit aromas, with herbal and minty scents, fully supported by sweet oak. Medium-full bodied. The wine enters the mouth supple, with generous fruit flavors and a full measure of oak throughout. I particularly like this wine, and have enjoyed it with meals on several occasions. Best with well-seasoned meat dishes. Excellent value.

Las Montanas Natural, 1984 Sonoma County

$12.00

Dark ruby color. Rich, ripe, fruity aromas, with spicy scents. Full bodied. Lush sweet fruit on the palate, with moderate tannins. Best with meats in rich sauces.

 ### Laurel Glen Vineyard, 1985 Sonoma Mountain

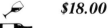 **$18.00**

Very attractive aromas of ripe cherries, with scents of cocoa and herbs, fully supported by sweet oak. Medium-full bodied. Wonderful flavors of cherries, currants, chocolate, and spice on the palate, with oak and tannin in perfect balance. I have tasted this wine a number of times, from the summer of 1987 through late fall of 1988. It has come around beautifully. Just enjoy!

☆☆☆ **_Laurel Glen Vineyard, 1984 Sonoma Mountain_** 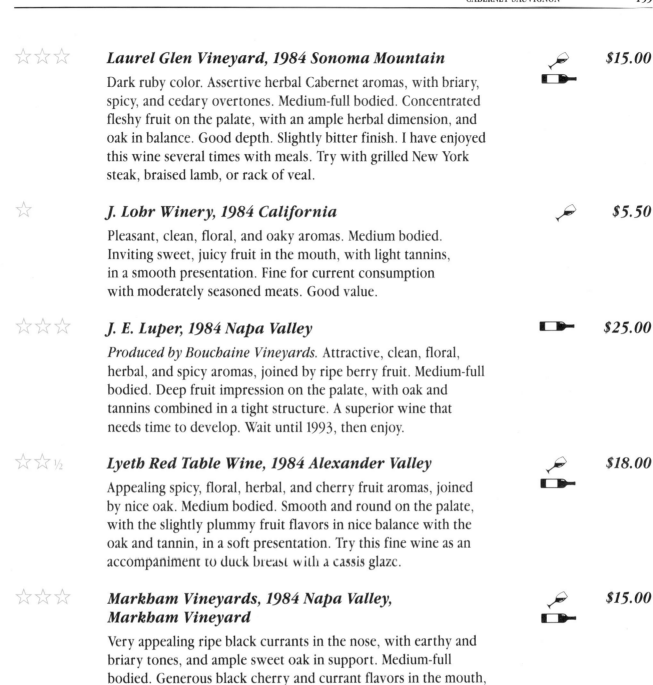 **_$15.00_**

Dark ruby color. Assertive herbal Cabernet aromas, with briary, spicy, and cedary overtones. Medium-full bodied. Concentrated fleshy fruit on the palate, with an ample herbal dimension, and oak in balance. Good depth. Slightly bitter finish. I have enjoyed this wine several times with meals. Try with grilled New York steak, braised lamb, or rack of veal.

☆ **_J. Lohr Winery, 1984 California_** **_$5.50_**

Pleasant, clean, floral, and oaky aromas. Medium bodied. Inviting sweet, juicy fruit in the mouth, with light tannins, in a smooth presentation. Fine for current consumption with moderately seasoned meats. Good value.

☆☆☆ **_J. E. Luper, 1984 Napa Valley_** **_$25.00_**

Produced by Bouchaine Vineyards. Attractive, clean, floral, herbal, and spicy aromas, joined by ripe berry fruit. Medium-full bodied. Deep fruit impression on the palate, with oak and tannins combined in a tight structure. A superior wine that needs time to develop. Wait until 1993, then enjoy.

☆☆½ **_Lyeth Red Table Wine, 1984 Alexander Valley_** **_$18.00_**

Appealing spicy, floral, herbal, and cherry fruit aromas, joined by nice oak. Medium bodied. Smooth and round on the palate, with the slightly plummy fruit flavors in nice balance with the oak and tannin, in a soft presentation. Try this fine wine as an accompaniment to duck breast with a cassis glaze.

☆☆☆ **_Markham Vineyards, 1984 Napa Valley, Markham Vineyard_** **_$15.00_**

Very appealing ripe black currants in the nose, with earthy and briary tones, and ample sweet oak in support. Medium-full bodied. Generous black cherry and currant flavors in the mouth, with ample oak and tannins in perfect balance. Plenty of fruit and tannin in the finish. Although delicious now, I would suggest waiting until 1993 or so. Then enjoy.

☆☆☆ **_Markham Vineyards, 1982 Napa Valley, Markham Vineyard, Yountville_** **_$13.00_**

Intense oak, spice, and berry fruit in the nose. Medium-full bodied. Deep, ripe currant fruit on the palate, with a full dimension of tannin through the finish. Give this wine a couple of years to smooth out further, then enjoy with red meats or strong cheeses.

Louis M. Martini Winery, 1985 North Coast   **$8.00**

Medium-intense herbal-scented varietal fruit in the nose.
Medium bodied. Moderately intense herbal fruit flavors on the
palate, with mild tannins. A well-made wine in a lighter style.
Fine for current consumption with fowl, veal, or light meats.
Good value.

 Louis M. Martini Winery, 1984 North Coast   **$8.00**

Nice ruby color. Medium-intense cherry fruit in the nose, with
herbal and oaky tones. The wine has a soft feel in the mouth,
with the moderate cherry fruit in balance with soft tannins.
Enjoy with a wide range of moderately seasoned meat dishes.
Good value.

 McDowell Valley Vineyards, 1983 McDowell Valley   **$10.50**

Forward toasty oak in the nose, joined by somewhat subdued
ripe cherry and spicy tones. Medium bodied. Generous fruit
flavors in the mouth, with a long dimension of oak and tannin.
Astringent finish. Give this wine a few years to smooth out,
then enjoy with savory foods.

 Meeker Vineyard, 1984 Dry Creek Valley   **$18.00**

Forward ripe cherry fruit and oak in the nose, joined by scents
of spice and anise. Medium-full bodied. Generous curranty fruit
and oak flavors in the mouth, with ample tannins. Give this wine
a couple of years to smooth out, then enjoy with well-seasoned
beef or lamb dishes.

 Robert Mondavi Reserve, 1984 Napa Valley   **$37.50**

Here is another great wine! Most attractive, complex aromas of
cherries, cassis, and spice, with loads of sweet oak in support.
Medium bodied. Soft and smooth in the mouth, with the rich
fruit, spice, and oak flavors in perfect balance with medium
tannins. This is an elegant wine that is very tasty now, and
will improve for years. Just enjoy.

 Robert Mondavi Reserve, 1983 Napa Valley   **$25.00**

Wonderful, complex aromas of spice, flowers, mint, and
eucalyptus, nicely supported by rich fruit and sweet oak.
Medium-full bodied. The wine enters the mouth supple, with
the rich fruit, acid, and oak in perfect balance, in a good
structure. Very pleasant now, and will improve for the next ten
years. Try as an accompaniment to duck breast with cherry-
peppercorn sauce or rack of lamb with Cabernet sauce.

Robert Mondavi Winery, 1985 Napa Valley

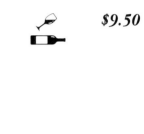

$14.00

Very attractive sweet fruit and creamy oak in the nose, with herbal nuances. Medium bodied. Supple on entry, with the moderately intense fruit and sweet oak in balance with mild tannins. A nicely styled Cabernet that is very enjoyable now, and will improve for several years. Try with saddle of veal, grilled quail, or roast lamb.

Robert Mondavi Winery, 1984 Napa Valley

$12.00

Pleasant aromas of curranty fruit and sweet oak, with floral and herbal tones. Medium bodied. Soft and gentle in the mouth, with the ripe fruit and oak flavors nicely balanced with mild tannins, in a smooth presentation. A refined wine that can be enjoyed with roast duck, rack of lamb, or veal medallions.

Robert Mondavi Winery, 1983 Napa Valley

$9.50

Pleasant varietal fruit in the nose, with herbal and olive overtones. Medium-bodied. The wine is supple on the palate, with the fruit and oak flavors in perfect balance. Lingering aftertaste. This is a very attractive wine for current consumption, and will improve for a few years. Enjoy with roast duck, saddle of veal, or leg of lamb.

Montali Aubudon Collection, 1984 Napa Valley

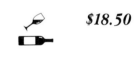

$11.00

Medium-intense aromas of plummy fruit, chocolate, and tobacco. Medium-full bodied. Attractive sweetish fruit on the palate, with herbal and oaky nuances, and moderate tannins. Will go well with beef or lamb dishes.

Monticello Corley Reserve, 1984 Napa Valley

$18.50

Concentrated, sweet, plummy fruit, with scents of black currants, spice, and chocolate. Medium-full bodied. Rich, extracted ripe fruit on the palate, with ample acid and tannins for aging potential. Needs a little time to smooth out. Enjoy with well-seasoned meat dishes.

Monticello Jefferson Cuvée, 1985 Napa Valley

$12.00

Pleasant ripe black currant aromas, with spicy and cedary tones. Medium-full bodied. Medium concentration of fruit on the palate, with ample oak and tannins. This is a fine wine that needs a little time to smooth out. Enjoy with well-seasoned meat dishes.

Monticello Jefferson Cuvée, 1984 Napa Valley   *$10.00*

Forward berry fruit aromas, with scents of currants, spice, chocolate, and cedar. Medium-full bodied. Moderately intense fruit flavors in the mouth, with an ample tannic dimension. Tart finish. The wine needs a few years to blossom. Best with beef or lamb dishes.

 Mount Eden Vineyards, 1984 Santa Cruz Mountains   *$22.50*

Intense rich spicy oak and herbs in the nose, with hints of cherries and coffee in the background. Medium-full bodied. Generous cassislike flavors on the palate, with nice spicy oak, and ample tannins, in a good structure. Astringent finish. Should reach an elegant level in five years. Then enjoy.

 Newton Vineyard, 1984 Napa Valley   *$13.50*

Attractive, complex aromas of black cherries, currants, and herbs, with hints of tobacco and cedar. Medium-full bodied. Rich grape flavors in the mouth, with chocolaty nuances, and ample tannins, in a firm structure. Accessible now, and will improve for several years. Best with well-seasoned meat dishes.

Newton Vineyard, 1983 Napa Valley   *$12.50*

Attractive plummy fruit aromas, with complex elements of spice, cedar, herbs and olives. Medium-full bodied. Deep fruit impression on the palate, with nice oak and herbal flavors and moderate tannins. The wine is accessible now, and will improve for several years. Try with rack of lamb, grilled quail with currant jelly, or roast beef au jus.

 Neyers Winery, 1984 Napa Valley   *$12.00*

Ripe, plummy fruit aromas, with briary, herbal, and earthy tones. Medium bodied. The wine enters the mouth soft and smooth, with the moderate fruit flavors and tannins in balance. Give this wine a year or so to round out. Best with moderately seasoned meat dishes.

Neyers Winery, 1983 Napa Valley   *$12.00*

Dark ruby color. Moderately intense ripe fruit aromas, with considerable oak in support. Medium-full bodied. Deep fruit impression on the palate, with herbal nuances, and considerable tannin. Tart finish. Give this wine a couple of years to smooth out, then enjoy with well-seasoned meat dishes.

☆☆½ **Optima Wine Cellars, 1985 Sonoma County** $18.50

Intense aromas of cherries and oak, with tarry tones. Full bodied. Rich and dense on the palate, with the solid fruit, generous oak, and tannin, in good balance. Briary and tarry elements add interest. Tannic finish. This fine wine needs at least five more years of aging for optimum enjoyment.

☆☆½ **Optima Wine Cellars, 1984 Sonoma County** $16.50

Appealing ripe currant aromas, joined by nice toasty oak. Medium-full bodied. Generous ripe fruit flavors fill the mouth, with oak and tannins in perfect balance. The wine is enjoyable now, and will improve for a number of years. Best with well-seasoned meat dishes.

☆☆☆☆ **Opus One, 1984 Napa Valley** $50.00

Winning streak continues. Beautiful ripe currants and toasty oak aromas, with floral and spicy tones. Medium-full bodied. The fruit flavors are rich and complex in the mouth, enhanced with plenty of sweet oak, and ample tannins for aging. And all this in an elegant structure. Although this exceptional wine is delicious now, I would suggest a wait of several years for even further improvement.

☆☆☆☆ **Opus One, 1983 Napa Valley** $50.00

Continues a string of winners! Most attractive spicy, cedary, curranty fruit aromas, delicately laced in sweet oak. Medium-full bodied. Elegant fruit on the palate, perfectly balanced with oak flavors. My comments regarding the prior vintage also apply to this bottling. This is simply a great wine, and is very enjoyable now. In addition, it has long aging potential. It is not necessary to wait for that special occasion; this wine will make any occasion special.

☆☆½ **Palisades Vineyards, 1984 Napa Valley, Hewitt Vineyards** $12.00

Forward ripe fruit in the nose, with a full dimension of spicy, briary, and oaky aromas in support. Medium-full bodied. Lush fruit on the palate, with strong herbal and oaky elements, and modest tannins. Will improve for several years. Best with savory foods.

☆☆ **Parducci Wine Cellars, 1984 Mendocino County** $8.50

Very appealing cherry fruit in the nose, with nice smoky, herbal, and tealike tones. Medium bodied. Supple on entry, with fairly ripe fruit on the palate, and a touch of cocoa, in a good structure. A fine wine for early consumption with moderately seasoned beef or lamb dishes.

Pat Paulsen Vineyards, 1985 Sonoma County $11.00

Assertive briary, herbaceous, and smoky aromas, joined by
cherry fruit and sweet oak. Medium-full bodied. Generous
herbal fruit on the palate, with briary nuances, and ample tannins. Astringent finish. Best with well-seasoned meat dishes.

Robert Pecota Winery, 1983 Napa Valley $12.00

Rich curranty fruit in the nose, with spicy, herbal, and oaky
overtones. Medium-full bodied. Generous fruit on the palate,
with herbal nuances, and ample tannins. Finishes a bit sharp.
Will improve for a number of years. However, it can be enjoyed
now with roast beef au jus or rack of lamb.

Robert Pecota Winery, 1985 Napa Valley, Kara's Vineyard $16.00

Appealing cherry fruit in the nose, with herbal and floral scents,
in a nice oaky framework. Medium-full bodied. Nice concentration of ripe currant and plum flavors on the palate, with
ample tannins, in a firm structure. This elegant wine grows on
you with each tasting. Its early charms notwithstanding, I suggest
a wait of several years for further improvement. Then enjoy!

Robert Pecota Winery, 1984 Napa Valley, Kara's Vineyard $14.00

Medium-intense ripe, sweet, berry fruit aromas, with an
added dimension of spice and rich oak. Medium-full bodied.
Moderately rich cherry and currant flavors on the palate, nicely
balanced with tangy acid and tannins, in a solid structure. Nice,
sharp finish. Accessible now, and will improve for a number of
years. Enjoy with beef Wellington, leg of lamb, or veal Oscar.

J. Pedroncelli Winery, 1985 Sonoma County $7.00

Medium-intense herbal-scented cherry fruit and oak in the nose.
Medium bodied. The fruit is somewhat lean on the palate, with a
nice touch of oak. Slightly astringent finish. Try with moderately
seasoned beef or lamb dishes.

Robert Pepi Winery, 1983 Napa Valley, Vine Hill Ranch $16.00

Pleasant cassis aromas, with floral and herbal tones. Medium-full
bodied. Generous varietal fruit on the palate, with oak and
tannins in balance, in a good structure. Slightly astringent in
the finish. Try this fine wine with roast beef au jus or roast
leg of lamb.

Joseph Phelps Insignia, 1984 Napa Valley $30.00

Intense, complex aromas of raspberries, eucalyptus, spice, and sweet oak. Medium-full bodied. Deep impression of ripe cherry fruit on the palate, with a nice minty dimension, and ample tannins. Lots of fruit and tannins in a long finish. Simply a great wine. Try it in 1995.

Joseph Phelps Insignia, 1983 Napa Valley $25.00

Forward aromas of sweet oak, spice, and mint, joined by mild curranty scents. Medium bodied. Soft herbal fruit on the palate, with hints of cocoa and mint, and tannins in balance. Fine with sautéed duck or leg of lamb.

Joseph Phelps Vineyards, 1984 Napa Valley $14.00

Forward ripe fruit aromas, with herbal and peppery tones. Medium-full bodied. Generous herbal fruit flavors on the palate, with a good oak dimension, in a firm structure. Slightly harsh finish. Look for at least five years of improvement. Best with well-seasoned meat dishes.

Joseph Phelps Vineyards, 1983 Napa Valley $12.75

Very appealing aromas of ripe currants, spice, flowers, and sweet oak, with hints of mint and eucalyptus. Medium-full bodied. Rich fruit and oak on the palate, with ample tannin, in a good structure. The wine is complex and balanced. Try with rack of lamb or roast beef au jus.

Joseph Phelps Vineyards, 1985 Napa Valley, Backus Vineyard $27.50

Intense, complex aromas of cassis, spice, mint, and sweet oak. Medium-full bodied. Big and full on the palate, with concentrated minty Cabernet fruit flavors joined by a fair dimension of oak and tannins. Harsh finish. A powerful wine that should be cellared for a decade.

Joseph Phelps Vineyards, 1984 Napa Valley, Eisele Vineyard $35.00

Attractive aromas of spice, cedar, mint, herbs, and berry fruit. Medium-full bodied. Loads of ripe curranty fruit on the palate, with a heavy tannic dimension through the finish. This is a wine of the future, since the tannins are so powerful. I suggest a wait until 1995, then enjoy.

Joseph Phelps Vineyards, 1983 Napa Valley, Eisele Vineyard

$25.00

Dark ruby color. Forward rich oak, spice, and mint in the nose, joined by restrained fruit. Medium-full bodied. Rich fruit flavors in the mouth, with loads of tannin. This wine needs time to smooth out, say another five years. Best with well-seasoned beef dishes.

Pine Ridge Andrus Reserve, 1984 Napa Valley

$38.00

Pleasant curranty fruit in the nose, with spicy and piney tones. Medium-full bodied. Rich blackberry and cassis flavors, with spicy elements, are nicely balanced with sweet oak. This is a chewy wine with big tannins, which will take some years to resolve. I would suggest a wait of five years or so, then match with highly seasoned foods.

Pine Ridge Andrus Reserve, Cuvée Duet, 1985 Napa Valley

$40.00

Attractive aromas of cassislike fruit and toasty oak. Medium-full bodied. Silky texture in the mouth, with the ripe fruit and rich oak in nice balance with the tannins. Slightly astringent in the finish, with the fruit carrying through. Although the wine is tasty now, better to wait a couple of years and enjoy at a higher level of elegance.

Pine Ridge Private Reserve, 1985 Napa Valley, Pine Ridge Stag's Leap Vineyard

$26.00

Very attractive cassislike Cabernet fruit in the nose, with herbal tones, and nice oak in support. Medium-full bodied. Loads of ripe fruit on the palate, enriched by sweet oak, and good tannins for aging. Wait five years or so for this wine to reach a high level of elegance, then enjoy.

Pine Ridge Rutherford Cuvée, 1985 Napa Valley

$15.00

Medium-intense Cabernet fruit aromas, with herbal and cedary tones. Rich and supple, with the generous cassislike fruit flavors nicely balanced with oak and medium tannins. Lingering finish. Will improve for at least five years. Try with roast beef au jus or rack of lamb.

Pine Ridge Winery, 1983 Napa Valley, Pine Ridge Stag's Leap Vineyard

$20.00

Attractive aromas of ripe berry fruit, herbs, olives, and oak. Medium bodied. Sharp, lean berry fruit on the palate, with ample acid and tannins. This wine needs time for the flavors to emerge. Give it a few years, then enjoy with veal scallops, sweetbreads, or roast rabbit.

★★★ *Plam Vineyards, 1985 Napa Valley* $24.00

Forward aromas of ripe curranty fruit and sweet oak, with green olive and spicy tones. Full bodied. Heavy ripe grape flavors fill the mouth, with peppery and tarry nuances, and a full dimension of sweet oak. Long finish. This is a big wine of superior quality that is enjoyable now, and will improve for a few years. Try with grilled New York steak, leg of lamb, or venison.

★★½ *Preston Vineyards, 1985 Dry Creek Valley* $11.00

Pleasant aromas of black cherry, cedars, and tea in the nose, with overtones of anise and herbs. Medium bodied. Medium-intense cherry fruit flavors on the palate, with herbal nuances, in a firm structure. Finishes slightly astringent. Will improve for a few years. Try with roast beef au jus or rolled leg of lamb with rosemary.

★★½ *Preston Vineyards, 1984 Dry Creek Valley* $11.00

Medium-intense aromas of rich, jammy fruit and herbs, with earthy and briary scents. Medium-full bodied. Plummy blackberry fruit on the palate, with earthy nuances, and ample sweet oak. Tangy finish. Enjoy this fine wine with beef stew, roast veal, or leg of lamb.

★★½ *Quail Ridge Cellars, 1983 Napa Valley* $15.00

Pleasant cherry fruit aromas, with herbal and oaky overtones. Medium-full bodied. The wine enters the mouth soft, with the fleshy fruit in nice balance with oak and herbal flavors. Pleasant, fruity finish. Try with veal scallops or sweetbreads.

★★½ *Ravenswood, 1986 Sonoma County* $12.00

Concentrated spicy Cabernet fruit in the nose, with herbal overtones. Medium-full bodied. Lots of ripe cherry fruit and spice flavors on the palate, with abundant oak, and sufficient tannins. This is a substantial wine that will improve for at least five more years. Try with roast beef au jus or rack of lamb.

★★½ *Ravenswood, 1985 Sonoma County* $12.00

Attractive, medium-intense aromas of blackberry fruit and oak, with earthy tones. Medium-full bodied. Deep fruit impression on the palate, with ample oak and tannins, in a firm structure. Will improve for at least five years. Enjoyed with well-seasoned meat dishes.

Raymond Private Reserve, 1983 Napa Valley

$18.00

Attractive curranty fruit in the nose, with blackberry and olive scents, nicely framed in oak. Medium-full bodied. Generous cherry, chocolate, and cedar flavors on the palate, with ample tannins. Astringent finish. Accessible now, and will improve for at least five more years. Try with veal Orloff or braised lamb.

Raymond Private Reserve, 1982 Napa Valley

$16.00

Most attractive ripe curranty aromas, supported by elements of mint, cocoa, and coconut, laced with spicy oak scents through-out. Medium-full bodied. Rich, complex fruit flavors in the mouth, with a nice dimension of spicy oak. This is a superior wine that is accessible now, and will improve for at least five more years. Enjoy with filet mignon, roast leg of lamb, or saddle of veal.

Raymond Vineyard, 1983 Napa Valley

$12.00

Pleasant aromas of cherry fruit, cedar, spice, and pine. Medium-full bodied. Generous ripe fruit on the palate, with ample oak and tannin, in a good structure. Slightly tannic finish. Enjoy with roast leg of lamb or roast beef.

Richardson Vineyards, 1985 Sonoma Valley

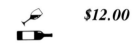

$12.00

Dark ruby color, with purple tinges. Pleasant ripe berry fruit in the nose, with spicy scents. Medium-full bodied. Concentrated berry fruit on the palate, with peppery nuances, supported by creamy oak. Fruity finish. Best with spicy foods.

Ridge Vineyards, 1984 California, York Creek Vineyards

$14.00

Somewhat sweet, jammy fruit in the nose, with oaky and herbal scents and a slightly weedy element. Medium bodied. The wine is supple in the mouth, with the slightly rich fruit flavors nicely balanced with oak and moderate tannins. A fine wine for early consumption with moderately seasoned meat dishes.

Ridge Vineyards, 1985 Santa Cruz Mountains, Monte Bello Vineyard

$40.00

A big winner here! Intense aromas of currants and plums, laced in toasty oak. Full bodied. Loads of ripe curranty fruit on the palate, with minty and chocolaty nuances, with abundant oak, and medium tannins, in an elegant presentation. A superior wine in every respect. Will live into the next century.

☆☆   ***Rodney Strong, 1982 Alexander Valley,*** $12.00
Alexander's Crown Vineyard

Medium intense cherry fruit aromas, with herbal and weedy
tones. Medium bodied. Generous cherry fruit flavors on the
palate, with mild tannins, in a smooth presentation. A fine wine
for early consumption with moderately seasoned meat dishes.

☆☆☆   ***Rombauer Vineyards, 1985 Napa Valley*** $13.50

Attractive ripe currants and sweet oak in the nose, with minty
and earthy tones. Medium-full bodied. Full and rich on the
palate, with the cassislike fruit nicely balanced with rich oak and
moderate tannins. Long, fruity finish. This superior wine is
delicious now, and will improve for several years. Just enjoy.

☆☆½   ***Rombauer Vineyards, 1984 Napa Valley*** $13.50

Attractive, medium-intense aromas of ripe cherries, currants,
and herbs. Medium-full bodied. Soft and round at entry, with the
rich fruit flavors in balance with oak and tannins, in a good
structure. Very enjoyable now, with good aging potential.
Try with rack of lamb or grilled quail with currant jelly.

☆   ***Round Hill Vineyards, 1986 Napa Valley*** $8.00

Medium intense cherry fruit in the nose, with oaky scents.
Medium bodied. Pleasant fruit flavors on the palate, in a good
structure. A well-made wine that can best accompany moderately
seasoned meat dishes.

☆☆   ***Rustridge Vineyards, 1986 Napa Valley,*** $13.00
Priest Ranch

Ruby color. Very attractive cherry fruit and spice in the nose,
with cedary tones. Medium bodied. Moderate cherry fruit
flavors on the palate, nicely balanced with oak and tannins,
in a good structure. A claret-style wine that will improve for
five more years. Try with roast beef or leg of lamb.

☆☆½   ***Rutherford Hill Winery, 1984 Napa Valley*** $12.50

Attractive aromas of ripe blackberries and toasty oak, with
herbal and olivey tones. Medium-full bodied. Fleshy feel in the
mouth, with the ripe fruit nicely supported by oak, acid, and
moderate tannins. Long, fruity finish. Fine with beef or
lamb dishes.

☆☆½   ***Rutherford Hill Winery, 1983 Napa Valley*** $11.00

Attractive rich, plummy fruit aromas, with hints of cedar and
herbs. Medium-full bodied. Ripe Cabernet fruit in the mouth,
with ample oak and moderate tannins. Pleasant, lingering
aftertaste. Best with well-seasoned lamb or beef dishes.

St. Andrew's Winery, 1984 Napa Valley **$9.00**

Attractive aromas of cherries and cassis, with hints of spice and mint. Medium bodied. The wine enters the mouth supple, with the generous cherry fruit aromas nicely balanced with oak. This is a fine wine for early consumption, and will improve for a couple of years. Fine with fowl or lamb.

 St. Clement Vineyards, 1984 Napa Valley 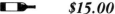 **$15.00**

Forward sweet oak aromas, joined by cherry and currant scents, and a nice touch of spice. Medium-full bodied. Rich, somewhat plummy fruit on the palate, with ample oak, and a fair tannic dimension through the finish. This superior wine needs time for further development. Patience will reward you. Wait until 1995, then enjoy.

 St. Francis Winery, 1985 California  **$10.00**

Intense ripe cherry fruit aromas, fully supported by rich oak. Medium-full bodied. The wine is deep and firm on the palate, with the ripe fruit in nice balance with spicy, herbal, and chocolaty elements, and ample toasty oak. A tasty wine that will improve for several years. Fine with a wide range of beef or lamb dishes. Good value.

 Sausal Winery, 1985 Alexander Valley **$11.00**

Appealing, medium-intense cherry fruit and vanillin aromas, with herbal and spicy tones. Medium-full bodied. Pleasant and relatively smooth on the palate, with the cherrylike fruit and sweet oak flavors in nice balance with tannins. Slightly rough finish. Try with well-seasoned fowl or veal dishes.

 Sausal Winery, 1984 Alexander Valley **$10.00**

Intense ripe fruit in the nose, with strong herbal, earthy, and chocolaty tones. Medium-full bodied. The rich fruit flavors are lush and expansive on the palate, with moderate oak and tannins. Finishes a bit hot. Best with spicy foods. Good value.

 Sequoia Grove Vineyards, 1985 Napa Valley **$15.00**

Beautiful curranty aromas, with nice tobacco and earthy scents. Medium bodied. Most attractive currant, flower, and oak flavors fill the mouth, in a good structure. This is a wonderful wine for current consumption and for several more years. Just enjoy!

Sequoia Grove Vineyards, Estate Bottled, 1985 Napa Valley

$28.00

Attractive, intense ripe curranty fruit in the nose, with spicy scents, and a nice dimension of sweet oak. Medium-full bodied. Supple in the mouth, with loads of rich, fleshy fruit, perfectly balanced with oak and tannin, in a smooth presentation. A great wine for early consumption, and will improve for a number of years. Try as an accompaniment to duck breast with a cherry-peppercorn sauce.

Shafer Vineyards, 1985 Napa Valley

$15.50

Appealing cherrylike fruit aromas, with cedary and chocolaty overtones. Medium bodied. Lean and elegant on the palate, with the cherry and cedar flavors in nice balance with firming acid. Quite smooth for a young wine, and will improve for a couple of years. Try as an accompaniment to duck breast with an olive sauce.

Shafer Vineyards, 1984 Napa Valley

$14.00

Medium-intense cherry and currant fruit aromas, with minty and spicy scents, and toasty oak in the background. Medium bodied. Round and soft at entry, with the cherry fruit, oak, and tannin in nice balance. A fine wine for current consumption with game, fowl, or lamb.

Sierra Vista Winery, 1984 El Dorado

$9.00

Medium-intense aromas of ripe currants, briar, and sweet oak. Medium-full bodied. Rounded in the mouth, with the generous cherry fruit in good balance with the oak and tannin. Slightly astringent finish. Fine with moderately seasoned meat dishes. Good value.

Silver Oak Cellars, 1984 Alexander Valley

$22.00

Very appealing aromas of cherries, herbs, and vanillin spice, with scents of tobacco and violets. Medium-full bodied. Supple on entry, with the slightly plummy fruit flavors in nice balance with vanillin oak and moderate tannins. An elegant wine that can be enjoyed now and for years to come.

Silver Oak Cellars, 1983 Alexander Valley

$21.00

Attractive ripe cherry and currant fruit aromas, with floral and herbal scents, supported by rich oak. Medium bodied. Generous fleshy fruit on the palate, with herbal nuances, rich oak, and moderate tannins, in a soft structure. This is an excellent wine for current consumption and for the next few years. Try as an accompaniment to duck breast with a cherry-peppercorn sauce.

Silver Oak Cellars, 1984 Napa Valley **$22.00**

Very attractive, complex aromas of currants, herbs, spice, and sweet oak. Medium-full bodied. Loads of rich cassislike fruit on the palate, beautifully balanced with rich vanillin oak and moderate tannins. Nice fruit and oak through a long finish. A superior wine that can be enjoyed now, and will improve for at least five more years.

 Silver Oak Cellars, 1983 Napa Valley **$21.00**

Moderately aggressive ripe fruit in the nose, with herbal and weedy scents, supported by rich oak. Medium-full bodied. Deep cherry and currant fruit flavors on the palate, with cedary nuances, and ample tannins. Will improve for at least another five years. Try as an accompaniment to rack of lamb with Cabernet sauce.

 Silverado Vineyards, 1985 Napa Valley **$11.50**

Attractive herbal Cabernet aromas, with bell pepper tones, and nice oak in support. Medium-full bodied. Generous curranty fruit on the palate, balanced with moderate oak and tannins. Try as an accompaniment to duck breast with an olive sauce or grilled veal chops.

 Simi Winery, 1984 Sonoma County **$12.00**

Appealing, clean varietal fruit and creamy oak in the nose. Medium-full bodied. Generous curranty fruit and oak flavors on the palate, in a good structure. This is a very well-made wine that will improve for at least five more years. Try with rack of lamb or roast beef au jus.

 Smith and Hook, 1983 Monterey **$13.00**

Attractive ripe, plummy fruit in the nose, with herbal and earthy scents, framed in creamy oak. Medium-full bodied. Abundant spicy fruit flavors in the mouth, with a full dimension of oak, acid, and tannins. Wait a couple of years for it to smooth out, then enjoy with savory foods.

 Smith-Madrone, 1984 Napa Valley **$14.00**

Very attractive aromas of ripe plums and black cherries, with a nice dimension of creamy oak in support. Medium-full bodied. Big and forward on the palate, with the rich curranty fruit beautifully balanced with oak, and with ample tannins in support. Somewhat hard finish. This is a wine of the future. Wait until 1994 or so for optimum enjoyment.

☆☆☆ **Spottswoode, 1985 Napa Valley** $26.00

Very attractive, intense aromas of ripe currants and sweet oak, with scents of tar and anise. Medium-full bodied. Substantial currant and berry flavors on the palate, with ample oak, and a full tannic dimension, in a firm structure. This is a superior wine that needs more time to develop; say, at least five more years.

☆☆½ **Spring Mountain Vineyards, 1983 Napa Valley** $16.00

Forward ripe curranty fruit in the nose, with rich oak in support. Medium-full bodied. Generous fruit on the palate, with oaky nuances, and abundant tannins. Astringent finish. Give this wine several years to smooth out, then enjoy with highly seasoned meat dishes.

☆☆☆ **Stag's Leap Wine Cellars, 1985 Napa Valley** $26.00

Very appealing ripe cherry fruit and sweet oak in the nose. Medium-full bodied. Deep and flavorful in the mouth, with the cherry and plum flavors nicely balanced with creamy oak, in a good structure. Long, fruity finish. A wonderful wine for current consumption and for years to come. Try as an accompaniment to rack of lamb with Cabernet sauce, duck breast with an olive sauce, or medallions of veal.

☆☆½ **Stag's Leap Wine Cellars, 1984 Napa Valley** $15.00

Ruby-brick color. Attractive ripe herbal fruit in the nose, with floral and oaky scents. Medium-full bodied. Rounded feel in the mouth, with the rich, soft fruit nicely balanced with oak and light tannins. This is a fine wine for early consumption with moderately seasoned meats.

☆☆½ **Stag's Leap Wine Cellars Cask 23, 1983 Napa Valley** $35.00

Dark ruby color. Moderately aggressive aromas of blackberry fruit and herbs, with smoky tones, and hints of tobacco and coffee. Medium-full bodied. Round and supple in the mouth, with ripe herbal fruit flavors, and moderate tannins, in a soft structure. The wine is enjoyable now. Try with well-seasoned meat dishes.

☆☆½ **Steltzner Vineyards, 1985 Napa Valley** $15.00

Intense, very ripe fruit in the nose, with spicy, weedy, and resiny scents. Full bodied. Substantial in the mouth, with the generous cherry and currant flavors joined by a fair dimension of oak, acid, and tannins. Tart finish. Allow several years of further development, then enjoy with highly seasoned meat dishes.

☆☆ ½   ***Steltzner Vineyards, 1984 Napa Valley*** $15.00

Forward aromas of spicy oak, joined by restrained fruit.
Medium-full bodied. Rounded feel in the mouth, with the deep,
ripe fruit flavors balanced with abundant tannins. Needs time.
Wait until 1994, then enjoy with highly spiced foods.

☆☆ ½   ***Sterling Vineyards, 1985 Napa Valley*** $14.00

Very appealing, medium-intense aromas of sweet currants, spice,
violets, and oak. Medium-full bodied. Moderately concentrated
fruit flavors on the palate, with oak and tannins in balance,
in a lean and elegant style. An excellent wine for current
consumption, and will improve for a few years. Try as an
accompaniment to grilled quail with mushrooms.

☆☆ ½   ***Sterling Vineyards, 1984 Napa Valley,
Diamond Mountain Ranch*** $15.00

Medium-intense ripe cherry fruit aromas, with briary and spicy
scents. Medium-full bodied. Rich blackberry and oak flavors on
the palate, with ample tannins. Astringent finish. Give this wine
several years to smooth out, then enjoy with spicy food.

☆☆☆   ***Sterling Vineyards Reserve, 1983 Napa Valley*** $22.50

Attractive ripe cherry and cassis aromas, elegantly perfumed
with sweet oak. Medium bodied. Rich and nicely textured on the
palate, with the curranty fruit and oak in perfect balance, and
ample tannin for aging. This is a superior wine that needs several
years to reach its potential. Enjoy!

☆☆ ½   ***Sterling Vineyards Reserve, 1982 Napa Valley*** $22.50

Moderately intense curranty fruit aromas, with spicy and oaky
overtones. Medium-full bodied. Combined flavors of currants,
cedar, and green olives in the mouth, with ample oak and
tannins. Astringent finish. Give this wine a couple of years
to smooth out, then enjoy with spicy foods.

☆☆   ***Stonegate Winery, 1984 Napa Valley*** $13.00

Dark ruby color. Medium-intense ripe berry fruit aromas, with
briary tones. Medium-full bodied. Moderately intense berry fruit
flavors on the palate, with oak and tannins in balance. Slightly
coarse in the finish. Fine with beef or lamb dishes.

☆☆   ***Sunny St. Helena Winery, 1985 Napa Valley*** $9.00

Forward herbal grounds, joined by ripe fruit and oak. Medium-
full bodied. Appealing, moderately deep sweet cherry flavors on
the palate, with chocolaty nuances, and ample oak, in a good
structure. Slightly bitter finish. Best with well-seasoned
meat dishes.

☆ **Sutter Home Winery, 1985 California** $5.50

Moderately intense ripe fruit in the nose. Medium bodied.
Generous ripe fruit in the mouth, with mild tannins.
Fine with veal or fowl dishes. Good value.

☆☆ **Taft Street, 1985 California** $7.50

Nicely focused berry fruit aromas, with oaky scents. Medium
bodied. Attractive curranty fruit, spice, and oak flavors on the
palate, nicely balanced with tannins, giving some structure.
Best with moderately seasoned beef or lamb dishes. Good value.

☆ **Taft Street, 1984 Sonoma/Mendocino** $6.00

Moderately intense cherrylike aromas, with toasty oak scents.
Medium bodied. The wine is supple in the mouth, with the nice
cherry flavors somewhat diminished by a stemmy quality.
But still, a good wine. Best with moderately seasoned meats.
Good value.

☆☆½ **Topolos at Russian River, 1981 Sonoma County,
Limited Edition, Artist Series** $10.00

Intense, complex aromas of currants, spice, and oak. Medium-
full bodied. Deep, lively fruit impression on the palate, with
ample oak flavors and firm acid. Somewhat astringent in the
finish. Wait until 1991, then enjoy this very fine wine with highly
seasoned meat dishes. Good value.

☆☆ **Trefethen Vineyards, 1983 Napa Valley** $11.75

Medium-intense ripe cherry fruit in the nose, with herbal and
spicy scents. Medium bodied. Rich herbal fruit and oak flavors,
with ample tannins. Astringent finish. Best with well-seasoned
beef dishes.

☆☆½ **Tudal Winery, 1984 Napa Valley** $12.50

Moderately intense ripe cherry aromas, with herbal scents, and
spicy oak in full support Medium-full bodied. The ripe fruit is
deep and firm on the palate, with ample acid and tannins. This is
a well-structured wine that needs several years of cellaring.
Best with savory dishes.

☆☆½ **Viansa Cellars, 1984 Sonoma/Napa** $12.50

Attractive, medium-intense berry fruit, oaky, and herbal aromas.
Medium-full bodied. Nice black cherry and cassislike flavors on
the palate, with herbal nuances, and medium tannins, in a clean
presentation. Very enjoyable to drink now, and will improve for
a few years. Try with roast beef au jus or grilled quail with
Cabernet sauce.

Vichon Winery, 1985 Napa Valley **$14.00**

Forward ripe berry fruit and oaky aromas. Medium-full bodied. Generous, very ripe curranty fruit and sweet oak flavors are in perfect harmony with the tannins. Long, fruity finish. Best with highly seasoned beef or lamb dishes.

 ### *Vichon Winery SLD, 1985 Napa Valley* **$20.00**

Intense black cherry and currant aromas, with herbal, spicy, and oaky overtones. Medium-full bodied. Supple on entry, with generous ripe fruit flavors joined by vanillin oak, in a good structure. Slightly tannic finish. This is a superior wine that will improve for at least five more years.

 ### *Wente Bros., 1984 Napa Valley* **$7.00**

Medium-intense cherry fruit in the nose, with a touch of oak. Medium bodied. Moderately intense sweetish cherry fruit flavors on the palate, with pleasant oak, in a clean presentation. This is a well-made wine, in a light style, that will go well with moderately seasoned poultry, veal, or light meats. Good value.

 ### *Wm. Wheeler Vineyards, 1984 Dry Creek Valley* **$11.00**

Dark ruby color. Attractive ripe blackberry fruit in the nose, with herbal and spicy oak overtones. Medium-full bodied. Lush feel in the mouth, with rich fruit and oak flavors, and ample tannins, in a firm structure. Astringent finish. Best with highly seasoned meat dishes.

 ### *White Oak Vineyards, 1984 Alexander Valley, Myers Vineyard* **$11.50**

Medium-intense curranty aromas, with earthy tones and herbal scents, and a nice oak dimension. Medium-full bodied. Ripe fruit and rich oak flavors on the palate, with ample tannins, in a firm structure. Astringent finish. Best with highly spiced meat dishes.

 ### *Whitehall Lane Winery, 1985 Napa Valley* **$16.00**

Attractive ripe cherry fruit in the nose, with tobacco, tea, and minty scents in support. Medium-full bodied. Generous minty fruit on the palate, with spicy and herbal nuances, in a good structure. Slightly astringent in the finish. Try this superior wine with rolled leg of lamb or duck breast with a cherry-peppercorn sauce.

 ### *Zaca Mesa, 1984 Santa Barbara County* **$8.00**

Medium intense berry fruit in the nose, with smoky tones. Medium bodied. Generous fruit on the palate, with ample oak and tannin, in a firm structure. Slightly bitter finish. Best with well-seasoned meat dishes. Good value.

Zaca Mesa American Reserve, 1983 Santa Barbara **$12.75**

Intense black cherry and currant aromas, with tobacco and cedar overtones. Medium-full bodied. Generous ripe fruit flavors fill the mouth, with a nice dimension of spice and oak. Will improve for several years. Best with highly seasoned meat dishes.

 ### *ZD, 1983 Napa Valley* **$14.00**

Complex aromas of cherries, currants, spice, bell peppers, and herbs, with nice oak in support. Medium-full bodied. Layers of ripe fruit fill the mouth with plenty of tannins. Harsh finish. The wine will age well. Wait until 1992, then enjoy with savory dishes.

Z I N F A N D E L

 ½ | ### Alexander Valley Vineyards, Wetzel Family Estate, 1985 Alexander Valley | | **$7.50**

Dark garnet color. Lots of ripe raspberry fruit in the nose, with toasty oak tones. Medium-full bodied. Loads of plummy fruit on the palate, with oak and tannin in good balance. Good aging potential. Best with well-seasoned meat dishes. Good value.

 | ### Buehler Vineyards, 1985 Napa Valley | | **$8.00**

Loads of very ripe fruit in the nose, fully supported by spice and oak. Full bodied. Rich, briary, toasty fruit flavors fill the mouth, with ample oak and tannin, in a good structure. Slightly harsh finish. Improvement for at least five more years. Best with rich foods. Excellent value.

 ½ | ### Burgess Cellars, 1984 Napa Valley | | **$8.00**

Dark ruby-purple color. Forward plummy fruit in the nose, with earthy and briary scents, and toasty oak in the background. Medium-full bodied. Rich, ripe berry fruit flavors, with peppery tones, and moderate tannins. An excellent Zinfandel that will do best with highly seasoned meat dishes. Good value.

 ½ | ### Caymus Vineyards, 1984 Napa Valley | | **$8.00**

Pleasant, medium-intense raspberry fruit aromas, with briary and peppery scents, and creamy oak in support. Medium bodied. Attractive, moderately intense berry fruit in the mouth, with a nice oak dimension. Lingering aftertaste. Try with blackened red snapper or duck ragout with polenta. Good value.

 ½ | ### Chateau Montelena, 1985 Napa Valley | | **$10.00**

Medium-intense berry, spicy, and herbal aromas, joined by a full dimension of sweet oak. Medium-full bodied. Ripe, jammy fruit in the mouth, with peppery elements, and ample tannins, in a firm structure. Slightly harsh finish. Give this wine a couple of years for further development, then enjoy with well seasoned meat dishes.

 | ### Chateau Montelena, 1984 Napa Valley, John Rolleri Reserve | | **$10.00**

Most attractive aromas of ripe raspberries and cassis, with nice oaky overtones. Medium-full bodied. The fruit impression on the palate is deep and rich, with oak in balance, and soft tannins. Finishes a bit hot. This wine will improve for several years. Try this excellent wine with marinated lamb kabobs or grilled chicken with Salsa Verde. Good value.

The Christian Brothers, 1986 Napa Valley $6.25

Pronounced earthy, herbal, and briary aromas. Medium bodied. The wine enters the mouth full and round, with nice herbal fruit through the finish. Fine for current consumption with fowl or veal dishes.

Clos du Val, 1985 Napa Valley $12.00

Heavy, complex aromas of herbs, spice, and ripe blackberries, with briary overtones. Medium-full bodied. Beautifully focused varietal fruit on the palate, with ample tannins, in a firm structure. This is a reasonably big Zinfandel that will improve for at least five more years. Best with spicy dishes.

Cuvaison, 1985 Napa Valley $7.50

Attractive ripe, spicy berry fruit aromas, with peppery scents, and rich oak in full support. Medium-full bodied. The fruit is deep and firm on the palate, and is nicely balanced with ample oak and moderate tannins. All components are in perfect proportion. Enjoy this excellent wine with savory dishes. Good value.

De Loach Vineyards, 1986 Russian River Valley $9.00

Very appealing, forward aromas of raspberry fruit and sweet oak, with herbal tones. Medium-full bodied. Supple on entry, with the ripe fruit flavors, oak, and tannins in good balance. The wine is enjoyable now, and will improve for several years. Enjoy with roast lamb or chicken cacciatore.

De Moor Winery, 1984 Napa Valley $8.00

Abundant rich oak, spice, and ripe fruit aromas, with peppery and briary scents. Medium-full bodied. Loads of berry fruit in the mouth, with a full dimension of oak and tannin. Tart finish. Give this wine a couple of years to smooth out, then enjoy with savory dishes.

Dehlinger Winery, 1983 Sonoma County $8.00

Very attractive berry fruit aromas, with peppery, spicy, briary scents, and a full dimension of sweet vanillin oak. Medium-full bodied. The wine enters the mouth round and full, with the rich berry fruit and oak in perfect balance. Soft tannins. This is the last-planned Zinfandel from this winery, ending on a high note. Enjoy this excellent wine with spicy meat and potato ragout, roast lamb with garlic sauce, or barbecued chicken. Excellent value.

☆☆ ½ **Gary Farrell, 1985 Sonoma County** $10.00

Dark ruby-purple color, medium-intense aromas of jammy fruit, briar, and herbs. Medium-full bodied. Loads of young fruit on the palate, with a strong herbaceous element, in a firm structure. Sharp finish. Best with spicy foods.

☆☆ **Fetzer Special Reserve, 1986 Mendocino** $9.00

Medium intense young berry fruit in the nose, joined by a nice dimension of spicy oak. Medium-full bodied. Deep fruit flavors on the palate, with abundant tannins. Best with hearty dishes.

☆☆☆ **Fetzer Special Reserve, 1984 Mendocino** $8.50

Beautifully focused blackberry and oak aromas, with a delicate spicy/briary dimension. Medium-full bodied. Deep fruit impression in the mouth, with spicy and cedary nuances, and tannins in balance. This excellent wine is accessible now, and will improve for several years. Best with savory dishes. Super value.

☆ **Fetzer Vineyards, 1986 Lake County** $5.00

Light raspberry fruit and oak in the nose. Medium bodied. Moderate raspberry fruit flavors, with cedary nuances, and mild tannins. A very enjoyable wine for current consumption with moderately seasoned meats.

☆ **Fetzer Vineyards, 1985 Lake County** $5.00

Restrained berry fruit aromas, with briary and herbal overtones. Medium bodied. Nice plummy fruit in the mouth, with minty nuances. Astringent finish. Enjoy with moderately seasoned meats.

☆☆ ½ **Fritz Cellars, 1984 Dry Creek Valley** $7.00

Abundant raspberry fruit in the nose with nice sweet oak in support. Medium-full bodied. The wine enters the mouth smooth and round, with the rich fruit, oak, and mild tannins in perfect balance. The Zins from this winery have been consistently good over the years. Enjoy with savory foods. Fine value.

☆☆ ½ **Frog's Leap, 1985 Napa Valley** $8.50

Very appealing ripe berry fruit and sweet oak in the nose. Medium-full bodied. The generous fruit flavors are nicely complemented with sweet oak and ample tannins, in a good structure. Try with well-seasoned beef or lamb dishes.

Grgich Hills Cellar, 1984 Alexander Valley

 $10.00

Assertive ripe berry fruit aroma, with chocolaty overtones. Medium-full bodied. Rich, plummy fruit flavors fill the mouth, with soft tannins, in a balanced presentation. This is a big Zinfandel. Try with blackened red snapper, duck ragout with polenta, or roast lamb with garlic sauce.

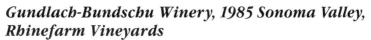 ### Gundlach-Bundschu Winery, 1985 Sonoma Valley, Rhinefarm Vineyards

 $8.00

Forward ripe berry fruit in the nose, with weedy overtones. Full bodied. Loads of rich fruit on the palate, with a briary dimension, and ample rich oak. High alcohol (13.6%) does not intrude. This is a big Zinfandel that will go well with spicy foods. Good value.

Haywood Winery, 1985 Sonoma Valley

 $9.50

Medium-intense cherry fruit aromas, with herbal scents. Medium bodied. Moderate cherry flavor on the palate, enriched by vanillin oak, in a clean presentation. This is a pleasant wine for early consumption with moderately seasoned meat dishes.

Hop Kiln Winery, 1984 Russian River Valley

 $8.50

Pleasant berry fruit in the nose, with a full oaky dimension in support. Medium bodied. The fruit and oak flavors are nicely balanced in the mouth with light tannins. A touch of spice in the lingering finish. Enjoy this fine wine with savory dishes.

Hop Kiln Winery Primitivo, 1985 Russian River Valley

 $12.00

A big, powerful wine. Deep purple color. Intense, complex aromas of raspberries, black cherries, peppery spice, and oak. Full bodied. Loads of ripe, concentrated fruit flavors fill the mouth, with ample oak and tannin, in a harmonious combination. High alcohol (14.5%) does not intrude. A remarkable wine that needs time for further development. Improvement will continue for at least ten years. Enjoy beginning in 1994. Excellent value.

Karly, 1984 Amador County

 $7.50

Moderately intense ripe berry fruit and oak in the nose, with earthy overtones. Medium-full bodied. The wine is supple in the mouth, with medium intense grape flavors, and an earthy element throughout. Slightly astringent finish. Best with spicy foods.

Kendall-Jackson Vineyards, 1986 Mendocino County, Ciapusci Vineyard *$10.00*

Attractive, medium-intense ripe berry fruit aromas, with floral and spicy scents, and oaky overtones. Medium bodied. Appealing berry flavors on the palate, with oak in balance, and soft tannins. Enjoy with roast veal or sautéed chicken.

 Kendall-Jackson Vineyards, 1984 Mendocino County, Du Pratt-De Patie Vineyard *$12.00*

Beautiful, ripe cherry fruit and sweet oak in the nose. Medium bodied. Moderately concentrated soft fruit in the mouth, perfectly balanced with modest tannins. The wine is exceptionally well made. Enjoy with veal roast or sautéed chicken.

 Kendall-Jackson Vineyards, 1986 Mendocino County, Mariah Vineyard *$10.00*

Dark ruby color. Pleasant aromas of spicy fruit, herbs, and toasty oak, with smoky overtones. Medium-full bodied. Moderate lean berry fruit in the mouth, with oak in balance. Tart finish. Try with moderately seasoned beef or lamb dishes.

 Kendall-Jackson Vineyards, 1986 Mendocino County, Pacini and Lolonis Vineyards *$8.00*

Pleasant cherry fruit and toasty oak in the nose, with herbal overtones. Medium bodied. Moderate fruit flavors on the palate, with oak and tannins in balance, in a good structure. Tart finish. Try with beef or lamb dishes.

 Kenwood Vineyards, 1985 Sonoma Valley *$9.00*

Attractive ripe berry fruit aromas, with spicy and briary nuances, and nice oak in support. Medium-full bodied. Loads of rich fruit on the palate, ample oak, and moderate tannins. A well-balanced Zinfandel that is currently delicious, and can be enjoyed for years to come. Best with spicy dishes. Good value.

 Kenwood Vineyards, 1984 Sonoma Valley *$8.50*

Enticing, forward raspberry and sweet oak aromas, with spicy herbal and peppery scents as an added attraction. Medium-full bodied. Generous clean berry fruit fills the mouth, with nice cedary nuances, in a refined presentation. I have had this Zin a number of times and never tire of it. Just enjoy! Fine value.

 La Jota Vineyard, 1984 Howell Mountain, Napa Valley *$10.00*

Attractive spicy, jammy raspberry fruit aromas, with briary, spicy, and oaky overtones. Medium-full bodied. Generous, complex fruit flavors in the mouth, with a fair tannic/oaky dimension. Finishes a bit rough. This wine needs time. Give it a couple of years to smooth out, then enjoy with beef or lamb dishes.

Lytton Springs Winery, 1985 Sonoma County **$9.00**

Beautiful raspberry fruit and expansive oak in the nose, with nice orange peel and spicy scents. Full bodied. The rich flavors in the mouth follow consistently from the aromas. This is a big, ripe, delicious Zinfandel, very similar to their previous bottling. Enjoy with highly spiced meat dishes. Good value.

 Mark West Vineyards, 1985 Sonoma County, Robert Rue Vineyard **$12.00**

Attractive, medium-intense ripe berry fruit aromas, with spicy oak in support. Medium-full bodied. Deep fruit impression on the palate, with ample acid and oak, and moderate tannins, in a good structure. Finishes a bit rough. Try with well-seasoned meat dishes.

 Mark West Vineyards, 1984 Sonoma County, Robert Rue Vineyard **$14.00**

Dark ruby color. Intense herbal-scented ripe fruit aromas, with briary and peppery overtones, and a full oak dimension. Full bodied. Loads of mature fruit flavors, balanced with powerful oak. This is a big wine from old vines. Give this wine several years to soften, then enjoy with hearty meals.

 Louis M. Martini Winery, 1985 North Coast **$6.00**

Nice ruby-purple color. Appealing medium-intense aromas of raspberries, chocolate, and mint. Medium bodied. Nice spicy fruit on the palate, in perfect balance with oak and tannins. A very tasty wine. Excellent with moderately seasoned red meats. Good value.

 Louis M. Martini Winery, 1984 North Coast **$6.00**

Moderate aromas of cherries and raspberries, with a nice touch of vanillin oak in the background. Medium-full bodied. Medium-intense cherry fruit flavors on the palate, in a smooth, nicely balanced presentation. Fine for current consumption and for several years to come with moderately seasoned meat dishes. Good value.

 Meeker Vineyard, 1985 Dry Creek Valley **$8.00**

Appealing, medium-intense, clean, ripe berry fruit in the nose, with nice oak in support. Medium bodied. Generous ripe fruit and oak flavors fill the mouth, with tannins under control, in a good structure. Try as an accompaniment to roast lamb with garlic sauce. Good value.

Meeker Vineyard, 1984 Dry Creek Valley **$7.00**

Nicely focused berry, spice, and oak in the nose. Medium-full bodied. Abundant extracted fruit flavors fill the mouth, with ample oak and tannin, in a firm structure. This fine wine will improve for at least five more years. Enjoy with beef or lamb dishes. Good value.

 Monteviña Winemaker's Choice, 1984 Shenandoah Valley **$9.00**

Restrained aromas of ripe raspberries and mint, balanced with oak. Medium-full bodied. Deep fruit impression on the palate, with ample tannins. Astringent finish. Give this wine a couple of years to smooth out, then enjoy with savory dishes.

 Nalle Winery, 1986 Dry Creek Valley **$9.00**

Intense, youthful raspberry fruit in the nose, with cranberry and spicy scents, supported by nice vanillin oak. Medium-full bodied. Supple on the palate, with the tasty raspberry and blackberry fruit flavors dominant throughout, in a good structure. Long, fruity finish. Just enjoy. Good value.

 Nalle Winery, 1985 Dry Creek Valley **$8.00**

Attractive rich, ripe raspberry fruit and oak aromas. Medium bodied. Generous cherry fruit flavors on the palate, with oak and tannin in balance. This is a very appealing wine for current consumption. Enjoy with a wide range of moderately seasoned meat dishes. Good value.

 Parducci Wine Cellars, 1986 Mendocino County **$5.50**

Moderate aromas of blackberry fruit, with spicy and cedary scents. Medium bodied. Appealing blackberry flavors on the palate, in a soft structure. A fine wine for current consumption with light foods.

 J. Pedroncelli Winery, 1984 Sonoma County, Dry Creek Valley **$5.50**

Very attractive plummy, sweet fruit in the nose, with a nice touch of oak. Medium-full bodied. Generous ripe fruit in the mouth, enhanced by sweet oak, with mild tannins, in a smooth structure. Best with moderately seasoned meat dishes. Good value.

 Joseph Phelps Vineyards, 1985 Alexander Valley **$10.00**

Attractive cherry, minty, and chocolaty aromas, with earthy tones, and ample oak in support. Medium-full bodied. Plummy fruit on the palate, with herbal nuances, and modest tannins, in a soft structure. Lingering aftertaste. Fine with moderately seasoned meats.

Preston Vineyards, 1985 Dry Creek Valley *$8.00*

Medium-intense berry fruit in the nose, with spicy, briary, and oaky scents. Medium bodied. Moderately rich fruit on the palate, enhanced by nice oak, with moderate tannins, in a good structure. Slightly coarse finish. Try with chicken cacciatore, duck ragout with polenta, or lamb kabobs. Good value.

 Quivira Vineyards, 1986 Dry Creek Valley *$9.00*

Most appealing ripe raspberry aromas, with peppery tones, and sweet oak in the background. Medium bodied. Deep impression on the palate, with raspberry fruit and sweet oak flavors in nice balance with soft tannins. High alcohol (13.5%) does not intrude. This is a superior claret-style Zin. Good value. Just enjoy.

 Quivira Vineyards, 1985 Dry Creek Valley *$8.00*

Medium-intense ripe berry fruit aromas, with herbal and earthy scents, framed in oak. Medium-full bodied. Rich fruit on the palate, with ample oak and tannins. High alcohol (13.5%) does not intrude. Try this excellent wine as an accompaniment to duck ragout with polenta or cioppino. Good value.

 A. Rafanelli Winery, 1986 Dry Creek Valley *$8.00*

This is a superior wine by any standard. Loads of beautifully focused berry fruit fill the nose—and it lingers, pleasantly. Medium-full bodied. The nose follows through to the palate. Plenty of bright fruit, in a balanced presentation. Will continue to develop for several more years. Try as an accompaniment to chicken breasts with oregano, basil, and red peppers. Super value.

 A. Rafanelli Winery, 1985 Dry Creek Valley *$7.00*

Appealing ripe blackberry fruit aromas, with briary and toasty oak tones. Medium-full bodied. Very ripe fruit flavors on the palate, with a substantial oak dimension in balance. This wine will improve for several years. Best with well seasoned beef or lamb dishes. Good value.

 Ravenswood, 1985 Napa Valley, Dickenson Vineyard *$10.50*

Forward aromas of berrylike fruit, spice, and oak, with smoky tones. Medium-full bodied. Deep impression on the palate, with the generous ripe fruit supported by ample tannins. A bit rough in the finish. This is an excellent wine that needs a few years to smooth out. Enjoy with spicy dishes.

Ravenswood, 1985 Sonoma County **_$9.00_**

Dark ruby color, with a purple tinge. Intense, rich fruit, herbs, and spice in the nose, nicely supported by creamy oak. Full bodied. Loads of well-extracted fruit on the palate, with ample tannin for good structure. This is a very tasty, big, brawny Zin. Fine for current consumption with highly spiced foods, and will improve for at least another five years. Good value.

 Ravenswood Limited Edition, 1985 Sonoma Valley, Old Hill Vineyard **_$12.00_**

A superior wine, and a worthy successor to the equally outstanding 1984 bottling. Beautiful blackberry fruit aromas, with herbal and creamy oak components in perfect balance. Medium-full bodied. Loads of rich fruit flavors fill the mouth, with ample oak in support. Long, pleasant finish. A great wine. It will pay handsome dividends if allowed to develop several years before being consumed. Enjoy. Good value.

 Ravenswood Vintners Blend, 1985 Napa Valley **_$5.00_**

Rich, ripe berry fruit in the nose, with briary, cedary, and melony scents, and a touch of sweet oak. Medium bodied. Nice raspberry fruit flavors in the mouth, with a spicy/oaky dimension. Finishes slightly astringent. Fine with spicy foods. Good value.

 Ravenswood Vintners Blend, 1986 Sonoma/Napa, 50% Sonoma County, 50% Napa County **_$5.50_**

Medium ruby color. Very appealing. Medium-intense cherry fruit in the nose, with herbal and chocolaty scents. Medium-full bodied. Round feel in the mouth, with the herbal fruit in nice balance with light tannins. Excellent with barbecued meats or pasta in a red sauce. Fine value.

 Richardson Vineyards, 1985 Sonoma Valley **_$8.50_**

Medium-intense cherrylike fruit aromas, nicely supported by toasty oak. Medium-full bodied. Rich fruit flavors on the palate, with oak and tannin in balance. A flavorful Zinfandel from old vines. Enjoy this fine wine with a wide range of well-seasoned meats.

 Ridge Vineyards, 1985 Howell Mountain, Beatty, Park-Muscatine, and Stout Vineyards **_$9.00_**

Ripe berry fruit and toasty oak in the nose, with spicy and earthy tones. Medium bodied. Dense, well-ripened fruit on the palate, with briary nuances, and moderate tannins. Slightly coarse finish. Enjoy with well-seasoned meat dishes.

Ridge Vineyards, 1984 Howell Mountain, Beatty, Park-Muscatine, and Stout Vineyards $9.00

Rich, intense raspberry fruit, spice, and oak in the nose. Medium-full bodied. Complex berry fruit flavors in the mouth, with peppery nuances, and a nice dimension of oak, in a well-defined presentation. Smooth finish. Enjoy this superior wine with well-seasoned meat dishes. Good value.

  Ridge Vineyards, 1985 Napa County, York Creek Vineyards $10.50

Intense ripe currant aromas, with briary scents, all framed in nice tangy oak. Medium-full bodied. Generous blackberry fruit on the palate, with ample oak and tannin. A substantial Zin that is drinkable now, and will improve for a number of years. Enjoy with savory dishes.

  Ridge Vineyards, 1984 Napa County, York Creek Vineyards $10.50

Beautiful, intense blackberry fruit in the nose, with briary, spicy, and herbal tones, and an ample oaky dimension. Medium-full bodied. The wine is big and rich in the mouth, with a nice spicy element, ample oak, and tannins under control. This is a superior wine by any standard, and will improve for at least five more years. Enjoy!

  Ridge Vineyards, 1984 Paso Robles, Dusi Ranch $8.00

Pleasant, medium intense berry fruit aromas, with black pepper, earthy, and oaky overtones. Medium-full bodied. Generous fruit in the mouth, with noticeable tannins. Give this wine a year or so to smooth out, then enjoy with spicy foods.

  Ridge Vineyards, 1985 Sonoma County, Geyserville Vineyards $12.00

Dark ruby color, with purple tinges. Ripe berry fruit in the nose, with herbal scents, and nice roasty oak in support. Medium full bodied. Supple on entry, with the ripe blackberry fruit flavors in balance with oak and tannins, in a good structure. Best with spicy dishes.

  Ridge Vineyards, 1985 Sonoma County, Lytton Springs Vineyard $9.00

Forward ripe berries in the nose, with ample vanillin oak in support. Generous tasty fruit on the palate, with spicy nuances, and creamy oak in perfect balance. Very pleasant, lingering aftertaste. Good aging potential. Try with marinated lamb kabobs or barbecued chicken. Good value.

⯨⯨ ½   *Riverside Farm Winery, 1984 Sonoma County* $4.00

Forward ripe fruit in the nose, with earthy scents, and nice oak in support. Medium-full bodied. Loads of rich fruit in the mouth, with mild tannins. Long, pleasant finish. Try with pasta in a red sauce. Super value.

⯨⯨ ½   *Rosenblum Cellars, 1985 Napa Valley* $8.50

Attractive, deep berry fruit, spice, and sweet oak in the nose. Medium bodied. The wine enters the mouth full and round, with sweet oak and tannin in nice balance. Lingering Zin aftertaste. Enjoy with well-seasoned meat dishes.

⯨⯨ ½   *Rosenblum Cellars, 1985 Sonoma Valley, Cullinan Vineyard* $8.50

Rich blackberry fruit in the nose, with herbal, spicy, and oaky overtones. Medium bodied. Generous peppery fruit in the mouth, with considerable tannin. Astringent finish. Give this wine a year or so to smooth out, then enjoy with blackened red snapper or spicy barbecued chicken.

⯨⯨   *Round Hill Vineyards, 1985 Napa Valley* $5.50

Medium-intense aromas of oak, spice, and berry fruit. Medium bodied. Moderately deep fruit on the palate, with ample oak, in a tight structure. Good aging potential. Best with beef or lamb dishes. Good value.

⯨⯨   *Round Hill Vineyards, 1984 Napa Valley* $5.00

Appealing aromas of very ripe fruit, with peppery overtones. Medium-full bodied. Mature plum and blackberry fruit flavors fill the mouth. High alcohol (14.1%) does not intrude. This is a big Zinfandel, with late-harvest characteristics. Best with highly spiced meats. Good value.

⯨⯨ ½   *Rustridge Vineyards, 1986 Napa Valley* $8.25

Nice dark ruby color. Appealing sweet cherry fruit in the nose, with minty tones. Medium bodied. Supple on entry, with the generous cherry fruit, oak, and tannins in perfect balance. Very enjoyable for current consumption, and will improve for several years. Try with chicken cacciatore or duck ragout with polenta.

⯨⯨⯨   *Rustridge Vineyards, 1985 Napa Valley* $7.50

Most attractive dark ruby color. Has nice sparkle. Loads of very ripe raspberry and plum aromas, with peppery tones. Medium-full bodied. Deep fruit impression on the palate, with the rich fruit flavors nicely complemented with briary, cedary, and tannic elements, in a good structure. Long, fruity finish. An excellent Zin that will improve for at least five more years. Just enjoy. Fine value.

Rutherford Ranch Vineyards, 1985 Napa Valley — $7.75

½ ★★

Very appealing, intense raspberry fruit and creamy oak in the nose. Full bodied. Loads of dense, ripe Zin flavors on the palate, with plenty of tannins in support. Good aging potential. This is a big wine that requires highly spiced foods. Good value.

Rutherford Ranch Vineyards, 1984 Napa Valley — $6.25

★★

Medium-intense aromas of cherries and sweet oak. Medium-full bodied. Deep fruit impression on the palate, with ample acid, and a fair tannic dimension. Coarse finish. Give this wine a couple of years to smooth out, then enjoy with spicy dishes.

Santa Barbara Winery, 1985 Santa Ynez Valley — $6.50

★

Fresh, simple berry aromas, with spicy and oaky scents. Medium bodied. Moderate cherry fruit flavors. Finishes with a slight tannic stiffness. Best with a light luncheon fare.

Sausal Winery, 1984 Alexander Valley — $6.50

★★ ½

Forward ripe fruit and attractive oak in the nose. Medium-full bodied. Round and full on entry, with the fleshy fruit in balance with mild tannins. Try with barbecued chicken or baked lasagna. Good value.

Sausal Winery, 1983 Alexander Valley — $5.75

★★★

Beautiful ripe raspberry aromas, with a nice briary dimension, and oaky overtones. Medium bodied. Loads of rich, jammy fruit fill the mouth, with sufficient acid for good structure. Try this superior wine with marinated lamb kabobs, duck ragout with polenta, or blackened red snapper. Super value.

Sbarboro Winery, 1984 Sonoma County — $10.00

★★ ½

Appealing, moderately intense berrylike fruit aromas, with a nice oaky dimension. Medium bodied. The wine enters the mouth smooth and round, with the generous tasty fruit nicely balanced with oak and tannin. A slight astringency in the finish. The wine is very pleasant now, and will improve for a few years. Try with chicken cacciatore or duck ragout with polenta.

Sea Ridge Winery, 1985 Sonoma Coast, Porter-Bass Vineyards — $9.75

★★

Clear. Light ruby color. Ripe raspberry aromas, with spicy overtones. Medium bodied. Generous ripe fruit flavors on the palate, with spicy and briary nuances, and good oak for structure. Long, pleasant finish. Best with well-seasoned meat dishes.

☆ ☆ ½   *Sea Ridge Winery, Cazadero Late Harvest,*   *$9.75*
             1984 Sonoma County   *375 ml.*

Very dark red-inky color. Lots of raisiny fruit in the nose, with woody tones. Medium-full bodied. Weighty, sweetish fruit fills the mouth, in a smooth presentation. Pleasant, lingering finish. Has special appeal for Port lovers. Just enjoy.

☆   *Stevenot Winery, 1984 Calaveras County*   *$6.00*

Moderate berry fruit aromas. Medium-light body. Modest fruit flavors on the palate, in a soft structure. Best served slightly chilled as a quaff, or at a picnic.

☆ ☆ ½   *Storybook Mountain Vineyards, 1985 Napa Valley*   *$10.00*

Intense blackberry fruit, spice, and oak in the nose. Medium-full bodied. The fruit sits firm and deep on the palate, with ample acid and a full dimension of tannin. Astringent finish.
Cellar until 1994, then enjoy with spicy meats.

☆ ☆ ½   *Sutter Home Reserve, 1984 Amador County*   *$8.00*

This is a big wine, similar to the popular style of the early 1970s. Loads of ripe fruit in the nose. Full bodied. Rich and deep on the palate, with high alcohol (15.0%) and substantial tannins. Requires highly spiced foods. Good value.

☆   *Sutter Home Winery, 1985 California*   *$4.00*

Attractive cherry fruit and oaky aromas. Medium-full bodied. The appealing young fruit on the palate is nicely balanced with sweet oak and mild tannins. Try with fowl or veal dishes.
Good value.

P I N O T   N O I R

 Acacia Winery, 1985 Napa Valley—Carneros **_$12.00_**

Light ruby color. Moderate aromas of cherry fruit, spice, and sweet oak, with weedy and peppery tones. Medium-light bodied. Supple on entry, with the moderately intense fruit flavors in nice balance with the oak and tannins. Pleasant fruity finish. Best with delicately seasoned meat dishes.

 Acacia Winery, 1984 Napa Valley—Carneros **_$11.00_**

Moderate cherry aromas, with herbal and smoky scents. Medium bodied. Generous ripe fruit in the mouth, with toasty oak and tannins in balance. This is a fine wine for early consumption with moderately seasoned beef or lamb dishes.

 Acacia Winery, 1985 Napa Valley—Carneros, Lund Vineyard **_$16.00_**

Nicely focused cherry fruit in the nose, with herbal and earthy tones, and sweet oak in support. Medium-full bodied. Generous ripe fruit on the palate, with a herbaceous element through the finish, in a good structure. Best with well-seasoned meat dishes.

 Acacia Winery, 1984 Napa Valley—Carneros, Lund Vineyard **_$15.00_**

Moderately intense cherry fruit aromas, with earthy scents, nicely supported by spicy oak. Medium-full bodied. The wine is supple upon entry, with the well-defined varietal fruit balanced with ample oak and low tannins. The wine is very accessible now, and will improve for a number of years. Try as an accompaniment to grilled quail with mushrooms or hickory-smoked grilled salmon.

 Acacia Winery, 1985 Napa Valley—Carneros, Madonna Vineyard **_$16.00_**

Pleasant, medium-intense fresh cherry fruit aromas, with spicy and herbal tones and rich oak in full support. Medium bodied. Moderate fruit flavors on the palate, with herbal elements through the finish, in a good structure. Fine with fowl or veal dishes.

 Acacia Winery, 1984 Napa Valley—Carneros, Madonna Vineyard **_$15.00_**

Forward cherry aromas, with earthy scents and ample oak. Medium bodied. The wine is supple in the mouth, with moderate cherry fruit and a musty element underlying the fruit. The wine will hold for several years. Best with well-seasoned meat dishes.

***

Acacia Winery, 1985 Napa Valley—Carneros, St. Clair Vineyard

 $16.00

Attractive, forward ripe fruit, smoky spice, and sweet oak in the nose, with earthy tones. Medium-full bodied. Generous ripe cherry flavors on the palate, with earthy, oaky, and spicy nuances, and moderate tannins, in good balance. Lingering finish. It is a nicely focused wine that can be enjoyed now or can be held for a number of years. A fine accompaniment to duck breast with currants or stuffed breast of veal.

 ***

Acacia Winery, 1984 Napa Valley—Carneros, St. Clair Vineyard

 $15.00

Lovely aromas of ripe cherries, with orange peel scents, and nice spicy oak in support. Medium-full bodied. This is a well-proportioned wine, with the ripe cherry fruit and floral nuances nicely balanced with oak and moderate tannins. This excellent wine will improve for a number of years. A fine accompaniment to duck breast with currants, stuffed breast of veal, or lamb stuffed with goat cheese and herbs.

☆

Adams Vineyard, 1984 Yamhill County, Oregon

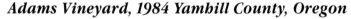 $12.00

Medium-intense cherry fruit in the nose, with minty and earthy tones. Medium bodied. Moderate cherry fruit flavors on the palate, with good acid, in a clean presentation. Sweet fruit aftertaste. Fine with fowl, veal, or light meals.

 **

Adelsheim Vineyard, 1985 Oregon, 62% Adelsheim Vineyard

 $16.00

Dark ruby color. Appealing, medium-intense cherry/currant fruit aromas, with herbal tones, nicely supported by sweet oak. Generous fruit on the palate, with ample tannins for aging. Best with well-seasoned beef or lamb dishes.

 ☆

Adelsheim Vineyard, 1984 Yamhill County, Oregon

$10.50

Medium-intense ripe fruit aromas, with herbal and minty scents, and a touch of sweet oak. Medium bodied. Lean cherry fruit flavors on the palate, with an ample oak dimension, and light tannins. Finishes slightly harsh. I liked the 1983 bottling more; however, this wine is fine for early consumption with veal, fowl, or light meats.

 **½

Alexander Valley Vineyards, 1984 Alexander Valley

 $8.00

Appealing aromas of rich, ripe fruit, with herbal, cedary, and chocolaty overtones. Medium-full bodied. Lush, deep fruit impression on the palate, with ample oak, fully enhanced by acid and tannin in balance. Nice potential for improvement in the next few years. A great wine with savory foods. Good value.

☆☆   ***Alexander Valley Vineyards, Wetzel Family Estate, 1985 Alexander Valley*** $7.00

Dark ruby color. Forward ripe curranty fruit in the nose, with earthy, weedy, and tarry tones, and ample oak in support. Medium-full bodied. Very ripe fruit on the palate, with tarry and earthy elements through the finish. Finishes a bit hot. Best with spicy dishes.

☆☆ ½   ***Amity Vineyards, 1985 Willamette Valley, Oregon*** $20.00

Dark garnet color. Appealing cherry fruit and mint in the nose, with herbal and vanillin tones. Medium bodied. Nice curranty and spicy flavors on the palate, with tannins in balance. Slightly astringent finish. Try with veal Oscar or sautéed guinea hen.

☆☆ ½   ***Amity Vineyards, Winemakers Reserve, 1983 Oregon*** $30.00

Dark ruby color. Intense, very ripe cherry fruit aromas, with nutty tones. Medium-full bodied. Weighty, mature fruit on the palate, with a briary dimension, and ample tannin. Good structure. Try with beef or lamb dishes.

☆☆   ***Beaulieu Reserve, 1986 Los Carneros—Napa Valley*** $11.00

Light ruby color. Appealing, medium-intense cherry fruit aromas, with spicy tones. Medium bodied. Nice young fruit flavor in the mouth, with an interesting herbal dimension. A fine wine for early consumption with fowl or veal dishes.

☆☆   ***Beaulieu Reserve, 1985 Los Carneros—Napa Valley*** $9.50

Nice cherry aromas, joined by sweet oak. Medium bodied. The moderately deep cherry fruit and oak flavors are in good balance, in a smooth presentation. Lingering aftertaste. Try as an accompaniment to duck breast with currants.

☆☆   ***Beaulieu Reserve, 1984 Los Carneros—Napa Valley*** $9.00

Attractive, delicate aromas of ripe currants and spice, with floral scents. Medium bodied. The wine enters the mouth smooth and round, with the bright cherry fruit flavors in nice harmony with the light oak and tannins. A fine wine for early consumption with moderately seasoned meats.

☆   ***Beaulieu Vineyard Beaumont, 1985 Napa Valley*** $6.50

Forward ripe cherry fruit and sweet oak in the nose. Medium bodied. Moderately intense ripe cherry fruit sits firmly on the palate, in a somewhat austere presentation. Finishes slightly hot. Best with beef or lamb dishes.

☆☆   ### Beringer Vineyards, 1984 Sonoma Valley   **$6.00**

Forward aromas of ripe cherry fruit and sweet oak, with herbal and earthy tones. Medium bodied. Supple on entry, with the ripe fruit and oaky flavors in balance, and an ample tannic dimension. Finishes slightly astringent. Best with beef or lamb dishes. Good value.

☆☆   ### Bethel Heights Vineyard, 1986 Willamette Valley, Oregon   **$15.00**

Brick-garnet color. Very mature cherry fruit aromas, with spice, currant, and bell pepper tones. Medium bodied. Lots of ripe, spicy fruit on the palate, with oak and tannin in balance. Enjoy with well-seasoned meat dishes.

☆☆☆   ### Bethel Heights Vineyard, 1985 Willamette Valley, Oregon   **$15.00**

Beautiful aromas of sweet cherry fruit, with vanillin and bacony overtones. Medium bodied. Rich, sweet fruit fills the mouth, with nice floral nuances. This is an easy-drinking wine with good character. Try as an accompaniment to roast turkey with a pine nut and rice dressing or tenderloin of beef with herbs.

☆☆☆   ### Bonny Doon Vineyard, 1985 Oregon, Bethel Heights Vineyard   **$16.00**

Abundant ripe black cherry fruit in the nose, with earthy and herbal tones. Medium-full bodied. Deep fruit impression on the palate, with the rich fruit flavors, spicy oak, and tannins in balance, in a good structure. This wine will improve for a number of years. Try as an accompaniment to game-marinated rabbit with wild mushrooms.

☆☆   ### Bouchaine, 1985 Los Carneros   **$7.50**

Medium-intense black cherry aromas, with some earthy scents. Medium bodied. Moderate cherry flavors, with tannins in balance. A pleasant wine that will go well with poultry or veal dishes. Good value.

☆☆   ### Bouchaine, 1984 Napa Valley   **$7.50**

Light ruby color. Moderate cherrylike aromas, with floral scents. Medium bodied. Medium-intense cherry and plum flavors, with low tannin. This is a well-made wine, best for early consumption with moderately seasoned meats. Good value.

☆☆   ### Broadley Vineyards Reserve, 1986 Oregon   **$12.00**

Dark garnet-brick color. Moderately intense cherry and currant aromas, with herbal scents. Medium-full bodied. Deep fruit impression on the palate, with the spicy fruit in balance with oak and tannins. Slightly astringent finish. Best with well-seasoned meat dishes.

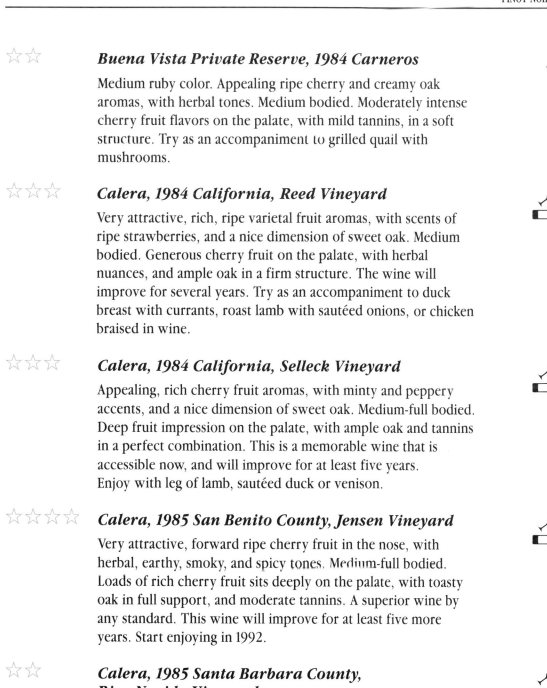

☆☆   ***Buena Vista Private Reserve, 1984 Carneros*** $14.50

Medium ruby color. Appealing ripe cherry and creamy oak aromas, with herbal tones. Medium bodied. Moderately intense cherry fruit flavors on the palate, with mild tannins, in a soft structure. Try as an accompaniment to grilled quail with mushrooms.

☆☆☆   ***Calera, 1984 California, Reed Vineyard*** $23.00

Very attractive, rich, ripe varietal fruit aromas, with scents of ripe strawberries, and a nice dimension of sweet oak. Medium bodied. Generous cherry fruit on the palate, with herbal nuances, and ample oak in a firm structure. The wine will improve for several years. Try as an accompaniment to duck breast with currants, roast lamb with sautéed onions, or chicken braised in wine.

☆☆☆   ***Calera, 1984 California, Selleck Vineyard*** $25.00

Appealing, rich cherry fruit aromas, with minty and peppery accents, and a nice dimension of sweet oak. Medium-full bodied. Deep fruit impression on the palate, with ample oak and tannins in a perfect combination. This is a memorable wine that is accessible now, and will improve for at least five years. Enjoy with leg of lamb, sautéed duck or venison.

☆☆☆☆   ***Calera, 1985 San Benito County, Jensen Vineyard*** $25.00

Very attractive, forward ripe cherry fruit in the nose, with herbal, earthy, smoky, and spicy tones. Medium-full bodied. Loads of rich cherry fruit sits deeply on the palate, with toasty oak in full support, and moderate tannins. A superior wine by any standard. This wine will improve for at least five more years. Start enjoying in 1992.

☆☆   ***Calera, 1985 Santa Barbara County, Bien Nacido Vineyards*** $14.00

Moderately intense cherry fruit in the nose, joined by herbal and piny scents. Medium bodied. Generous fruit in the mouth, with ample oak, and an herbal dimension that carries through the finish. Best with well-seasoned meat dishes.

☆☆☆   ***Carneros Alliance, 1985 Carneros*** $25.00

Intense aromas of spice, oak, and smoke in the nose, joined by scents of ripe cherries, juniper, and chocolate. Medium-full bodied. Generous cherry/berry fruit flavors on the palate, with ample tannins. Astringent finish. This wine will improve for at least five more years. Best with savory dishes.

Carneros Creek Winery, 1985 Los Carneros   *$13.00*

Forward ripe cherry aromas, with spicy scents. Nicely supported by sweet oak. Medium-full bodied. Loads of fleshy fruit fill the mouth, with attractive oak and spice in support, and well-proportioned tannins, in a clean presentation. Pleasant finish. This tasty wine will improve for a number of years. Enjoy with venison, leg of lamb, braised veal, or sautéed duck.

 Carneros Creek Winery, 1984 Los Carneros   *$15.00*

Restrained aromas of fresh, sweet varietal fruit, with modest oaky overtones. Medium bodied. The wine enters the mouth soft and round, with the fruit and minimal tannins in nice balance. This is an easy wine to drink. Best with moderately seasoned meats.

 Caymus Special Selection, 1984 Napa Valley   *$12.50*

Dark ruby color. Loads of rich, ripe cherry aromas, with spicy, smoky, and oaky tones in full support. Medium-full bodied. Deep and full on the palate, with the concentrated fruit flavors balanced with ample oak, and medium tannins. An excellent wine that will improve for at least five more years. Enjoy with leg of lamb, venison, roast veal, or chicken braised in wine.

 Caymus Special Selection, 1983 Napa Valley   *$12.50*

Rich cherry fruit aromas with mint, tobacco, and cinnamon in a complex mixture, plus a full measure of creamy oak. Medium-full bodied. Loads of cherry and cassis flavors fill the mouth, with plenty of tannin for aging. Give the wine a couple of years to smooth out and improve, then enjoy on that special occasion with savory dishes.

 Chalone Vineyard, 1984 Chalone   *$18.50*

Medium-intense spicy and earthy aromas, joined by scents of ripe fruit and tobacco. Medium-full bodied. Generous spicy fruit on the palate, with ample oak, and a full tannic dimension. Astringent finish. Best with spicy meat dishes.

 Chalone Vineyard, 1983 Chalone   *$18.00*

Moderately intense ripe varietal fruit aromas, supported by a complex array of scents including spice, herbs, smoke, and oak. Medium-full bodied. Rich fruit flavors fill the mouth, with ample oak and a fair dimension of tannins for aging. This wine will improve for well over five years. Enjoy with medallions of beef, braised guinea hen, leg of lamb, or Camembert.

☆   ***Chateau Ste. Michelle, 1985 Washington*** $9.00

Medium-intense cherry fruit aromas, with earthy scents. Medium bodied. Appealing cherry fruit on the palate, with moderate oak and tannins, in a soft presentation. Fine with fowl or veal dishes.

☆☆½   ***Clos du Bois, 1985 Sonoma County*** $10.50

Very appealing sweet cherry fruit aromas, with mild oak in support. Medium-full bodied. Round and full in the mouth, with the ripe cherry and sweet oak flavors in nice balance. Mild tannins. Try as an accompaniment to warm duck salad with peppers or roast pork.

☆☆   ***Clos du Val, 1985 Napa Valley*** $12.00

Clean, nicely focused cherry fruit in the nose, with spicy and herbal notes, and creamy oak in support. Medium bodied. Generous young cherry fruit and oak in balance, in a good structure. Enjoy with moderately seasoned meat dishes.

☆☆   ***Clos du Val, 1984 Napa Valley*** $11.50

Medium-intense spicy oak in the nose, joined by ripe cherry and herbal scents. Medium bodied. Moderate fruit flavors on the palate, with ample oak and considerable tannins. Astringent finish. Best with well-seasoned meat dishes.

☆☆½   ***Congress Springs Vineyards, 1985 Santa Clara County*** $12.00

Attractive floral and cherrylike aromas, with earthy overtones. Medium bodied. Moderately deep black cherry flavors on the palate, with light acid and tannins. A very enjoyable wine to drink now, it will gain additional appeal with a couple of years of aging. Try with duck breasts or roast lamb.

☆☆½   ***De Loach Vineyards, 1984 Russian River Valley*** $12.00

Moderately deep, ripe cherries and oak in the nose, with earthy scents. Medium-full bodied. Abundant rich fruit and oak flavors fill the mouth, with a full tannic dimension. Slightly bitter finish. Best with highly spiced dishes.

☆☆½   ***Dehlinger Winery, 1985 Russian River Valley*** $12.00

Intense ripe fruit and spicy oak aromas, with herbal and earthy scents. Medium-full bodied. Loads of rich fruit flavors fill the mouth, joined by abundant spicy oak and moderate tannins. Will improve for at least five more years. Try as an accompaniment to roast lamb with sautéed onions or tenderloin of beef and herbs.

Dehlinger Winery, 1984 Russian River Valley   **$11.00**

This wine has most attractive aromas of ripe black cherries, with nice scents of herbs and tobacco, supported by sweet oak. Medium-full bodied. Loads of ripe fruit fill the mouth, with ample oak flavors and light acid and tannins. This is simply a delicious Pinot Noir that will improve for several years. Just enjoy!

 Edna Valley Vineyard, 1984 Edna Valley   **$10.00**

Ruby-brick color. Forward ripe blackberry fruit aromas, with floral, spicy, and earthy scents. Medium bodied. Rich varietal fruit on the palate, with smoky and herbal nuances, and nice toasty oak. Moderate tannins. Enjoy with well-seasoned meat dishes. Good value.

 Elk Cove Vineyards, 1985 Willamette Valley, Oregon   **$15.00**

Bright. Tea-ruby color. Medium-intense cherry and currant aromas, with spicy and mushroomy scents. Medium-light bodied. Moderately intense curranty and figgy flavors on the palate, balanced with mild oak and tannins. A fine wine for early consumption with light meats.

 Etude, 1985 Napa Valley   **$12.00**

Beautiful, deep, ripe berry fruit and sweet oak aromas, with spicy scents. Medium-full bodied. Velvety feel in the mouth, with the rich, jammy fruit flavors nicely balanced with sweet oak. Pleasant, lingering aftertaste. Try this excellent wine with beef Bourguignon or lamb stuffed with herbs. Good value.

 Etude, 1984 Napa Valley   **$12.00**

Very nice sweet cherry and strawberry fruit aromas, with creamy oak in full support. Medium bodied. The wine enters the mouth smooth and supple, with the rich cherry fruit in nice balance with the oak flavors and acid. Low tannins. Fine as an accompaniment to grilled quail with mushrooms or beef Bourguignon.

 The Eyrie Vineyards, 1985 Willamette Valley, Yamhill County, Oregon   **$21.00**

Clear. Nice ruby color. Refined cherry, currant, and spicy aromas. Medium bodied. The flavors of currants, spice, and mint are in perfect balance with moderate oak. Smooth finish. Classic style. Try with seetbreads, veal piccata, or duck breast with currants.

☆☆ ½   ***Gary Farrell, 1985 Russian River Valley***   **$12.00**

Appealing cherry fruit aromas, with earthy scents, and nice toasty oak in support. Medium bodied. Moderately deep plumlike fruit on the palate, with a mushroomy element, and abundant oak through the finish. Best with beef or lamb dishes.

☆☆☆   ***Gary Farrell, 1984 Russian River Valley***   **$12.00**

Intense ripe blackberry fruit aromas, with strong scents of oak and herbs. Medium-full bodied. Rich, fleshy fruit flavors fill the mouth, with ample spice and oak, in a firm structure. The finish is slightly astringent. This is a great wine that will improve for at least five years. Just enjoy! Good value.

☆☆ ½   ***Gary Farrell, 1985 Sonoma County, Howard Allen Vineyard***   **$15.00**

Medium ruby color. Moderately intense aromas of cherry fruit, spice, herbs, and oak. Medium bodied. Generous cherry fruit flavors on the palate, with strong, earthy nuances, and ample oak, in a good structure. Try as an accompaniment to lamb stuffed with goat cheese and herbs.

☆☆ ½   ***Fetzer Special Reserve, 1985 Mendocino County, C. Barra Vineyard***   **$14.00**

Very appealing blackberry fruit aromas, with floral scents, and rich oak in support. Medium-full bodied. Generous fruit and oak flavors sit deeply on the palate, in a firm structure. Finishes a bit rough. Allow this wine several years of further development, then enjoy with well-seasoned meat dishes.

☆☆   ***Fetzer Special Reserve, 1984 Mendocino County, Decesare Vineyard***   **$14.00**

Forward ripe fruit and smoky tones in the nose. Medium-full bodied. Appealing cherry fruit and oak flavors on entry, following into a tart finish. Best served with spicy dishes.

☆☆   ***Gundlach-Bundschu Winery, 1985 Sonoma Valley, Rhinefarm Vineyards***   **$10.00**

Medium-intense ripe cherries and oak in the nose, with smoky tones. Medium-full bodied. Loads of rich fruit fill the mouth, with ample oak in support, and moderate tannins. Try with roast leg of lamb.

☆☆   ***Hanzell Vineyards, 1985 Sonoma Valley***   **$17.00**

Medium-intense smoky and earthy aromas, joined by scents of ripe fruit. Medium-full bodied. Moderate cherry fruit on the palate, with a full dimension of tannins throughout. Astringent finish. Best with highly spiced dishes.

★★ ½ ***Kistler Vineyards, 1985 California, Dutton Ranch***   *$13.50*

Intense ripe black cherry aromas, joined by cassis and herbal scents. Medium-full bodied. Generous cherry fruit flavors on the palate, with herbal nuances, and ample tannins. Astringent finish. Best with well-seasoned beef or lamb dishes.

★★ ½ ***Kistler Vineyards, 1984 California, Dutton Ranch***   *$16.00*

Appealing spicy Pinot Noir aromas, with herbal and cedary overtones. Medium bodied. Generous cherry fruit flavors on the palate, with ample oak, and a tart finish. Give this fine wine a couple of years to smooth out, then enjoy with well-seasoned meat dishes.

★★ ½ ***Charles Krug Winery, 1985 Napa Valley—Carneros***   *$6.50*

Nice sweetish cherry fruit in the nose, with herbal nuances, and a touch of oak. Medium bodied. The wine enters the mouth supple, with the sweetish fruit and oak flavors in perfect balance with tannins, in a smooth presentation. Excellent for early consumption, and will improve for several years. Enjoy with sweetbreads, veal cutlets, or linguine and clams. Excellent value.

★★ ***La Crema, 1985 California***   *$11.00*

Loads of ripe cherry fruit in the nose, with sweet oak in support. Medium-full bodied. Abundant fleshy fruit fills the mouth, which is nicely balanced with oak. Finishes slightly hot. Best with spicy foods.

★★ ***La Crema, 1984 California***   *$10.00*

Moderately intense ripe cherry aromas, with spicy and earthy scents. Medium bodied. Generous fruit in the mouth, with toasty oak and light tannins. A fine wine for early consumption with moderately seasoned meat dishes.

★★ ½ ***La Crema Reserve, 1985 California***   *$17.50*

Abundant deep oak in the nose, joined by ripe blackberry fruit, with herbal, smoky, and briary scents. Medium-full bodied. Loads of ripe fruit flavors fill the mouth, matched with a long oak dimension. Finishes a bit coarse. Try with breast of veal or rack of lamb.

★★ ***Mark West Vineyards, 1984 Russian River Valley, Ellis Vineyard***   *$10.00*

Forward, concentrated fruit in the nose, with ample spicy and oaky scents. Medium bodied. Generous cherry fruit flavors in the mouth, with a full dimension of oak and tannins. Enjoy with beef or lamb dishes.

Louis M. Martini Winery, 1986 Napa Valley

$7.00

Clear. Light ruby color. Medium-intense aromas of currants, mint, and sweet oak. Medium bodied. Moderately intense currant and mint flavors on the palate, perfectly balanced with oak and mild tannins. Smooth finish. Fine with moderately seasoned poultry or veal dishes. Good value.

Louis M. Martini Winery, 1984 Napa Valley

$6.00

Pleasant, medium-intense cherry fruit aromas, with floral scents. Medium-light bodied. Moderate fruit flavors on the palate, with mild tannins. Long finish. A very appealing wine that can be served with light luncheon dishes. Good value.

Louis M. Martini Winery, 1983 Napa Valley

$6.00

Pleasant, moderately intense cherry fruit aromas, with oaky overtones that follow consistently into the flavors. Medium bodied. The wine is supple in the mouth, with a nice touch of oak and light tannins. Fine with fowl or veal dishes. Good value.

Robert Mondavi Reserve, 1983 Napa Valley

$19.00

Intense aromas of ripe cherries, with herbal scents, and toasty oak in support. Medium-full bodied. Deep fruit impression on the palate, with the ripe fruit flavors in balance with ample oak and tannins, in a good structure. This excellent wine will improve for a number of years. Try with crown roast of lamb, wild boar, or breast of veal.

Robert Mondavi Winery, 1984 Napa Valley

$8.25

Nicely focused varietal fruit in the nose, joined by delicate oak. Medium bodied. Supple on entry, with the medium-intense ripe fruit and oak flavors in perfect balance with mild tannins. A fine wine to be enjoyed now with veal piccata or roast pork. Good value.

Mount Eden Vineyards, 1984 Santa Cruz Mountains

$20.00

Intense black cherry fruit and toasty oak aromas, with scents of coffee and smoke. Medium-full bodied. The fruit is dense and full in the mouth, with ample oak and medium tannins, in a firm structure. Slightly bitter finish. This is a superior wine that needs time to develop further. Starting in 1993, enjoy with well-seasoned beef or lamb dishes.

Parducci Wine Cellars, 1985 Mendocino County

$6.00

Appealing, fresh, sweet cherry and strawberry fruit aromas. Medium bodied. Supple on entry, with the young, zesty fruit nicely balanced with modest tannins. Enjoy this fine wine with light luncheon foods. Good value.

Qupe, 1984 Santa Barbara, Sierra Madre Vineyards $8.50

Attractive cherry fruit aromas, with strong herbal and oaky overtones. Medium bodied. Fairly rich, with a long herbal dimension, and nice oak. Moderate tannins. The wine will improve for several years. Enjoy with beef or lamb dishes. Good value.

Rex Hill, 1985 Oregon, Dundee Hills Vineyards $20.00

Bright. Brick-garnet color. Intense, ripe cherryfruit in the nose, with earthy tones. Medium-full bodied. Loads of mature cherry fruit flavors on the palate, with minty nuances, and ample oak, in a good structure. Has some power. Best with savory dishes.

Rex Hill, 1985 Oregon, Maresh Vineyards $20.00

Deep ruby color. Ripe cherry and currant aromas, with briary scents. Medium-full bodied. Lots of ripe, almost raisiny fruit on the palate, with a woody dimension, and moderate tannins. Slightly harsh finish. Best with well-seasoned meat dishes.

Richardson Vineyards, 1986 Sonoma Valley, Sangiacomo Vineyards $12.00

Very attractive, intense floral, spicy, and herbal aromas. Medium bodied. Generous, clean fruit on the palate, with spicy and toasty nuances. Fine for current consumption, and will improve for a few years. Try as an accompaniment to duck breast with currants.

J. Rochioli Vineyards, 1984 Russian River Valley $12.00

Appealing cherry fruit in the nose, with herbal and earthy scents, and nice oak in support. Medium bodied. Generous fruit in the mouth, with an astringent dimension that carries through the finish. Will improve for a number of years. Try with roast lamb and sautéed onions.

Rodney Strong, 1984 Russian River Valley, River East Vineyard $8.00

Light ruby color. Medium-intense cherry fruit aromas, with hints of herbs and bacon. Medium bodied. Soft in the mouth, with the moderate herbal fruit flavors in balance with oak and mild tannins. This is an easy-drinking wine that will go well with lightly seasoned poultry or veal dishes.

Roudon-Smith Vineyards, 1985 Santa Cruz Mountains $15.00

Medium-intense cherry fruit and sweet oak aromas. Medium bodied. Moderate fruit flavors in the mouth, with tannins in balance. Best with fowl or veal dishes.

Saintsbury, 1986 Carneros

$14.00

Very appealing, medium-intense aromas of cherry and raspberry, with nice scents of chocolate and oak. Medium bodied. Soft and round in the mouth, with a nice depth of clean cherry fruit. Most enjoyable now, and will age well for a few years. Try this superior wine with grilled quail and mushrooms, veal roast, or sweetbreads.

Saintsbury, 1985 Carneros

$13.00

Very attractive cherry-raspberry aromas, with nice herbal scents. Medium bodied. The wine enters the mouth clean and supple, with the cherry fruit dominating. This is a lovely wine for early consumption. Suggest duck breast with currants or sweetbreads.

Sanford Winery, 1985 Santa Barbara County

$11.00

Medium-intense cherry fruit aromas, with spicy tones. Medium bodied. Silky feel in the mouth, with the moderate fruit in good balance with the oak. Slightly tart in the finish. Best with fowl or veal dishes.

Sea Ridge Winery, 1983 Sonoma County

$11.50

Light ruby color, with amber edges. Medium-intense aromas of currants and spice. Medium bodied. Generous spicy fruit on the palate, with tannins in balance. Try with sweetbreads or roast duck.

Sebastiani Black Beauty, 1985 Sonoma County

$6.00

Moderate cherry and sweet oak in the nose. Medium bodied. Supple on entry, with the fruit and mild tannins in balance. Fine with poultry or veal dishes.

Seghesio Winery, 1984 Sonoma/Mendocino

$5.50

Medium-intense cherry fruit in the nose, with oaky tones. Medium bodied. Moderate fruit flavors on the palate, in nice balance with oak and tannins. Best with fowl or veal dishes. Good value.

Robert Stemmler Winery, 1985 Sonoma County

$18.00

Attractive, intense cherry fruit and sweet oak in the nose, with spicy and earthy scents. Medium-full bodied. Deep fruit impression on the palate, with the generous fruit flavors, oak, and tannins in good balance. This is a substantial wine that will go well with highly seasoned meat dishes.

Trefethen Vineyards, 1984 Napa Valley

$9.25

Medium-intense ripe, plummy fruit in the nose, with earthy tones. Medium-full bodied. Quite intense oaky fruit in the mouth, with smoky nuances, and a fair tannic dimension. Astringent finish. Best with spicy meat dishes.

Tualatin Vineyards Private Reserve, 1985 Willamette Valley, Oregon

$13.00

Fresh, lively cherries and sweet oak in the nose. Medium bodied. The cherry flavors are clean and nicely focused, with a nice touch of oak. Ample acidity gives the wine good structure. Try as an accompaniment to grilled quail with a cassis glaze or grilled veal chops with mushrooms.

Williams Selyem, 1986 Sonoma County

$16.00

Forward earthy, weedy, and spicy aromas. Medium bodied. The wine is supple on entry, with the generous rich varietal fruit flavors filling the mouth through the finish. This is not a typical Pinot Noir. Best with savory dishes.

Williams Selyem, 1985 Sonoma County

$12.50

Ruby-brick color. Forward cherry fruit in the nose, supported by spicy, smoky, and herbal scents. Medium-full bodied. Lush plummy fruit in the mouth, with earthy nuances. This is a big Pinot Noir. Best with well-seasoned meat dishes.

Zaca Mesa American Reserve, 1984 Santa Barbara County

$12.75

Ruby-brick color. Slightly spicy fruit aromas, with herbal and earthy scents. Medium-full bodied. Lots of heavy fruit flavors fill the mouth, carrying through the finish. This wine has depth, and is best with highly spiced foods.

ZD, 1983 Napa Valley

$12.50

Very appealing cherry fruit aromas, with a nice dimension of creamy oak in support. Medium bodied. Generous fleshy fruit on the palate, with coconut nuances, and ample oak. Fruity finish. Try with beef Bourguignon or roast lamb with sautéed onions.

M E R L O T

Acacia Winery, 1984 Napa Valley $15.00

Attractive ripe fruit and herbal aromas, with green olive and oaky scents. Medium bodied. Rich fruit flavors in the mouth, with moderate acidity and tannins. A very fine wine for current consumption, and will improve for a couple of years. Goes well with grilled veal chops or grilled quail.

Alexander Valley Vineyards, Wetzel Family Selection, 1985 Alexander Valley $11.00

Appealing ripe fruit aromas, with briary scents. Medium-full bodied. Rich curranty fruit flavors on the palate, with ample oak and tannin. Slightly harsh finish. Enjoy with roast leg of lamb or grilled veal chops with wild mushrooms.

Carneros Creek Winery, 1985 Napa Valley $12.00

Moderately intense aromas of black cherries, clove, and tobacco. Medium-full bodied. Rich cherry fruit on the palate, with woody nuances. Somewhat rough finish. Will improve for several years. Enjoy with well-seasoned meat dishes.

Carneros Creek Winery, 1984 Napa Valley $10.50

Forward black currant and cherry aromas, with herbal and briary tones. Medium-full bodied. Generous fleshy fruit on the palate, with earthy nuances, and ample oak. Try with rack of lamb or roast beef au jus.

Chateau Chevre Reserve, 1984 Napa Valley $15.00

Aggressive cherry fruit aromas, with chocolaty, briary, and earthy scents. Medium bodied. Expansive fruit flavors on the palate, with earthy nuances, and medium tannins. This wine will improve for several years. Enjoy with beef or lamb dishes.

Chateau Ste. Michelle, Chateau Reserve, 1983 River Ridge Vineyards, Washington $15.00

Dark ruby color. Intense aromas of ripe cherries and raspberries, with herbal scents. Medium-full bodied. Loads of jammy fruit fill the mouth, with spicy and chocolaty nuances, and sufficient acid for structure. This is a great wine that will improve for at least another five years. Try as an accompaniment to grilled quail with a cassis glaze.

Chateau Souverain, 1984 Sonoma County $8.00

Medium-intense cherry fruit in the nose, with smoky and herbal nuances, and a touch of oak. Medium bodied. Nicely textured fruit on the palate, with moderate tannins. A fine wine for early consumption with moderately seasoned meat dishes.

Chestnut Hill, 1985 North Coast

☆☆ $8.00

Moderately intense cherry fruit aromas, with spicy oak in support. Medium bodied. Somewhat deep fruit impression on the palate, with ample oak and light tannins. Will improve for a few years. Enjoy with roast duck or veal.

The Christian Brothers, 1985 Napa Valley

☆☆½ $9.00

Appealing, medium-intense ripe fruit aromas, with smoky overtones. Medium bodied. Soft on the palate, with the herbal fruit flavors, oak, and tannin in nice balance. A well-made wine that is enjoyable now, and will hold for several years. Best with moderately seasoned meat dishes.

Clos du Bois, 1986 Sonoma County

☆☆☆ $11.00

Appealing ripe cherry fruit aromas, with herbal and oaky tones. Medium-full bodied. Generous berry and herb flavors on the palate, perfectly balanced with vanillin oak and moderate tannins, in a smooth presentation. Continues the string of superior Merlots from this winery. Will improve for several more years. Enjoy.

Clos du Bois, 1985 Sonoma County

☆☆☆ $10.00

Attractive ruby color. Pleasant cherry aromas, with spicy scents. Medium-full bodied. Lively currant and spice flavors, perfectly balanced with oak and soft tannins, in an elegant presentation. Long finish. Enjoy this superior wine with sweetbreads, sautéed duck, saddle of veal, or rack of lamb. Good value.

Clos du Val, 1984 Napa Valley

☆☆ $15.00

Forward aromas of ripe fruit, joined by a full dimension of sweet oak. Medium-full bodied. Generous ripe fruit and oak in the mouth, with abundant tannin. Astringent finish. Best with well-seasoned beef or lamb dishes.

Conn Creek Limited Bottling, 1985 Napa Valley, Collins Vineyard

☆☆½ $14.00

Appealing ripe raspberry/cherry fruit aromas, with a nice touch of oak in support. Deep fruit impression on the palate, with oak and tannin in balance, in a firm structure. This excellent wine will improve for at least another five years. Try as an accompaniment to roast leg of lamb with herbs or grilled veal chops with wild mushrooms.

Covey Run Vineyards, 1984 Yakima Valley, Washington

 *$8.50*

Medium-intense aromas of cherries, with scents of tea and oak. Medium bodied. Moderately intense cherry fruit flavors on the palate, with herbal and oaky nuances, in a firm presentation. Slightly astringent finish. Best with fowl or light meats.

Cuvaison, 1985 Napa Valley

 *$19.00*

Attractive, somewhat restrained, nicely focused ripe varietal fruit aromas. Complexity develops with airing. Medium-full bodied. Loads of rich, ripe, tasty fruit flavors fill the mouth, with sufficient oak and tannin, in a good structure. A superior wine for current consumption, and will improve for several years. Try as an accompaniment to crown roast of lamb rubbed with herbs.

Cuvaison Anniversary Release, 1984 Napa Valley

 *$18.00*

Intense rich fruit in the nose, with herbal scents. Medium bodied. Expansive, ripe blackberry fruit flavors fill the mouth, and continues through the aftertaste. Slightly astringent finish. This is a substantial wine that will improve for at least five more years. Best with highly spiced meat dishes.

Dehlinger Winery, 1985 Sonoma County

 *$13.00*

Attractive ripe fruit and rich oak aromas, with herbal scents. Medium-full bodied. Deep fruit impression on the palate, with the generous fruit, oak, and tannin in perfect balance. Long, fruity finish, with a touch of astringency. Will improve for at least five years. Enjoy.

Dehlinger Winery, 1984 Sonoma County

$12.00

Appealing aromas of oak, cherry fruit, and herbs. Medium-full bodied. Soft and supple in the mouth, with the fruit flavors, oak, and tannin in balance, in a good structure. Fine with beef or lamb dishes.

Devlin Wine Cellars, 1984 Central Coast

$8.50

Appealing, moderately intense ripe fruit and sweet oak aromas, with herbal tones. Medium-full bodied. Supple in the mouth, with a good depth of varietal fruit, ample oak, and tannin in good balance. This wine is well made. Enjoy with beef and lamb dishes.

Dry Creek Vineyard, 1985 Dry Creek Valley

$10.00

Pleasant, medium-intense aromas of cherries, flowers, spice, and herbs. Medium bodied. Generous, soft fruit on the palate, with chocolaty nuances. A very attractive wine to consume now and for several more years. Enjoy with moderately seasoned beef or lamb dishes.

Duckhorn Vineyards, 1985 Napa Valley $16.00

Medium-intense, ripe, plummy fruit in the nose, with cedary and earthy scents. Medium-full bodied. Deep, juicy fruit on the palate, with ample oak and tannin, in a firm structure. Astringent finish. This is a tannic wine that needs time to develop further. Wait until 1994, then enjoy with highly seasoned meat dishes.

Duckhorn Vineyards, 1985 Napa Valley, Three Palms Vineyard $20.00

Assertive, youthful aromas of rich fruit, spice, and oak. Full bodied. Plenty of depth on the palate, with the ripe fruit and oak flavors in balance, and a full tannin dimension, in a firm structure. This is a big wine that needs time to develop. I have a few bottles at home that I have tagged for opening beginning in 1993. Be patient, and enjoy.

Duckhorn Vineyards, 1984 Napa Valley, Three Palms Vineyard $18.00

Another big winner! Deep, yet restrained, aromas of fresh fruit, rich oak, and spice. Medium bodied. The wine is round and supple on the palate, with the deep fruit and rich oak in perfect balance, with abundant tannins. This is a great wine, and you will be rewarded if you are patient. Give it several years to develop further, then enjoy.

Duckhorn Vineyards, 1985 Napa Valley, Vine Hill Vineyard $16.00

Attractive aromas of ripe plums, spice, and oak, with hints of violets and mint. Medium-full bodied. The ripe fruit sits firmly on the palate, nicely balanced with herbal and oaky flavors, in a good structure. The wine is accessible now, and will improve for several years. Enjoy with beef or lamb dishes. Very limited availability.

Fenestra Winery, 1984 Napa Valley $9.50

Forward rich berry aromas, with floral and herbal scents, and ample oak in support. Medium bodied. Generous ripe fruit in the mouth, in a soft texture. Nicely balanced. This is a rich wine that will go well with highly spiced dishes.

The Firestone Vineyard, 1985 Santa Ynez Valley $9.00

Clean, medium-intense cherry fruit aromas, with herbal scents. Medium bodied. Light cherry and oaky flavors on the palate, with a nice herbal dimension. Enjoy with moderately seasoned lamb or veal dishes.

The Firestone Vineyard, 1984 Santa Ynez Valley   *$9.00*

Medium-intense cherry, herbal, and oaky aromas. Medium
bodied. Moderate fruit on the palate, with modest tannins, in a
well-balanced presentation. Fine for early consumption with
fowl or light meats.

Flora Springs, 1985 Napa Valley   *$15.00*

Moderately intense cherry fruit in the nose, with herbal tones,
and a nice touch of spice. Medium-full bodied. Generous berry
fruit flavors on the palate, in a good structure. Slightly tart
finish. Try with warm duck salad and peppers.

Franciscan Vineyards, 1985 Napa Valley, Oakville Estate   *$9.25*

Appealing, medium-intense floral and earthy aromas. Medium
bodied. Generous herbal fruit flavors on the palate, with smoky
nuances, and oak/tannin in balance. Slightly tart finish. Enjoyable now and for the next few years. Best with savory dishes.

Franciscan Vineyards, 1984 Napa Valley, Oakville Estate   *$8.50*

Assertive ripe fruit aromas, with herbal scents, and ample oak in
support. Full bodied. Very generous rich, plummy fruit fills the
mouth, with ample oak and tannins. Astringent finish. This is a
heavy wine that requires matching with highly spiced foods.

Geyser Peak, 1984 Alexander Valley   *$7.00*

Produced by Trione Vineyards. Clean, moderate fruit aromas,
with herbal scents. Medium bodied. Soft on entry, with modest
fruit flavors, and a slight tannic bitterness in the finish. Fine with
fowl or veal.

Glen Ellen Proprietor's Reserve, 1984 California   *$6.00*

Attractive cherry, spicy, and herbal aromas. Medium bodied.
Somewhat rich, sweetish fruit on the palate, with a touch of oak,
in a pleasing presentation. Fine with fowl and light meats.
Good value.

Gundlach-Bundschu Winery, 1985 Sonoma Valley, Rhinefarm Vineyards   *$12.00*

Attractive rich, smoky, and herbal aromas. Medium-full bodied.
Deep, ripe fruit impression on the palate, with herbal nuances
and ample tannin, in a firm structure. Slightly bitter aftertaste.
Good aging potential. Give this wine a couple of years to
develop further, then enjoy with spicy dishes.

Gundlach-Bundschu Winery, 1984 Sonoma Valley, Rhinefarm Vineyards **$12.00**

Appealing rich, sweet cherry aromas, with herbal scents. Medium-full bodied. Generous ripe fruit flavors on the palate, with a good structure. High alcohol (13.7%) does not intrude. A nice wine for early consumption, and will improve for several years. Enjoy with well-seasoned meat dishes.

 Hogue Cellars, 1985 Washington **$12.00**

Forward cherry fruit and sweet oak aromas. Medium bodied. Very appealing young fruit flavors on the palate, with oak in balance, in a firm structure. A lively young red that will go well with pasta or veal dishes.

 Hogue Cellars Reserve, 1984 Washington **$15.00**

An abundance of creamy oak in the nose, joined by deep cherry fruit. Medium-full bodied. Generous deep fruit and oak flavors on the palate, with spicy nuances and good tannin, in a firm structure. This excellent wine is accessible now, and will improve for at least five additional years. Try with crown roast of lamb rubbed with herbs.

 Jaeger Cellar, 1983 Napa Valley, Inglewood Vineyard **$14.00**

Beautiful, rich aromas of flowers, spice, and berry fruit. Medium-full bodied. Generous cherry fruit flavors fill the mouth, with medium tannins, in a firm structure. Enjoyable now, and will improve for several years. Try as an accompaniment to grilled quail with cassis glaze.

 Robert Keenan Winery, 1985 Napa Valley **$18.00**

Appealing herbal-scented fruit in the nose, with earthy scents, and nice oak in the background. Medium-full bodied. Generous berry fruit in the mouth, with nice oak, and ample tannins. Tart finish. Enjoy with well-seasoned meat dishes.

 Robert Keenan Winery, 1984 Napa Valley **$16.50**

Forward aromas of cherries, currants, and sweet oak, with spicy scents. Medium-full bodied. Round and full on entry, with the ripe fruit, oak, and tannins in perfect balance, all in a firm structure. An elegant wine. A fine accompaniment to roast lamb with herbs.

 Lakespring Winery, 1985 Napa Valley **$12.00**

Moderately intense ripe currant aromas, with herbal and spicy scents. Medium bodied. Nicely textured herbal fruit flavors on the palate, with medium tannins. Slightly bitter in the finish. Fine with moderately seasoned beef or lamb dishes.

Lakespring Winery, 1984 Napa Valley

 $11.50

Very appealing cherry and sweet oak aromas. Medium-full bodied. Supple on entry, with the generous fruit, oak, and tannins in perfect balance. Accessible now, and will improve for several years. Try with grilled duck breasts.

Markham Vineyards, 1985 Napa Valley

$9.00

The nose opens wide with wonderful fruit aromas, joined by toasty oak tones throughout. Medium bodied. Generous cherry and blackberry fruit flavors fill the mouth, with spicy nuances, and just enough tannin for a firm structure. This is an exceptional wine. Just enjoy! Great value.

Markham Vineyards, 1984 Napa Valley

$10.00

Appealing cherry fruit aromas, with oaky overtones. Medium-full bodied. Concentrated currant and cherry flavors on the palate, with ample oak and tannins. Slightly rough finish. Give this fine wine a couple of years to smooth out, then enjoy with well-seasoned beef or lamb.

Louis M. Martini Vineyard Selection, 1984 Russian River Valley, Los Vinedos del Rio

$12.00

Appealing cherry fruit aromas, with hints of mint and oak. Medium-full bodied. The cherry fruit is firm and deep on the palate, with herbal nuances, and ample tannins, in a firm structure. Astringent finish. This wine will improve for several years. Try with saddle of veal, roast rabbit, country style pâté, or Fontina.

Louis M. Martini Winery, 1984 North Coast

$5.75

Pleasant, medium-intense cherry fruit aromas. Medium bodied. Round and supple on the palate, with the moderate fruit flavors in nice balance with soft tannins. This is a lighter-style wine for current consumption. Can be enjoyed with a wide range of moderately seasoned light meats. Good value.

Matanzas Creek Winery, 1985 Sonoma Valley

 $18.00

Attractive, rich, ripe berry, herbal, and spicy aromas. Medium bodied. Generous ripe fruit flavors on the palate, with nuances of herbs and tobacco, nicely balanced with tannins, in a firm structure. Lingering aftertaste. Try as an accompaniment to roast lamb rubbed with herbs.

Matanzas Creek Winery, 1984 Sonoma Valley — $14.50

Intense ripe cherry fruit in the nose, with hints of herbs and tobacco, and oaky tones throughout. Medium bodied. Supple on entry, with the ripe cherry fruit flavors in nice balance with oak, in a firm structure. Good aging potential. Try as an accompaniment to game marinated rabbit with wild mushrooms.

Monterey Peninsula Winery, Doctors' Reserve, 1984 Monterey County — $12.00

Beautiful aromas of ripe cherries and sweet oak. Medium-full bodied. Generous ripe fruit flavors fill the mouth, with ample oak and moderate tannins, in a firm structure. Enjoyable now, and will improve for several years. Fine as an accompaniment to roast lamb with pepper sauce.

Newton Vineyard, 1984 Napa Valley — $14.00

Appealing black currant aromas, with orange rind scents, and oaky tones in the background. Medium bodied. Supple on entry, with the ripe fruit and oak flavors in nice balance. Fruity finish. Try with warm duck salad and peppers.

Pagor, 1984 Santa Maria Valley — $9.00

Deep ruby color, with amber edges. Appealing ripe cherry fruit aromas, with figgy scents. Medium bodied. Lots of ripe raisiny fruit on the palate, in nice balance with oak and tannins. Fine with well-seasoned meat dishes.

Pine Ridge Selected Cuvée, 1984 Napa Valley — $13.00

Medium-intense ripe varietal fruit aromas, with briary and smoky tones, and ample oak throughout. Medium-full bodied. Generous ripe fruit on the palate, with herbal/weedy elements, and a fair tannic dimension. Astringent finish. Give this wine a couple of years to smooth out, then enjoy with savory foods.

Ravenswood, 1985 Sonoma County — $15.00

Plenty of rich, plummy fruit aromas, with nice sweet oak in support. Medium-full bodied. Loads of ripe fruit flavors on the palate, with oaky and chocolaty elements, and moderate tannins. This is a powerful wine that is best suited for savory dishes.

Ravenswood, 1984 Sonoma County — $12.00

Attractive, clean berry fruit, with minty scents. Medium-full bodied. Rich, ripe cherrylike flavors fill the mouth, with a moderate acid compound. Finishes a bit rough. Enjoy with pheasant or roast quail.

Round Hill Reserve, 1985 Napa Valley

$10.00

Pleasant, medium-intense ripe fruit in the nose, with earthy scents. Medium bodied. Moderate fruit flavors in the mouth, with oak and tannin in balance. Slightly tart finish. Enjoyable now, and will improve for a couple of years. Try with moderately seasoned meat dishes.

Round Hill Vineyards, 1984 Napa Valley

$9.00

Forward plummy fruit aromas, with smoky and weedy scents. Medium-full bodied. Round and full in the mouth, with the ripe cherry flavors in nice balance with oak and tannins. Slightly bitter in the finish. Good aging potential. Best with spicy foods.

Rutherford Hill Winery, 1984 Napa Valley

$10.50

Forward aromas of sweet oak, joined by nicely focused fruit, with herbal and earthy overtones. Medium-full bodied. Generous ripe fruit on the palate, balanced with ample toasty oak, and moderate tannins. Long, lingering finish. Enjoy with veal roast or leg of lamb.

Rutherford Hill Winery, 1983 Napa Valley

$10.50

Medium-intense ripe varietal fruit aromas, with nice spicy oak in support. Medium-full bodied. Round and full on the palate, with generous rich fruit flavors throughout. Finishes slightly coarse. A very fine wine for consumption in the next few years with spicy foods.

St. Clement Vineyards, 1983 Napa Valley

$14.50

Forward ripe fruit aromas, with chocolaty scents, fully supported by rich oak throughout. Medium-full bodied. Abundant ripe fruit flavors fill the mouth, with ample oak and tannins. Tart finish. This wine will improve for several years. Enjoy with crown roast of lamb or marinated rabbit.

St. Francis Reserve, 1984 Sonoma Valley

$16.00

Nicely focused fruit aromas, joined by a full dimension of sweet oak. Medium-full bodied. Deep fruit impression on the palate, with the generous fruit and ample oak flavors in nice balance, and considerable tannins through the finish. Give this fine wine several years to smooth out, then enjoy with pheasant or wild duck.

St. Francis Winery, 1985 Sonoma Valley

$12.00

Moderately intense ripe fruit aromas, with spicy, earthy, and oaky tones. Medium-full bodied. Loads of sweet fruit in the mouth. Enjoy this fine wine with braised rabbit, roast leg of lamb, or veal medallions.

St. Francis Winery, 1984 Sonoma Valley $12.00

Intense ripe fruit in the nose, with hints of bell peppers, spice, and tobacco, and a touch of oak. Medium-full bodied. Deep, mouth-filling flavors, with ample oak and tannin. Astringent finish. Give this wine several years to smooth out, then enjoy with saddle of veal or roast baby lamb.

Santa Cruz Mountain Vineyard, 1985 Central Coast $12.00

Forward aromas of cherry fruit, herbs, and oak. Medium-full bodied. The fruit flavors are firm on the palate, with spicy and chocolaty nuances, and a fair tannic dimension. Short, astringent finish. This wine needs several years to smooth out. Best with highly spiced foods.

Shafer Vineyards, 1985 Napa Valley $12.50

Appealing cherry fruit in the nose, with herbal and weedy scents. Medium bodied. Smooth and round in the mouth, with the rich fruit and oak in nice balance. A fine wine to consume now and for the next couple of years with moderately seasoned beef or lamb.

Silverado Vineyards, 1984 Napa Valley $12.50

Very appealing, well-focused cherry fruit aromas, with spicy and herbal scents, and nice oak in support. Medium bodied. Supple on entry, with the generous cherry fruit and oak flavors in balance, in a firm structure. Slightly astringent in the finish. Enjoy with beef or lamb dishes.

Stag's Leap Wine Cellars, 1985 Napa Valley $15.00

Medium-intense cherry fruit in the nose, with tealike and herbal scents, and nice clean oak in support. Medium bodied. Soft on the palate, with the textured fruit flavors and mild tannins in perfect balance. A very tasty wine that will go well with warm duck salad or veal chops with mushrooms.

Stag's Leap Wine Cellars, 1984 Napa Valley $15.00

Appealing floral, herbal, spicy, and smoky aromas. Medium bodied. Supple in the mouth, with the sweetish fruit flavors and soft tannins in balance. Fine for early consumption with chicken braised in wine or pork roast.

David S. Stare Reserve, 1983 Dry Creek Valley, 49% Merlot, 51% Cabernet Sauvignon $13.00

Produced by Dry Creek Vineyard. Moderately intense ripe fruit and rich oak aromas. Medium-full bodied. Loads of rich, ripe cherry fruit flavors fill the mouth, with ample sweet oak in support. High alcohol (14.2%) does not intrude. Enjoy this fine wine with savory dishes.

Sterling Vineyards, 1985 Napa Valley

$14.00

Attractive aromas of ripe cherries, spice, and tobacco, with nice oak throughout. Medium-full bodied. Generous fully ripened fruit flavors on the palate, with ample oak and tannin. Finishes slightly coarse. Give a couple of years to smooth out, then enjoy with savory dishes.

Sterling Vineyards, 1984 Napa Valley

$11.50

Moderately intense aromas of cherry fruit and vanillin oak, with herbal scents. Medium-full bodied. The soft cherry fruit is somewhat lean on the palate, with a fair tannic dimension. Slightly astringent finish. Fine for early consumption with hearty dishes.

Trentadue Winery, 1986 Alexander Valley

$11.00

Very dark ruby color. Intense aromas of blackberries, spice, chocolate, and cedar. Medium-full bodied. Loads of complex fruit flavors fill the mouth, with tannins in balance. High alcohol (13.7%) does not intrude. Needs time to reach an elegant level; say, five years. Just enjoy.

Vichon Winery, 1985 Napa Valley

$14.00

Intense aromas of ripe cherries, spice, and toasty oak. Medium-full bodied. Supple on entry, with the black cherry and sweet oak flavors in nice balance. Ample tannins bring an astringency to the finish. Give this wine a couple of years of to develop further, then enjoy with breast of veal or rack of lamb.

Waterbrook Winery, 1985 Washington

$10.00

Dark ruby color. Portlike aromas, with scents of anise and tobacco. Medium-full bodied. Intense black cherry fruit and spicy oak fill the mouth, with ample acid. Tart finish. Give this wine a couple of years to smooth out, then enjoy with spicy foods.

Waterbrook Winery, 1984 Washington

$13.00

Appealing, forward aromas of currants and blackberries, with briary and spicy scents. Medium-bodied. Generous ripe fruit flavors in the mouth, with a touch of astringency in the finish. A fine wine for early consumption with well-seasoned meat dishes.

Whitehall Lane Winery, 1984 Knights Valley

$14.00

Intense ripe varietal fruit in the nose, with chocolaty scents, and a nice dimension of spicy oak. Medium-full bodied. Loads of rich fruit flavors fill the mouth, with abundant oak and moderate tannins. The finish is slightly sharp. A relatively big wine that will improve for at least five more years. Best with savory dishes.

Bogle Vineyards, 1985 Clarksburg

$4.00

Very ripe berry aromas, with spicy and earthy nuances. Medium-full bodied. Enters the mouth soft, with a full dimension of jammy fruit. This wine should accompany spicy dishes. Good value.

Bonny Doon Vineyard Syrah, 1984 Paso Robles

$12.00

This is a winner! Intense aromas of raspberry and cherry fruit, supported by spicy and sweet oak scents. Medium-full bodied. An abundance of rich fruit fills the mouth, with added dimensions of pepper, herbs, and oak, in a smooth presentation. This is an exceptional wine for early consumption, and will improve for at least five years. Enjoy with the savory dish of your choice.

Concannon Vineyard, 1982 Livermore Valley

$8.00

Rich berry fruit in the nose, with piny wood scents. Medium bodied. Generous fruit on the palate, with a slightly bitter finish. Best with moderately seasoned meat dishes.

Fetzer Vineyards, 1985 Mendocino

$5.00

Nice aromas of blackberry fruit, cedar, and spice. Medium bodied. Deep cherry and plum flavors on the palate, with a pronounced peppery dimension. Long finish. Enjoy with highly seasoned meat dishes. Good value.

Louis J. Foppiano Winery, 1981 Russian River Valley

$7.00

Intense black cherry aromas, with ample spicy and oaky scents in support. Full bodied. Loads of rich fruit on the palate, with ample tannins. A bit coarse and astringent, but has enough fruit to improve for several years. Enjoy this excellent wine with beef or savory dishes. Good value.

Frey Vineyards Syrah, 1984 Mendocino, Butow Vineyards

$7.50

A young, dark, inky black wine, with dense ripe fruit in the nose. Full bodied. Loads of intense ripe fruit flavors fill the mouth, with ample rich oak in perfect balance. This is a great wine that is accessible now, and will improve for at least ten years. Enjoy with savory foods of your choice. Excellent value.

Frick Winery, 1983 Monterey County

$7.50

Intense grapy nose, with earthy nuances. Medium-full bodied. Concentrated, ripe fruit flavors in the mouth, with a tarry dimension. Best with well-seasoned meat dishes.

Granite Springs Winery, 1983 El Dorado, Granite Hill Vineyards **$7.00**

Intense, complex cherry, cedary, and spicy aromas. Full bodied. Deep fruit impression on the palate, with the cherry, black pepper, and vanillin characteristics in perfect balance. Try this superior wine with well-seasoned beef or lamb dishes. Excellent value.

 Guenoc Winery, 1983 Lake County **$5.50**

Attractive blackberry fruit in the nose, with smoky and oaky overtones. Medium-full bodied. Nice cherry fruit flavors on the palate, with oak in balance. Finishes a bit astringent. Try with standing rib of beef. Good value.

 McDowell Valley Vineyards Syrah, 1982 McDowell Valley **$10.00**

Intense ripe fruit in the nose, with complex smoky and oaky scents in support. Medium-full bodied. Deep, heavy fruit impression on the palate, with oak and tannins in balance. This wine is a favorite of mine. Enjoy this fine wine with spicy barbecued chicken or peppercorn steak.

 Palisades Vineyards, 1984 Napa Valley **$9.00**

Attractive purple-inky color. Powerful aromas of blueberries and plums, with spicy and earthy scents. Medium-full bodied. Lots of ripe raspberry fruit on the palate, with a nice dimension of clove, and ample tannins. A big wine with good aging potential. Best with highly seasoned foods. Good value.

 Parducci Wine Cellars, 1982 Mendocino County **$6.00**

Ripe fruit aromas in the nose, with earthy overtones. Medium-full bodied. The rich fruit flavors follow on the palate, with considerable tannins. The wine needs some time to smooth out. Try in a year or so with highly seasoned meat dishes. Good value.

 Parducci Wine Cellars, 1981 Mendocino County **$6.00**

Attractive, plummy, sweet grape aromas, with chocolaty and oaky scents. Medium-full bodied. Deep and ripe cherry flavors in the mouth, with nice oak and a fair tannin dimension. Try with spicy barbecued chicken.

 Joseph Phelps Vineyards Syrah, 1983 Napa Valley **$8.50**

Ripe blackberry fruit aromas, with a nice touch of pepper and oak. Medium bodied. The wine enters the mouth with a sense of rich, young fruit, followed by spicy elements and a fair tannic dimension. Astringent finish. A fine wine now, and will improve for a number of years. Enjoy this wine with well-seasoned meat dishes.

☆

Ridge Vineyards, 1983 Napa County, York Creek

$9.00

Moderately intense blackberry fruit in the nose, with oaky
scents. Medium bodied. The wine enters the mouth smooth and
round, with tannins under control. Finishes a bit short.
Best with beef or savory dishes.

☆☆☆

Rosenblum Cellars, 1984 Napa Valley, St. George Vineyard

$8.00

Very attractive blackberry fruit in the nose, with briary and
chocolaty tones in support. Medium bodied. Rich blackberry
fruit flavors fill the mouth, with a nice spicy/chocolaty
dimension. The wine is perfect for current consumption.
Try with savory foods of your choice. Good value.

☆

Roudon-Smith Vineyards, 1983 San Louis Obispo

$6.50

Soft, plummy aromas, with cedary and spicy tones. Medium
bodied. Moderately intense fruit on the palate, with oak and
tannin in balance. Fine with moderately seasoned meat dishes.

☆☆☆

Topolos, 1985 Sonoma County, Old Hill Ranch

$9.00

Beautiful, rich, deep blackberry fruit aromas, with ample oak in
support. Medium-full bodied. Loads of precise Petite Sirah
flavors in the mouth, with generous oak and tannin in perfect
balance. Drinkable now, and will improve for ten years.
Enjoy with savory foods of your choice. Good value.

☆☆☆

Trentadue Winery, 1985 Alexander Valley

$7.00

Purple-inky color. Appealing plummy fruit aromas, with smoky
tones. Medium-full bodied. Loads of spicy fruit flavors in the
mouth, with plenty of tannin for aging. A big wine that will
improve for years. Try with spicy barbecued chicken or lamb
shanks with garlic and herbs. Super value.

☆☆½

Zaca Mesa American Reserve Syrah, 1984 Santa Barbara County

$8.50

Deep cherrylike aromas, with strong earthy characteristics.
Medium-full bodied. Somewhat weighty grapy impression on the
palate, with light acid and a fair tannic dimension. Finishes a bit
rough. The wine will improve for a few years. Fine with spicy
barbecued chicken.

O T H E R   R E D   W I N E S

 ### Chateau Chevre, Cabernet Franc, 1985 Napa Valley **$16.00**

Pleasant berry fruit aromas, nicely framed in sweet oak. Medium-full bodied. Loads of clean raspberry fruit flavors fill the mouth, joined by sweet oak and tannins, in perfect balance. This fine wine will improve for at least five more years. Try with grilled quail in a cassis glaze.

 ### Chateau Chevre, Cabernet Franc, 1984 Napa Valley **$14.00**

Forward rich raspberry fruit in the nose, with spicy and earthy tones. Medium-full bodied. Generous, very ripe fruit flavors on the palate, with a full tannic dimension. Astringent finish. Good aging potential. Give this wine a couple of years to smooth out a bit, then enjoy with spicy dishes.

 ### Congress Springs Vineyards, Cabernet Franc, 1985 Santa Cruz Mountains **$18.00**

Intense aromas of ripe fruit and oak, with spicy and briary tones. Full bodied. Loads of heavy fruit flavors on the palate, with abundant oak and tannins. Harsh finish. Enjoy this very fine wine beginning in 1993 with well-seasoned meat dishes.

 ### Inglenook Reserve Cask, Cabernet Franc, 1983 Napa Valley **$18.50**

Very attractive aromas of sweet berries and oak, with hints of cocoa and herbs. Medium bodied. Moderately intense fruit flavors on the palate, with considerable tannins. Very astringent finish. Requires highly seasoned meat dishes.

Andrew Quady Elysium, Black Muscat, 1987 California **$11.00**

Very sweet (13% residual sugar). Intense, very pleasant roselike aromas that linger on and on. Lots of ripe raspberry fruit flavors fill the mouth, with ample acid, in a good structure. Try this superior wine as a complement to marzipan cake with berry sauce or blueberry pear tart. Good value.

 ### Trentadue Winery, Carignane, 1985 Alexander Valley **$6.50**

Striking bright appearance—almost fluorescent at edges, but very dark. Very ripe grapey, briary and spicy aromas. Medium-full bodied. Loads of rich, spicy fruit fills the mouth, with oak and tannin in balance. Long, fruity finish. Best with highly seasoned meat dishes. Great value.

W I N E R I E S

The following listing provides the mailing address and business office phone number for virtually all the wineries mentioned in the critiques.

C A L I F O R N I A

Acacia Winery
2750 Las Amigas Road
Napa, CA 94559
(707) 226-9991

Adler Fels
5325 Corrick Lane
Santa Rosa, CA 95405
(707) 539-3123

Ahlgren Vineyard
P.O. Box M
Boulder Creek, CA 95006
(408) 338-6071

Alderbrook Vineyards
2306 Magnolia Drive
Healdsburg, CA 95448
(707) 433-9154

Alexander Valley Vineyards
8644 Highway 128
Healdsburg, CA 95448
(707) 433-7209
(800) 248-8900 in CA

Almaden Vineyards
P.O. Box 99
Madera, CA 93639
(209) 673-7071

Amador Foothill Winery
12500 Steiner Road
Plymouth, CA 95669
(209) 245-6307

S. Anderson
1473 Yountville Crossroad
Napa, CA 94558
(707) 944-8642

Austin Cellars
P.O. Box 636
Los Olivos, CA 93441
(805) 688-9665
(800) 824-8584

Bargetto's Santa Cruz Winery
3535 North Main Street
Soquel, CA 95073
(408) 475-2258

Beaulieu Vineyard
1960 St. Helena Highway
Rutherford, CA 94573
(707) 963-1451

Bellerose Vineyard
435 West Dry Creek Road
Healdsburg, CA 95448
(707) 433-1637

Belvedere Winery
4035 Westside Road
Healdsburg, CA 95448
(707) 433-8236

Benziger
Glen Ellen Vineyards
1883 London Ranch Road
Glen Ellen, CA 95442
(707) 996-1066

Beringer Vineyards
P.O. Box 111
St. Helena, CA 94574
(707) 963-7115

Boeger Winery
1709 Carson Road
Placerville, CA 95667
(916) 622-8094

Bogle Vineyards
Route 1, Box 276
Clarksburg, CA 95612
(916) 744-1139

Bonny Doon Vineyard
P.O. Box 8381
Santa Cruz, CA 95061
(408) 425-3625

Bouchaine Vineyards
1075 Buchli Station Road
Napa, CA 94558
(707) 252-9065

Buehler Vineyards
820 Greenfield Road
St. Helena, CA 94574
(707) 963-2155

Buena Vista Winery and Vineyards
P.O. Box 182
Sonoma, CA 94576
(707) 938-8504

Burgess Cellars
P.O. Box 282
St. Helena, CA 94574
(707) 963-4766

Davis Bynum Winery
8075 Westside Road
Healdsburg, CA 95448
(707) 433-5852

Byron Vineyard
5230 Tepusquet Canyon Rd.
Santa Maria, CA 93454
(805) 937-7288

Cain Cellars
P.O. Box 509
St. Helena, CA 94574
(704) 963-1616
(800) 422-1111

Cakebread Cellars
P.O. Box 216
Rutherford, CA 94573
(707) 963-5221

Calera Wine Company
11300 Cienega Road
Hollister, CA 95023
(408) 637-9170

Callaway Vineyard
32720 Rancho California Rd.
Temecula, CA 92390
(714) 676-4001

J. Carey Vineyards
1711 Alamo Pintado Road
Solvang, CA 93463
(805) 688-8554

Carmenet Vineyard
101 Howard Street
San Francisco, CA 94105
(415) 546-7755

Carneros Creek Winery
1285 Dealy Lane
Napa, CA 94558
(707) 253-9463

Caymus Vineyards
P.O. Box 268
Rutherford, CA 94573
(707) 963-4204

Chalk Hill Winery
10300 Chalk Hill Road
Healdsburg, CA 95448
(707) 838-4306

Chalone
101 Howard Street
San Francisco, CA 94105
(415) 546-7755

Domaine Chandon
P.O. Box 2470
Yountville, CA 94599
(707) 944-8844

Chappellet Winery
1581 Sage Canyon Road
St. Helena, CA 94574
(707) 963-7136

Chateau Chevre Winery
2030 Hoffman Lane
Yountville, CA 94599
(707) 944-2184

Chateau Montelena Winery
1429 Tubbs Lane
Calistoga, CA 94515
(707) 942-5105

Chateau St. Jean
P.O. Box 293
Kenwood, CA 95452
(707) 833-4134

The Christian Brothers
P.O. Box 391
St. Helena, CA 94574
(707) 963-4480

Clos du Bois
Five Fitch Street
Healdsburg, CA 95448
(707) 433-5576

Clos du Val Wine Co.
5330 Silverado Trail
Napa, CA 94558
(707) 252-6711

Clos Pegase Winery
P.O. Box 305
Calistoga, CA 94515
(707) 942-4981

B. R. Cohn Winery
P.O. Box 1673
Sonoma, CA 95476
(707) 938-4064

Concannon Vineyards
4590 Tesla Road
Livermore, CA 94550
(415) 447-3760

Congress Springs Vineyards
23600 Congress Springs Road
Saratoga, CA 95070
(408) 867-1409

Conn Creek Winery
8711 Silverado Trail
St. Helena, CA 94574
(707) 963-9100/5133

R. J. Cook
P.O. Box 227
Clarksburg, CA 95612
(916) 775-1234

Corbett Canyon Vineyards
P.O. Box 3159
San Luis Obispo, CA 93403
(805) 544-5800

Cribari Winery
3223 East Church Avenue
Fresno, CA 93714
(209) 485-3080

Cronin Vineyards
11 Old La Honda Road
Woodside, CA 94062
(415) 851-1452

Cuvaison
P.O. Box 384
Napa, CA 94515
(707) 942-6266

De Loach Vineyards
1791 Olivet Road
Santa Rosa, CA 95401
(707) 526-9111

De Moor Winery
7481 St. Helena Highway
Oakville, CA 94562
(707) 944-2565

Deblinger Winery
6300 Guerneville Road
Sebastopol, CA 95472
(707) 823-2378

Devlin Wine Cellars
P.O. Box 728
Soquel, CA 95073
(408) 476-7288

Diamond Creek Vineyards
1500 Diamond Mountain Rd.
Calistoga, CA 94515
(707) 942-6926

Domaine Laurier Winery
P.O. Box 550
Forestville, CA 95436
(707) 887-2176

Domaine Michel
4155 Wine Creek Road
Healdsburg, CA 95448
(707) 433-7427

Domaine Mumm
8445 Silverado Trail
Rutherford, CA 94573
(707) 963-1133

Domaine St. George Winery
P.O. Box 548
Healdsburg, CA 95448
(707) 433-5508

Dry Creek Vineyard
P.O. Box T
Healdsburg, CA 95448
(707) 433-1000

Duckborn Vineyards
3027 Silverado Trail
St. Helena, CA 94574
(707) 963-7108

Dunn Vineyards
805 White Cottage Road
Angwin, CA 94508
(707) 965-3642

Durney Vineyard
P.O. Box 222016
Carmel, CA 93922
(408) 625-5433

Edmeades
5500 Highway 128
Philo, CA 95466
(707) 895-3232

Edna Valley Vineyard
101 Howard Street
San Francisco, CA 94105
(415) 546-7555

Ehlers Lane Winery
3222 Ehlers Lane
St. Helena, CA 94574
(707) 963-0144

Estancia
Franciscan Vineyards
P.O. Box 407
Rutherford, CA 94573
(707) 963-7111

Estate William Baccala
4611 Thomas Road at
Chalk Hill Road
Healdsburg, CA 95448
(707) 433-9463

Estrella River Winery
P.O. Box 96
Highway 46 East
Paso Robles, CA 93447-0096
(805) 238-6300

Far Niente Winery
P.O. Box 327
Oakville, CA 94562
(707) 944-2861

Fenestra Winery
14124 Buckner Drive
San Jose, CA 95127
(408) 258-1092

Ferrari-Carano Winery
P.O. Box 1549
Healdsburg, CA 95448
(707) 433-6700

Gloria Ferrer
Meadow Lark Lane at
Highway 121
Sonoma, CA 95476
(707) 996-6759

Fetzer Vineyards
P.O. Box 227
Redwood Valley, CA 95470
(707) 485-7634

Field Stone Winery
10075 Highway 128
Healdsburg, CA 95448
(707) 433-7266

Firestone Vineyard
P.O. Box 244
Los Olivos, CA 93441
(805) 688-3940

Fisher Vineyards
6200 St. Helena Road
Santa Rosa, CA 95404
(707) 539-7511

Flora Springs
1978 West Zinfandel Lane
St. Helena, CA 94574
(707) 963-5711

Thomas Fogarty Winery
5937 Alpine Road
Portola Valley, CA 94025
(415) 851-1946

Folie à Deux Vineyards
3070 St. Helena Highway
St. Helena, CA 94574
(707) 963-1160

Foppiano Winery
P.O. Box 606
Healdsburg, CA 95448
(707) 433-7272

Forman Vineyards
P.O. Box 343
St. Helena, CA 94574
(707) 963-0234

Franciscan Vineyards
P.O. Box 407
Rutherford, CA 94573
(707) 963-7111

Freemark Abbey
P.O. Box 410
St. Helena, CA 94574
(707) 963-9694

Frey Vineyards Ltd.
14000 Tomki Road
Redwood Valley, CA 95470
(707) 485-5177

Frick Winery
303 Potrero Street, #39
Santa Cruz, CA 95060
(408) 426-8623

Fritz Cellars
24691 Dutcher Creek Road
Cloverdale, CA 95425
(707) 894-3389

Frog's Leap Winery
3358 St. Helena Highway
St. Helena, CA 94574
(707) 963-4704

The Gainey Vineyard
P.O. Box 910
Santa Ynez, CA 93460
(805) 688-0558

Ernest & Julio Gallo Winery
P.O. Box 1130
Modesto, CA 95353
(209) 579-3111

Geyser Peak Winery
P.O. Box 25
Geyserville, CA 95441
(707) 433-6585

Girard Winery
P.O. Box 105
Oakville, CA 94562
(707) 944-8577

Glen Ellen Vineyards
1883 London Ranch Road
Glen Ellen, CA 95442
(707) 996-1066

Grace Family Vineyards
1210 Rockland Road
St. Helena, CA 94574
(707) 963-0808

Gran Val
Clos du Val Wine Co.
5330 Silverado Trail
Napa, CA 94558
(707) 252-6711

Grand Cru Vineyards
P.O. Box 789
Glen Ellen, CA 95442
(707) 996-8100

Granite Springs Winery
6060 Granite Springs Road
Somerset, CA 95684
(209) 245-6395

Grgich Hills Cellar
P.O. Box 450
Rutherford, CA 94573
(707) 963-2784

Groth Vineyards
P.O. Box 412
Oakville, CA 94562
(707) 255-7466

Guenoc Winery
P.O. Box 1146
Middletown, CA 95461
(707) 987-2385

Gundlach-Bundschu Winery
P.O. Box 1
Vineburg, CA 95487
(707) 938-5277

Hacienda Wine Cellars
P.O. Box 416
Sonoma, CA 95476
(707) 938-3220

Hafner
4280 Pine Flat Road
Healdsburg, CA 95448
(707) 433-4675

Hagafen Cellars
P.O. Box 3035
Napa, CA 94558
(707) 252-0781

Handley Cellars
P.O. Box 66
Philo, CA 95466
(707) 895-3876/2190

Hanna Winery
5345 Occidental Road
Santa Rosa, CA 95401
(707) 575-3330

Hanzell Vineyards
18596 Lomita Avenue
Sonoma, CA 95476
(707) 996-3860

Hawk Crest
Stag's Leap Wine Cellars
5766 Silverado Trail
Napa, CA 94558
(707) 944-2020

Haywood Winery
18701 Gehricke Road
Sonoma, CA 95476
(707) 996-4298

Heitz Wine Cellar
500 Taplin Road
St. Helena, CA 94574
(707) 963-3542

Hess Collection Winery
P.O. Box 4140
Napa, CA 94558
(707) 255-1144

William Hill Winery
P.O. Box 3989
Napa, CA 94558
(707) 224-6565

Louis Honig Cellars
P.O. Box 406
Rutherford, CA 94573
(707) 963-5618
(415) 921-8651

Hop Kiln Winery
6050 Westside Road
Healdsburg, CA 95448
(707) 433-6491

Husch Vineyards
4400 Highway 128
Philo, CA 95466
(707) 895-3216

Inglenook Vineyards
P.O. Box 402
Rutherford, CA 94573
(707) 967-3300

Innisfree
P.O. Box 1031
St. Helena, CA 94574
(707) 963-2745

Iron Horse Vineyards
9786 Ross Station Road
Sebastopol, CA 95472
(707) 887-1507

Jaeger Cellar
P.O. Box 322
St. Helena, CA 94574
(707) 963-1876

Jekel Vineyard
P.O. Box 336
Greenfield, CA 93927
(408) 674-5522

Jepson Vineyards
10400 South Highway 101
Ukiah, CA 95482
(707) 468-8936

Johnson-Turnbull Vineyards
P.O. Box 410
Oakville, CA 94562
(707) 963-5839

Jordan Vineyard
P.O. Box 878
Healdsburg, CA 95448
(707) 433-6955

Karly
P.O. Box 729
Plymouth, CA 95669
(209) 245-3922

Robert Keenan Winery
3660 Spring Mountain Road
St. Helena, CA 94574
(707) 963-9177

Kendall-Jackson Vineyards
700 Matthews Road
Lakeport, CA 95453
(707) 263-9333

Kathryn Kennedy Winery
13180 Pierce Road
Saratoga, CA 95070
(408) 867-4170

Kenwood Vineyards
P.O. Box 447
Sonoma Highway
Kenwood, CA 95452
(707) 833-5891

Kistler Vineyards
997 Madrone Road
Glen Ellen, CA 95442
(707) 996-5117

Konocti Winery
P.O. Box 890
Kelseyville, CA 95451
(707) 279-8861

F. Korbel & Bros.
13250 River Road
Guerneville, CA 95446
(707) 887-2294

Hanns Kornell Champagne Cellars
P.O. Box 249
St. Helena, CA 94574
(707) 963-2334

Charles Krug Winery
P.O. Box 191
St. Helena, CA 94574
(707) 963-2761

La Crema Vinera
P.O. Box 976
Petaluma, CA 94953
(707) 762-0393

Lakespring Winery
P.O. Box 2036
Yountville, CA 94599
(707) 944-2475

Lambert Bridge
4085 West Dry Creek Road
Healdsburg, CA 95448
(707) 433-5855
(800) 634-2680

Landmark Vineyards
9150 Los Amigos Road
Windsor, CA 95492
(707) 938-9708

Las Montanas
4400 Cavedale Road
Glen Ellen, CA 95442
(707) 996-2448

Laurel Glen Vineyard
P.O. Box 548
Glen Ellen, CA 95442
(707) 526-3914

Leeward Winery
2511 Victoria Avenue
Channel Islands Harbor
Oxnard, CA 93030
(805) 656-5054

J. Lohr Winery
1000 Lenzen Avenue
San Jose, CA 95126
(408) 288-5057

Lolonis Winery
3707 Mt. Diablo Boulevard
Lafayette, CA 94549
(415) 283-8066

Long Vineyards
P.O. Box 50
St. Helena, CA 94574
(707) 963-2496

Lyeth Vineyard
P.O. Box 558
Geyserville, CA 95441
(707) 857-3562

Lytton Springs Winery
650 Lytton Springs Road
Healdsburg, CA 95448
(707) 433-7721

Maison Deutz Winery
453 Deutz Drive
Arroyo Grande, CA 93420
(805) 481-1763

Mark West Vineyards
7000 Trenton-Healdsbrg. Rd.
Forestville, CA 95436
(707) 544-4813

Markham Winery
P.O. Box 636
St. Helena, CA 94574
(707) 963-5292

Louis M. Martini Winery
P.O. Box 112
St. Helena, CA 94574
(707) 963-2736

Masson Vineyards
P.O. Box 780
Gonzales, CA 93926
(408) 675-2481

Matanzas Creek Winery
P.O. Box 2555
Santa Rosa, CA 95404
(707) 528-6464

Mayacamas Vineyards
1155 Lokoya Road
Napa, CA 94558
(707) 224-4030

Mazzocco Vineyards
P.O. Box 49
Healdsburg, CA 95448
(707) 433-9035

McDowell Valley Vineyards
P.O. Box 449
Hopland, CA 95449
(707) 744-1053

The Meeker Vineyard
9711 West Dry Creek Road
Healdsburg, CA 95448
(707) 431-2148

Merlion Winery
P.O. Box 606
St. Helena, CA 94574
(707) 963-7100

Merryvale Vineyards
902 Main Street
St. Helena, CA 94574
(707) 963-2225

Milano Winery
14594 South 101
Hopland, CA 95449
(707) 744-1396

Mill Creek Vineyards
P.O. Box 758
Healdsburg, CA 95448
(707) 433-5098

Mirassou Vineyards
3000 Aborn Road
San Jose, CA 95135
(408) 274-4000

Robert Mondavi Winery
P.O. Box 106
Oakville, CA 94562
(707) 963-9611

R. Montali Winery
600 Addison Street at
Aquatic Park
Berkeley, CA 94710
(415) 540-5384

Monterey Peninsula Winery
467 Shasta Avenue
Sand City, CA 93955
(408) 394-2999

The Monterey Vineyard
P.O. Box 780
Gonzales, CA 93926
(408) 675-2481

Monteviña Wines
20680 Shenandoah
School Road
Plymouth, CA 95669
(209) 245-6942

Monticello Cellars
P.O. Box 2680
Yountville, CA 94599
(707) 253-2802

Morgan Winery
19301 Creekside Circle
Salinas, CA 93908
(408) 455-1382

Mount Eden Vineyards
22020 Mount Eden Road
Saratoga, CA 95070
(408) 867-5832

Mount Veeder Winery
1999 Mount Veeder Road
Napa, CA 94558
(707) 224-4039

Murphy-Goode
4001 Highway 128
Geyserville, CA 95441
(707) 578-9221

Nalle Winery
P.O. Box 454
Healdsburg, CA 95448
(707) 433-1040

Napa Creek Winery
1001 Silverado Trail
St. Helena, CA 94574
(707) 963-9456

Navarro Vineyards
P.O. Box 47
Philo, CA 95466
(707) 895-3686

Nevada City Winery
321 Spring Street
Nevada City, CA 95959
(916) 265-9463

Newton Vineyard
2555 Madrona Avenue
St. Helena, CA 94574
(707) 963-9000

Neyers Winery
P.O. Box 1028
St. Helena, CA 94574

Oak Ridge Vineyards
P.O. Box 440
Lodi, CA 95241
(209) 369-4768

Obester Winery
Route 1, Box 2Q
Half Moon Bay, CA 94019
(415) 726-9463

Opus One
Robert Mondavi Winery
P.O. Box 106
Oakville, CA 94562
(707) 963-9611

Pagor
Rolling Hills Vineyard
126 Wood Road, #106
Camarillo, CA 93010
(805) 484-8100

Palisades
P.O. Box 303
Calistoga, CA 94515
(707) 942-6625

Parducci Winery, Ltd.
501 Parducci Road
Ukiah, CA 95482
(707) 462-3828

Pat Paulsen Vineyards
P.O. Box 565
Cloverdale, CA 95425
(707) 894-3197

Robert Pecota Winery
3299 Bennett Lane, Box 303
Calistoga, CA 94515
(707) 942-6625

J. Pedroncelli Winery
1220 Canyon Road
Geyserville, CA 95441
(707) 857-3531

Robert Pepi Winery
P.O. Box 328
Oakville, CA 94562
(707) 944-2807

Joseph Phelps Vineyards
P.O. Box 1031
St. Helena, CA 94574
(707) 963-2745

**The R. H. Phillips
Vineyard**
P.O. Box 2468
Woodland, CA 95695
(916) 662-3215/661-6115

Pine Ridge Winery
P.O. Box 2508
Yountville, CA 94599
(707) 253-7500

Piper-Sonoma Cellars
P.O. Box 650
Windsor, CA 95492
(707) 433-8843

Plam Vineyards
6200 St. Helena Highway
Napa, CA 94558
(707) 944-1102

Preston Vineyards
9282 West Dry Creek Road
Healdsburg, CA 95448
(707) 433-3372

Quady Winery
P.O. Box 728
Madera, CA 93639
(209) 673-8068

Quail Ridge
1055 Atlas Peak Road
Napa, CA 94558
(707) 944-8128/257-1712

Quivira Vineyards
4900 West Dry Creek Road
Healdsburg, CA 95448
(707) 431-8333

A. Rafanelli Winery
4685 West Dry Creek Road
Healdsburg, CA 95448
(707) 433-1385

Ravenswood
21415 Broadway
Sonoma, CA 95476
(707) 938-1960

Raymond Vineyard
849 Zinfandel Lane
St. Helena, CA 94574
(707) 963-3141

Richardson Vineyards
2711 Knob Hill Road
Sonoma, CA 95476
(707) 938-2610

Ridge Vineyards
P.O. Box AI
Cupertino, CA 95015
(408) 867-3233

Riverside Farm Winery
P.O. Box 606
Healdsburg, CA 95448
(707) 433-7272

J. Rochioli Vineyards
6192 Westside Road
Healdsburg, CA 95448
(707) 433-2305

Rodney Strong
11455 Old Redwood Hwy.
Windsor, CA 95492
(707) 433-6511

Roederer U.S.
2211 McKinley Ave.
Berkeley, CA 94703
(415) 644-4437

Rombauer Vineyards
3522 Silverado Trail
St. Helena, CA 94574
(707) 963-5170

Rosenblum Cellars
2900 Main Street
Alameda, CA 94801
(415) 865-7007

Roudon-Smith Vineyards
2364 Bean Creek Road
Santa Cruz, CA 95066
(408) 438-1244

Round Hill Vineyards
1097 Lodi Lane
St. Helena, CA 94574
(707) 963-5251

Rustridge Vineyards
2910 Lower Chiles Valley Rd.
St. Helena, CA 94574
(707) 965-2871

Rutherford Hill Winery
200 Rutherford Hill Road
Rutherford, CA 94573
(707) 963-9694

Rutherford Vintners
P.O. Box 238
Rutherford, CA 94573
(707) 963-4117

St. Andrew's Winery
P.O. Box 4107
Napa, CA 94558
(707) 252-6748

St. Clement Vineyards
2867 St. Helena Hwy. N.
St. Helena, CA 94574
(707) 963-7221

St. Francis Winery
8450 Sonoma Highway
Kenwood, CA 95452
(707) 833-4666
(800) 221-1055

Saintsbury
1500 Los Carneros Avenue
Napa, CA 94559
(707) 252-0592

Sanford Winery
7250 Santa Rosa Road
Buellton, CA 93427
(805) 688-3300

Santa Barbara Winery
202 Anacapa Street
Santa Barbara, CA 93101
(805) 963-3633

**Santa Cruz Mountain
Vineyard**
2300 Jarvis Road
Santa Cruz, CA 95065
(408) 426-6209

Sarah's Vineyard
4005 Hecker Pass Highway
Gilroy, CA 95020
(408) 842-4278

Sausal Winery
7370 Highway 128
Healdsburg, CA 95448
(707) 433-2285

Scharffenberger Cellars
307 Talmage Road
Ukiah, CA 95482
(707) 895-2065

**Schramsberg
Vineyards Co.**
1400 Schramsberg Road
Calistoga, CA 94515
(707) 942-4558

Sea Ridge Winery
P.O. Box 287
Cazadero, CA 95421
(707) 847-3469

Sam J. Sebastiani
P.O. Box 1849
Sonoma, CA 95476
(707) 996-4448

Sebastiani Vineyards
389 Fourth Street, East
Sonoma, CA 95476
(707) 938-5532

Seghesio Winery
14730 Grove Street
Healdsburg, CA 95448
(707) 433-3579

Sequoia Grove Vineyards
8338 St. Helena Highway
Napa, CA 94558
(707) 944-2945

Shadow Creek
P.O. Box 2470
Yountville, CA 94599
(707) 944-8844

Shafer Vineyards
6154 Silverado Trail
Napa, CA 94558
(707) 944-2877

Sierra Vista Winery
4560 Cabernet Way
Placerville, CA 95667
(916) 622-7221

Silver Oak Wine Cellars
P.O. Box 414
Oakville, CA 94562
(707) 944-8808

Silverado Vineyards
6121 Silverado Trail
Napa, CA 94558
(707) 257-1770

Simi Winery
Box 698
Healdsburg, CA 95448
(707) 433-6981

Sky Vineyards
1500 Lakoya Road
Napa, CA 94558
(707) 255-7421

Smith & Hook Winery
Drawer C
Soledad, CA 93960
(408) 678-2132

**Smith-Madrone
Vineyards**
P.O. Box 451
St. Helena, CA 94574
(707) 963-2283

Sonoma-Cutrer Vineyards
4401 Slusser Road
Windsor, CA 95492
(707) 528-1181

Souverain Cellars
P.O. Box 528
Geyserville, CA 95441
(707) 433-8281

Spottswoode Winery
1401 Hudson Avenue
St. Helena, CA 94574
(707) 963-0134

**Spring Mountain
Vineyards**
2805 Spring Mountain Road
St. Helena, CA 94574
(707) 963-5233

Stag's Leap Wine Cellars
5766 Silverado Trail
Napa, CA 94558
(707) 944-2020

Stag's Leap Winery
6150 Silverado Trail
Napa, CA 94558
(707) 944-1303

David S. Stare
Dry Creek Vineyard
P.O. Box T
Healdsburg, CA 95448
(707) 433-1000

Steltzner Vineyards
5998 Silverado Trail
Napa, CA 94558
(707) 252-7272

Robert Stemmler Winery
3805 Lambert Bridge Road
Healdsburg, CA 95448
(707) 433-6334

Sterling Vineyards
P.O. Box 365
Calisotga, CA 94515
(707) 942-5151

Stevenot Winery
P.O. Box 548
Murphys, CA 95247
(209) 728-3436

Stonegate
1183 Dunaweal Lane
Calistoga, CA 94515
(707) 942-6500/5298

Story Vineyard
10525 Bell Road
Plymouth, CA 95669
(209) 245-6208

**Storybook Mountain
Vineyards**
3835 Highway 128
Calistoga, CA 94515
(707) 942-5310

Streblow Vineyards
P.O. Box 233
St. Helena, CA 94574
(707) 963-5892

Sunny St. Helena Winery
902 Main Street
St. Helena, CA 94574
(707) 963-2225

Sutter Home Winery
277 St. Helena Highway, S.
St. Helena, CA 94574
(707) 963-3104

Taft Street
P.O. Box 878
Forestville, CA 95436
(707) 887-2801

Topolos
P.O. Box 358
Forestville, CA 95436
(707) 887-2956

Trefethen Vineyards
P.O. Box 2460
Napa, CA 94558
(707) 255-7700

Trentadue Winery
19170 Redwood Highway
Geyserville, CA 95441
(707) 433-3104

Michel Tribaut
1005 Market Street, #305
San Francisco, CA 94103
(415) 864-1161

Tudal Winery
1015 Big Tree Road
St. Helena, CA 94574
(707) 963-3947

**Ventana Vineyards
Winery**
2999 Monterey-Salinas Hwy.
Monterey, CA 93940
(408) 678-2606/2306
(800) 237-8846

Viansa Winery
P.O. Box 1849
Sonoma, CA 95476
(707) 996-4448

Vicbon Winery
P.O. Box 363
Oakville, CA 94562
(707) 944-2811

Vina Vista Winery
925 Buckland Avenue
San Carlos, CA 94070
(707) 857-3722

Wente Bros.
5565 Tesla Road
Livermore, CA 94550
(415) 447-3603

William Wheeler Winery
P.O. Box 881
Healdsburg, CA 95448
(707) 433-8786/8894

White Oak Vineyards
208 Haydon Street
Healdsburg, CA 95448
(707) 433-8429

Whiteball Lane Winery
1563 St. Helena Highway
St. Helena, CA 94574
(707) 963-9454

Wiebel Vineyards
P.O. Box 3398
Mission San Jose, CA 94538
(415) 656-2340

Wild Horse Winery
P.O. Box 638
Templeton, CA 93465
(805) 434-2541

Williams Selyem
P.O. Box 195
Fulton, CA 95439
(707) 887-7480/823-9195

Winter Creek Winery
4142 Dry Creek Road
Napa, CA 94558
(707) 226-3148

Zaca Mesa Winery
P.O. Box 547
Los Olivos, CA 93441
(805) 688-9339

ZD Wines
8383 Silverado Trail
Napa, CA 94558
(707) 963-5188

I D A H O

St. Chapelle Winery
Route 4, Box 775
Caldwell, ID 83605
(208) 343-9463

O R E G O N

Adams Vineyard Winery
1922 N. W. Pettygrove Street
Portland, OR 97209
(503) 294-0606

Adelsheim Vineyard
22150 N. E. Quarter Mile Lane
Newberg, OR 97132
(503) 538-3652

Amity Vineyards
18150 Amity Vineyards Road
Amity, OR 97101
(503) 835-2362

Bethel Heights Vineyard
6060 Bethel Heights Rd., N.W.
Salem, OR 97304
(503) 581-2262

Elk Cove Vineyards
27751 N.W. Olsen Road
Gaston, OR 97119
(503) 985-7760

The Eyrie Vineyards
P.O. Box 204
Dundee, OR 97115
(503) 472-6315

Ponzi Vineyards
Route 1, Box 842
Beaverton, OR 97007
(503) 628-1227

Rex Hill Vineyards
30835 North Hwy. 99 W.
Newberg, OR 97132
(503) 538-0666

Sokol Blosser Winery
P.O. Box 199
Dundee, OR 97115
(503) 864-2282

Tualatin Vineyards
Route 1, Box 339
Forest Grove, OR 97116
(503) 357-5005

Veritas Vineyard
11322 S.W. Riverwood Road
Portland, OR 97219
(503) 538-1470

W A S H I N G T O N

Arbor Crest
East 4506 Buckeye
Spokane, WA 99207
(509) 927-9463

Chateau Ste. Michelle
One Stimson Lane
Woodinville, WA 98072
(206) 488-1133

Covey Run Wines
Quail Run Vintners
Route 2, P.O. Box 2287
Zillah, WA 98953
(509) 829-6235

The Hogue Cellars
Route 2, P.O. Box 2898
Prosser, WA 99350
(509) 786-4557

Preston Wine Cellars
502 East Vineyard Drive
Pasco, WA 99301
(509) 545-1990

Waterbrook Winery
Route 1, Box 46
Lowden, WA 99360
(509) 522-1918

Printed in Japan

Enjoy!